$\mathcal{T}$OP $\mathcal{R}$ETIREMENT $\mathcal{H}$AVENS

How to Relocate, Retire, and Increase Your Standard of Living

Edited by Margaret J. Goldstein

JOHN MUIR PUBLICATIONS
A Division of Avalon Travel Publishing

Look for these other retirement guides from JMP:

Live Well in Honduras

Live Well in Ireland

Live Well in Mexico

John Muir Publications

A Division of Avalon Travel Publishing

5855 Beaudry Street

Emeryville, CA 94608

Printed in .... rica

Secon ....

Library of Cong .... ition Data

World's top retirement havens / edited by Margaret J. Goldstein

p. cm.

ISBN 1-56261-377-4

1. Retirement, Places of. 2. Americans-Foreign countries.

I. Goldstein, Margaret J.

HQ1063.W67 1999

646.7'9-dc21   98-48393

CIP

Editors: Peg Goldstein, John Lyons-Gould

Production: Janine Lehmann

Design: Janine Lehmann

Typesetting: Melissa Tandysh

Printer: Publishers Press

Cover photos: Large photo—Unicorn Stock Photo/Phyllis Kedl

Inset photo—Leo de Wys, Inc./Clive Sawyer

Distributed to the book trade by

Publishers Group West

Berkeley, California

CONTENTS

Introduction

by KEN LUBOFF, SAN MIGUEL DE ALLENDE, MEXICO

Friends ask how my wife, Barbara, and I could just pick ourselves up and move to another country. They want to know how we can live so far away from our families, our friends, and our culture.

Our move to Mexico was really almost an accident. After I retired, we planned to spend a month or so in Mexico, trying to figure out our next move. A friend had kindly offered us the use of her house in San Miguel de Allende for this, our transition trip.

We thought the trip was a good idea. We were both only 52. Most of our friends were rigorously pursuing their careers. Everyone we knew was racing toward a goal that we no longer cared about. We knew we would be out of synch with our friends if we stayed in the United States. We felt that getting some distance from our former lives would give us a new perspective upon returning home.

So our expatriate life inadvertently began. We moved into our friend's house and tried to relax into our new lifestyle. Most days included a walk to the post office, then to the nearby outdoor market to buy flowers or fruit. We practiced yoga, read books, studied Spanish, and walked our dog in the country. We could do what we wanted, when we wanted. We iced the cake of our new lives by hiring a full-time cook and housekeeper, help we could never have afforded in the States. As time went by, it became clear that we had no inclination to return home. Who would?

Now family members love visiting us in a foreign country. The time we spend together is more relaxed and exciting and of much higher quality than when we were in the States. And though we may see our families less often, with e-mail we can "talk" with them almost every day—more often than we did in the States.

We learned quickly that in expatriate communities, friendships form easily. There is a special bond among those who have chosen to live in a foreign culture. Our former lives are behind us. What we did for a living and the amount of money we have no longer take on the importance they used to. We are in it together, like passengers on the same cruise ship. Living in a foreign land enriches us by showing us people in a different culture, with different values than our own. Seeing these differences can broaden and change our ideas of what is important.

And don't forget that we are living like kings (well, almost), on much less money than we needed in the States. We have a life we could only dream about before. We spend less because we need less—yet we want for nothing. I can't remember the last time I wore a suit, let alone bought one. Instead of buying clothes, we travel.

Of course, we experience frustrations as well: unheard of inefficiencies at banks and immigration offices, plumbers and servicepeople who make appointments, then fail to show up, electricity that shuts down at the most inconvenient times, and the constant effort to make ourselves understood.

Living in a foreign country takes some flexibility and may not be for everyone. Still, when all is said and done, for us the excitement and adventure of living in a foreign culture far outweigh the problems.

Our month in Mexico has now become almost five years. We speak Spanish well enough to get by in almost any situation, and we take great pleasure in learning new words and phrases. What a feeling of power and sense of accomplishment.

If you are considering relocating to a foreign county, let *World's Top Retirement Havens* be your guide. Each country described in this book is unique. Each has it own cultural point of view, traditions, and idiosyncrasies. Some countries are more exotic than our own, some are closer to the culture we grew up in. Some countries will cost more to live in, some are very inexpensive. Many are less expensive than the United States. Some countries will even let you work or start a business of your own. It is our hope that these pages will help you find a perfect place for your perfect retirement.

Before deciding to make the move, remember that nothing is more permanent than you want it to be. If your move doesn't work out, the States will always be there for you. But we believe that if you give your new home a fair chance, you will have the biggest and most enriching adventure of your life.

by Rosanne Knorr

Argentina offers incredible variety as it stretches 1,300 miles from north to south, encompassing lush tropical landscapes, glaciers, mountains, and wide-open prairies. Trek through rustic villages or go nightclubbing in lively Buenos Aires. Explore steamy jungles or ski the Andes. Retirees will never tire of this incredible country.

At roughly 1.1 million square miles (one-third the area of the United States), Argentina is the second largest country in South America—after Brazil. Bolivia and Paraguay make up Argentina's northern border, with Brazil and Uruguay to the east, Chile to the west, and the Atlantic Ocean to the south. Argentina even claims part of Antarctica, the Falkland Islands, and other southern Atlantic islands, though many nations, the United States among them, do not recognize these claims.

In Patagonia in the south, massive glaciers, deep lakes, and towering mountains attract adventure travelers from around the world. Typical Argentine prairies, complete with waving pampas grass and thistle, are home to the cattle industry and the country's own resident cowboys, called gauchos.

The Andes mountain range dramatically marks Argentina's western border. Southern altitudes are lush with trees, lakes, and

1

valleys, while Aconcagua, the tallest peak in the world outside the Himalayas, presides over the northern section.

Argentina extends from the scorching tropic of Capricorn (110-degree highs) to the frozen reaches of the Antarctic continent. But if you're living in the more populated and coastal regions, expect very mild conditions. Near Buenos Aires, the average annual temperature is a mild 61 degrees.

The biggest adjustment weatherwise for North Americans is an Argentine summer in January and winter in July. In Buenos Aires, January averages about 74 degrees; in July the average is 50 degrees.

The Culture and People of Argentina

Modern Argentina is a true melting pot of European and South American culture. Most North Americans, Europeans, and other English-speakers feel at home here and can travel relatively easily. Argentina also enjoys a rich Spanish heritage from its colonial period, which makes it attractive to travelers and retirees.

The Incas and other tribes dominated the region now known as Argentina until the Spanish arrived in the sixteenth century. Since the nineteenth century, the Argentine government has officially encouraged immigration from Italy and other European countries. As a result, you will encounter people with Spanish, Italian, French, British, German, Russian, and other European backgrounds, as well as immigrants from other South American countries.

More than 92 percent of the population is Roman Catholic. Judaism, Protestantism, and other religions are practiced here, though some sects are banned.

Lunch is the main meal of the day in most of the country. But Argentineans, like many South Americans, love the night life, so restaurants are often open for dinner until dawn the next day. Meat is popular, of course, in this country where cattle is king.

Speaking Spanish The official language of Argentina is Spanish. However, the Spanish most spoken here is the Castilian version (Spain's version), not the Mexican dialect so familiar to many North Americans. English is widely spoken, especially in the main tourist centers.

Spanish is one of the easier languages for North Americans to learn, so invest a little time in lessons before you travel. Just be sure to specify that you want Castilian Spanish or you may get some funny looks from your Argentine hosts.

You'll find language schools in Buenos Aires. One that offers a variety of levels, from basic to advanced, is the Instituto de Lengua Espanola Para Extranjeros at Lavalle 1619, Seventh C and Third E, (1048) Buenos Aires; tel. (54) (1) 375-0730, fax (54) (1) 864-4942.

You can also learn fairly quickly through less formal means. Since English is a popular language in Argentina, you may be able to trade English lessons for Spanish lessons. Ask your new neighbors or put a message on a local bulletin board.

A Brief History of Argentina The Incas reached northern sections of Argentina in pre-Columbian times. In 1516, Spanish navigator Juan Díaz de Solís reached the Río de la Plata and claimed that region in the name of Spain.

Spaniards began colonizing the region in 1535 and named Lima the capital city (later changed to Buenos Aires). Argentina declared independence from Spain in 1816 after Napoleon invaded the colonial superpower and weakened its ability to govern abroad.

By the twentieth century, Argentina had succeeded economically and beckoned Europeans. Some disruptions occurred as various factions representing immigrants established new political parties and vied for power. A military government took over in 1930 and a series of coups followed.

During the Juan Domingo Perón era, the Labor Party drew its

power from the working classes. But in 1955, dissidents overthrew Perón, who went into exile. He returned in 1973 and was elected president.

When Perón died, his wife, Isabel, succeeded him—making her the first female chief executive of a modern Latin American state. Despite this accomplishment, the era was known for terrorism, human-rights violations, political instability, and high inflation. A military junta seized power in 1976.

With a 1983 presidental election, democracy regained its strength in Argentina. Argentina reorganized its military and political structure and implemented monetary reforms. The result was a new period of stability, economic growth, and improved international relations.

Recommended Living Areas

Most people in Argentina live in urban areas, including more than one-third of the country's population that lives in or around the capital, Buenos Aires. Others choose provincial capitals such as Santa Fe or La Plata. The obvious reason for this is infrastructure: access to employment, services, and entertainment. Rustic ranches and mountain properties are available but relocating there involves much more research and a bona fide sense of adventure.

Buenos Aires   Called the "Paris of South America" because of its European flavor and culture, Buenos Aires is the focal point of tourism, trade, and almost everything else in Argentina. By some accounts the city has a population of almost 3 million, but adding the metropolitan area more than triples that figure to 10 million.

Despite its population density, the capital city is one of the safest in the world. So don't worry. Go nightclubbing or walk the bustling city sidewalks, especially the broad Avenida 9 de Julio with its towering obelisk. Or relax in the tranquil residential areas and enjoy Barrio

Norte's lovely historic homes. Stroll the parks and trails (even golf courses) that provide green spaces throughout the city.

Buenos Aires is home to many art galleries, museums, fine restaurants, and shopping districts. The La Boca neighborhood features brightly painted homes and fine Italian restaurants. Overall, the city's architecture is magnificent, especially the cathedral, the government house, Casa Rosada, and the famous Colon opera house.

The suburbs of northern Buenos Aires are divided into two sections: the coastal Rio de la Plata area and the section near the Pan-American highway. The suburbs near the coast are older, and there you'll find many Tudor-style homes built by British railroad workers. The properties have smaller gardens, due to the high price of the land here.

The suburbs are situated 6 to 20 miles from downtown Buenos Aires, but the local train line makes commuting easy. You don't have to travel into the capital for daily necessities; each suburb is essentially a small village with its own commercial center. Some of the best areas for retirees are Martínez, Acassuso, and San Isidro, although you will pay for the location.

A beautiful cathedral and historical monuments help define colonial San Isidro. You can rent small places—like the new riverside condos with marinas in San Isidro, Beccar, Punta Chica, and San Fernando for under $1,000 a month. In Acassuso, a sunny two-bedroom bungalow with living room, dining room, study, kitchen, maid's room, garden, pool, and barbecue hut rents for $2,500 a month. A large five-bedroom (two suites) home with large living and dining rooms, private garden, and pool rents for $6,000 a month.

The Lomas de San Isidro, Santa Rita, and La Horqueta suburbs near the Pan-American Highway are newer, offering larger gardens and new condominiums. In La Horqueta, an elegant four-bedroom home with large reception area, modern kitchen with breakfast area, and a total of 400 square meters of living space overlooking a spectacular 3,900-square-meter garden rents for about $5,000 a month.

Patagonia   Patagonia is a huge area beginning in central Argentina and extending to the tip of South America, where it points at the frozen Antarctic. Southern Patagonia is largely comprised of arid, desolate steppes. However, the northwestern region contains forests, lakes, mountains, and exotic flora and fauna. Here, wilderness is giving way in some places to exclusive country clubs and lodges that serve as jumping-off points for adventure travel.

Bariloce, in western Patagonia, is rich in woodlands, lakes, and mountains—to match its growing monetary riches. Wealthy Argentineans, Europeans, and Americans, including Ted Turner, have bought large *estancias* here. The town offers fine dining, theaters, nightlife, and a casino. Nearby, the Gran Catedral ski area, offers skiing for all levels, from beginner slopes to advanced runs, on snowfields above timberline.

The upscale town of San Martin de Los Andes has all the amenities you would expect from a fine resort with European flavor. The town is somewhat quieter and more family oriented than popular Bariloce, but it nonetheless boasts 33 restaurants and excellent vineyards. Five minutes from town in San Martin, a three-bedroom, two-bathroom, wood and brick home with pine, poplar, and peach trees and mountain views goes for about $150,000. For the same amount, you could find a 170-square-meter house on the outskirts of town, three minutes from the lake, with two dining rooms, two living rooms, three bedrooms, two bathrooms, a large fireplace, cathedral ceilings, and slate floors throughout.

Ranches in this area are beautiful and worth the extra price. In Acquinco, 20 minutes from San Martin, there is a ranch covering 22,000 acres that backs up to a 78,000-acre national park. A two-hour horseback ride into the park leads to 100-acre Lago Azul, a lake whose blue waters have rarely been touched by human hands. The only access is via horseback or helicopter. At $2 million, this property is truly exceptional.

As you leave the major cities, prices drop significantly. For example, in Belisle, a 30,000-acre ranch two hours northeast of San Martin features three rivers and gorgeous, rolling terrain that can handle 600 head of cattle. Situated on the property is a large four-bedroom, two-bathroom house.

The property also contains three houses for Belisle's gauchos. The cattle operation can reasonably gross $80,000 per year. Expenses should not exceed $40,000. At an asking price of $800,000, a 5 percent return isn't great, but that's $40,000 to pay for yearly visits and vacations.

Salta The striking city of Salta sits at nearly 4,000 feet in the foothills of the Andes mountains. The city was founded on the banks of the Rio Arias in the Lerma Valley in 1582 by the Spanish. Ironically, this town of beautiful colonial buildings is where Argentina fought its decisive battle for independence from Spain.

Not only is Salta picturesque in its own right, it also serves as the gateway to Argentina's famed northern area. The city of 370,000 people is a tourist and handicraft center, served via train and paved roads from Buenos Aires about 800 miles to the southwest. However, connections via rail may not be easy or often, depending on your destination within Argentina or nearby countries.

The cathedral here is one of the best preserved in Argentina. Built between 1858 and 1878, it houses the images of the Cristo del Milagro and the Virgin Mary, first sent from Spain in 1592. The Convent of San Bernardo also represents mid-nineteenth-century architecture.

The city offers several good museums to explore, including the Museo Arqueológico (Archaeological Museum) and the historic Museo Histórico del Norte (Museum of the North). Others include Museo de Bellas Artes, Museo Folclorico Pajarito Velarde, and Museo de Ciencias Naturales.

You can choose from countless restaurants in Salta that offer regional cuisine and casual to fine dining (the town is popular with conventions). Throughout the year enjoy festivals like Mardi Gras, with decorated floats and live entertainment. And if you're in the mood to relax and reflect on all that Salta has to offer, take the cable car from Parque San Martin up to Cerro San Bernardo for a bird's-eye view of the city.

You can take various excursions from Salta, including the Train to the Clouds, a 200-mile day trip along mountain gorges with beautiful scenery. El Rey National Park, about 55 miles east of Salta, offers a chance to visit exotic wildlife and birds in a subtropical forest.

Córdoba The hill section of Córdoba Province has an excellent climate and lovely views, so it's popular with retirees. It's also home to a large community of Europeans, notably British and Germans. The town of Córdoba, authentically colonial, features quaint old homes with wrought-iron grillwork and landscaped brick patios. The National University of Córdoba, founded in 1613, gives the city its youthful atmosphere despite its gentrified majority populace. Day trips are popular to the hill country, as well as to numerous year-round resorts scattered throughout the Sierras de Córdoba.

La Plata The 600,000 residents of La Plata enjoy a slow-paced lifestyle and quieter community than their counterparts in Buenos Aires, even though the capital city is just 33 miles northwest. Convenient train and bus transportation make trips back and forth easy.

The city's cathedral is one of the largest in South America, and the Museum of Natural Science, with its broad range of exhibits on the country and culture, is among the best in Argentina.

Mar del Plata For those who crave the ocean, Mar del Plata is situated on the Atlantida Argentina (Argentine Riviera) about 250 miles southeast of Buenos Aires. Here you'll discover 14 miles of beautiful Atlantic beaches—though the water is chilly even in summer—and excellent fishing. Naturally, many popular restaurants here serve excellent seafood. The city also is known throughout Argentina for its nightlife and showcases the world's largest casino.

RENTING IN ARGENTINA

Real estate agents in Argentina show rental properties and arrange contracts much like agents do in the United States. By law, rental contracts in Argentina are for 24 months. However, foreigners can sign a temporary lease.

You must hold a residence visa to rent property in Argentina. You must also provide a guarantee (co-signature) from your employer or from someone who owns property in the country.

Average Rental Costs and Listings Rentals are expensive in Argentina, but you can sometimes bargain for up to 10 percent less than the listed rate. A two-bedroom furnished apartment in Buenos Aires rents for about $1,200 a month, taxes and building maintenance fees included. Unfurnished, a two-bedroom apartment can cost from $450 to $700 a month. You will pay the gas, telephone, and electricity costs separately. A three-bedroom house with a nice garden and pool rents for about $2,500 a month; much smaller houses rent for about $700 to $1,200 a month. Prices can also go much higher. A luxury rental, such as a three-bedroom penthouse in Buenos Aires, might be listed for $4,200 or more a month.

Deposits and Fees When you sign your lease, you will pay one month's rent in advance, plus one or two months' rent as a security deposit. When renting through an agent, you will pay a 5 percent commission. In addition, you may be required to pay a 21 percent value-added tax if you need an official receipt. A .5 percent stamp tax applies to the contract. You may break a lease after six months, but you must give two months' notice. You must also agree to allow prospective tenants to look at the property on specified days.

Resources Check some of the more than 200 daily newspapers published in Argentina for classified listings. The principal newspapers are published in Buenos Aires and circulate throughout the country. Check the *Buenos Aires Herald,* the international English-language daily, which covers the capital region. You'll find ads for rentals and home sales, including listings by longtime expatriates now in the real estate or rental business in Argentina.

Outside Buenos Aires, the provincial capitals and secondary centers all have daily papers with local news and advertising sections. Also check with local real estate agents, who usually handle rentals as well as sales. (For names of recommended agents, see Buying Real Estate, below.)

ℬUYING ℛEAL ℰSTATE

Foreign investors can buy property in Argentina, though you will need to provide your birth certificate and other paperwork, including evidence of no criminal record. Some of these documents will need to be certified by the Argentine consulate.

The Buying Process   When you decide on a house, you will make your offer by providing a good-faith deposit called a *reserva,* which normally ranges between 5 and 10 percent of the total price you offer for the property. This sum commits both you and the seller. If the seller accepts the reserva but does not complete the next step by signing a *boleto* (purchase agreement), he or she must refund twice the amount of the reserva to you. If you don't sign the boleto after making an offer on a property, you forfeit the reserva. If the owner simply doesn't accept your price offer, your reserva is returned.

Once you and the seller sign the boleto, you will be required to pay approximately 30 percent of the total amount of the purchase up front. The remaining 70 percent is usually due within 30 to 45 days.

As in many Latin American countries, an Argentine notary public handles many of the functions Americans usually associate with a lawyer. The notary will research the title in the property registry to ensure that the title is clear. At the closing, the notary will testify to that fact and note that the purchase money was paid. He or she will inscribe your name in the registry as the new owner and collect money from you to pay property taxes. As soon as you sign and pay for your property, you receive the keys.

Financing, Taxes, and Fees   Mortgages are available through private lenders or banks in Argentina. Most banks will loan as much as 70 percent of the property valuation, with a loan term of up to 25 years. Interest rates are extremely high, however, ranging from 14 to 18 percent a year. For this reason, most people who purchase property pay cash.

Taxes, real estate commissions, and notary fees will add about 7 to 12 percent to the price of your property, depending on its location. Taxes are higher in Buenos Aires Province than in the capital city itself.

Closing costs due at the signing of the title deed amount to 8 percent of the purchase price for an unmortgaged property and an additional 1.5 percent of the loan for a mortgaged property. Note that when buying a new property you must pay a 21 percent IVA (value-added tax). In this case, the real estate commission fee is included or paid by the building company.

Finding Your Property   Below are some recommended real estate agents. Most of them handle both sales and rentals.

- Susana Ferrer, Luis Vernet 510, Fifth Floor, Apartment D, Vicente Lopez 1638, Buenos Aires; tel. (54) (1) 425-8556, (54) (1) 791-7996, (54) (1) 807-6042; sferrer@satlink.com.
- Jeanne Reynolds Propiedades, Roque Saenz Peña 1279, (1636) Buenos Aires; tel. (54) (1) 794-4100, (54) (1) 790-5950; fax (54) (1) 794-4044; reynolds@realestate.com.ar
- Jorge Trucco of Patagonia Outfitters, Pérez 662, 8370 San Martin de Los Andes, Neuquene, Argentina; tel. (54) (9) 727-7561; fax (54) (9) 722-9561; patout@smandes.datacop8.com.ar

COST OF LIVING

With its high taxes, Argentina can be expensive. Tobacco and some kinds of alcohol can be particularly costly. Steak and local wines, however, are amazingly low in cost. Here's an idea of what you will pay for everyday items and services in Argentina:

electricity	$35/month	lettuce	$.10/head
gasoline	$4.25/gallon	coffee	$4/pound
movie ticket	$7	milk	$2.30/gallon
bottle of wine	$2	chicken	$1.50/pound
maid service	$5/hour	fish	$1.50/pound
banana	$.25/pound	video rental	$3
bread	$.40/pound	compact disc	$20
steak	$1.50/pound		

DAY-TO-DAY LIVING CONCERNS

Democratic and social institutions are well established in Argentina, and retirees should feel relatively safe living here. The country boasts an annual crime rate that is lower than New York's daily rate.

Although the postal service extends throughout the country and is maintained by the government, it is not particularly reliable. Make sure you mail letters at the post office itself, rather than at a mailbox.

Argentina has an extensive telephone system of more than 3.6 million customers, though many families do not have private phones. The country's microwave radio system and satellite network are used to relay calls but the system often goes down, even in Buenos Aires.

Argentina is technologically advanced in South American terms, with 40 percent of its homes wired for cable television and new companies developing to meet rising needs. Electricity is 220/240 volts at

50 cycles AC, so you'll need adapter plugs, as well as converters or transformers, depending on the electrical appliance.

$\mathcal{T}$AXES

The personal and corporate tax rate in Argentina is a stiff 33 percent and is increasing to 35 percent. In addition, new excise taxes are planned. Taxes on alcoholic drinks will go up to nearly 25 percent from the current 4 to 12 percent. Tobacco taxes are rising from 60 to 70 percent.

Argentina's social security system was privatized within the past ten years. Social security taxes were so high (a total of 50 percent of wages) that the system was breaking down. The high taxes encouraged an underground economy, and its growth further eroded the ability of the government to earn income for the social security system. Now, workers (including foreigners) can place their old-age contributions, at no less than 11 percent of wages, into one of several private pension companies. These accounts accumulate interest and dividends to build retirement savings.

$\mathcal{M}$AKING THE $\mathcal{M}$OVE

American citizens will not need a visa to visit Argentina, just a passport. However, if you stay longer than 90 days, you will need to apply for a visa at the nearest Argentine embassy or consulate, or with the immigration authorities in Buenos Aires. They will answer questions and provide the specialized forms required.

You will need a valid passport, a completed visa application, a curriculum vitae (resume), and proof that you have no criminal record. You will also need to provide a completed health and psycho-physical examination certificate (form provided by consulate), certified copies of your birth certificate and marriage license (if applicable), three photos, and a letter from your employer if you intend to work.

The fee for the visa is $80, which you are expected to pay via money order to the Argentine consulate. Neither cash nor checks are accepted. You will be required to have a personal appointment to provide fingerprints and finalize your visa before you leave the United States.

For more information, contact the Argentine Embassy, 1600 New Hampshire Avenue, NW, Washington, D.C. 20009; 202/939-6400, fax 202/332-3171.

What to Bring, What to Leave Behind   Argentina's electrical current operates on 220 volts, 50 cycles versus 110 volts, 60 cycles in the United States. You can purchase adapters for electrical plugs, converters, or transformers to use with U.S. appliances. However, converters and transformers change only the current, not cycles, so computer printers or anything with a motor will not run properly. You'll need to buy these machines new or used in Argentina.

What About Pets?   To bring your dog or cat, you must have a certificate of good health issued by your pet's veterinarian and obtain a certification from the USDA Veterinarian Service Department. The USDA signature must be typed, and the raised seal must be visible. This certificate must then be legalized by the consulate.

You will also need a picture of your pet and a money order or cashier's check for $30, payable to the Argentine embassy or consulate through which you apply. Supply a postage-paid envelope in which the completed permit can be mailed back to you.

The certification process takes about 48 hours, but start at least 15 days prior to your date of departure to allow for mailing time and unexpected delays. If you have any questions, contact the Argentine embassy or consulate.

$\mathcal{M}$EDICAL $\mathcal{C}$ARE

Hospitals and medical care are of good quality and very accessible in Argentina's cities, while efforts are being made to improve medical facilities in rural areas. Unions provide Argentine workers with medical coverage, and others receive care at free clinics.

Health Insurance in Argentina Be aware that Medicare doesn't cover Americans in Argentina. However, even recent residents can participate in the country's national health-insurance program. Private plans are also available. Municipal hospitals offer free medical assistance, but the quality and number of services offered are not up to par with private options.

Health insurance, with very good coverage, costs about $350 a month for a family of four. Other plans are available for anywhere from $100 to $900 or more a month.

$\mathcal{F}$INANCIAL $\mathcal{M}$ATTERS

To an American, banking systems in Argentina may seem bureaucratic and downright impossible to deal with. However, after years of mismanagement and high inflation, general economic conditions have improved dramatically. Today the Argentine economy is strong and has grown vigorously based on strict fiscal policies implemented in 1990. Even with a recession in 1995, Argentine industry has grown by an average of 4.5 percent a year since 1991.

The country has enormous natural resources including hardwood forests, oil, natural gas, iron ore, and coal. Agriculture is the country's most important industry, producing primarily cereals, oilseeds, sugar, fruits, wine, tobacco, and cotton. Ranches raise cattle and sheep, and dairy production is growing due to foreign investment.

The Banking System   Banks are open from 10 to 3, but don't expect simply to walk in and open a checking account. The banking system is complicated and difficult even for Argentineans. To open a bank account you must present property titles and a tax declaration, among other documents.

The average Argentine pays his or her bills in cash. U.S. residents of Argentina often do the same by keeping accounts in the United States and changing money in Argentina as they need it. You can cash traveler's checks at some banks (not all) and the American Express office in Buenos Aires.

What Should Retirees Do with Their Money?   The basic monetary unit in Argentina is the peso, which is divided into 100 centavos. To exchange your dollars, you can go to a bank or exchange facility in most tourist centers. Occasionally some shops accept U.S. dollars, but don't count on it.

For the best rates, exchange your U.S. currency at a bank or use an automatic teller machine to withdraw cash from your U.S. bank account. Avoid changing money at hotels, restaurants, or shops, which often offer a less favorable exchange rate or charge high commissions. When you make a purchase in Argentina, don't expect change if it's less than 20 centavos. One- and five-centavo coins don't circulate anymore.

Advice for Entrepreneurs   Argentina's business-sector economy is exploding, and conditions are perfect for investment. Increasing numbers of middle-income consumers need products, and businesses—from high-tech computer firms to food processing plants—are on the rise here.

Import-export businesses, manufacturing, and other sectors are popular investments. In addition, Argentina is working with its neighbor nations to create a Southern Zone Common Market that could spark an explosion in Argentine business and commerce.

Many people predict that Argentina will be one of the hottest tourist destinations of the next decade, offering diverse activities and presenting entrepreneurs with excellent opportunities to serve the tourist trade. Projects like private dude ranches and ski resorts catering to American tourists are popular investments. Of foreign investment, 34 percent comes from U.S. sources.

$\mathcal{T}$RANSPORTATION

Public bus transportation is inexpensive in and around Buenos Aires, with routes to and from convenient points throughout the city and suburbs. Long-distance buses to other areas of the country are fast and comfortable, sometimes even offering meal service. Fares can be expensive, though, depending on distance and inflation rates.

Trains for areas outside Buenos Aires leave from Retiro Station. Argentina has an extensive rail network, though the system is not completely integrated. The system uses two different gauges of track, and two separate lines cross the Andes for connections with parts of Chile. The railroad also links Argentina with Bolivia, Paraguay, Uruguay, and Brazil—although service to some areas is limited or unavailable.

Aerolineas Argentinas offers flights to the United States and even has frequent-flier benefits. For more information on Aerolineas Argentinas call 800/333-0276. Other airlines, such as Austral Airlines, cover domestic routes only. Lineas Aereas del Estado operates mostly to and from Patagonia. Several other smaller airlines serve internal routes as well. Fares as a whole are expensive, though discounts and special passes are available.

Driving in Argentina Argentina has about 132,000 miles of roads, including a section of the Pan-American Highway that links capitals and principal cities of South and Central America with the United States. National and state routes are paved, but smaller roads are dirt and often in bad shape. A railroad tunnel through the Andes provides passage for vehicles.

A car will cost much more in Argentina than in the United States—as much as 100 percent more, though prices are starting to come down. Maintenance is difficult and costly. Insurance is obligatory, and premiums are typically higher than in the United States. Depending on the type of car, you can also expect to pay a monthly tax—up to $150.

*L*EISURE *T*IME

Deep in the tropical rain forest bordering Argentina and Brazil, Iguaçu Falls sends a curtain of water tumbling 200 feet to the valley floor. Its width expands to more than two miles during the intense rainy season. There is still plenty of unspoiled forest and jungle habitat in Argentina just waiting to be explored, and birders especially will find plenty to rave about.

For wildlife at its most exotic, visit the Patagonian coast and scan the beaches for Antarctic penguins, seals, sea lions, whales, herons, and albatross. Scuba diving and deep-sea fishing are also popular activities.

Visit the old colonial city of Salta in the Andes or any one of the other numerous small villages throughout Argentina. Explore La Quiaca and Humahuaca near the Bolivian border, a breathtaking place where local legend claims God found the colors to make the rest of the world.

Tierra del Fuego, the Land of Fire, sits on an island at the southern tip of South America. Here you can take in striking contrasts, from forests to desolate plains, from clear blue lakes to snowcapped mountain peaks. Wildlife viewing is plentiful on nearby islands that are accessible by ferry. Animals include sea lions, birds, and penguins.

Shopping Argentina's modern shops, especially those in Buenos Aires, come in all shapes and sizes and are open six days a week. In general, there are shopping centers and stores to match every taste and budget. Major credit cards are welcome in most stores.

The busy Florida pedestrian mall is popular, while fashionable and well-heeled window-shoppers can enjoy the upscale Avenida Santa Fe and Avenida Alvear. In particular, leather goods and woven cloth are outstanding in quality and price.

For antiques, visit the San Telmo Fair area in Buenos Aires. Visit regional gift shops for local handicrafts such as wood carvings, gaucho accessories, ceramics, and jewelry.

Large supermarkets are becoming popular in Buenos Aires and other provincial cities. The U.S. retailing giant Wal-Mart has even made its presence felt, with three Wal-Mart Supercenters and three Sam's Club discount warehouses. Other international retailers, such as France's Carrefour, are also opening stores here.

Sports and Hobbies Soccer is a national passion in Argentina, so you'll want to learn about the players and matches, if not kick a ball around yourself. You can attend a soccer match in Buenos Aires' 80,000-seat River Plata Stadium or countless other stadiums and fields throughout the country. Polo is another popular sport in Argentina, and its players rate among the best in the world.

If you enjoy winter sports, skiing in the Andes is some of the best in the world, offering opportunities for everyone from beginners to the most advanced. Mountaineering here is world-class and a chance of a lifetime for the really adventurous; make sure to work with an experienced guide.

The tango began almost a century ago in the dance halls and bordellos of Buenos Aires' working-class neighborhoods. The dance has yet to lose its allure in the city's nightclubs.

ADDITIONAL RESOURCES

Argentina Government Tourist Office, 12 W. 56th St., New York, NY 10019; 212/603-0443, fax 212/397-3523

Argentine Tourist Office, Buenos Aires, tel. (54) (1) 312-2232, fax
   (54) (1) 313-6834
Consulate General of the Argentine Republic, 205 N. Michigan
   Ave., Suite 4209, Chicago, IL 60601-5914; 312/819-2610, fax
   312/819-2612
Embassy of Argentina, 1600 New Hampshire Avenue, NW,
   Washington, D.C. 20009; 202/939-6400, fax 202/332-3171

Useful Web Sites
CityNet: www.city.net/countries/argentina/
Clarin newspaper: www.clarin.com.ar
Consulate General: fdigac@mrecic.gov.ar
Embassy newsletter:
   http://embeeuu.mrecic.gov.ar/news0497.htm
General information: http://emb-eeuu.mrecic.gov.ar/

by PARIS PERMENTER AND JOHN BIGLEY

No country has inspired more conflicting reports of life within its borders than Belize. Travelers return from this tiny Central American country praising it as a paradise on earth or damning it as the Calcutta of the Caribbean. The truth is Belize is neither heaven nor hell, but one of the most exciting, unusual, and intensely interesting countries on earth.

Situated on the Caribbean coast of Central America, Belize does not fit the stereotype people usually associate with neighboring countries in the region. For instance, there are no dictators and no armed forces in the streets. People trust their government officials. They smile at their police, who often smile in return. Yes, there is a bureaucracy, but it's relatively benign. Bribery and corruption are not ways of life in Belize.

For the most part Belize is a sleepy, developing, Third World country. The pace of life is slow, and foreigners arriving here via the fast lane must learn to downshift. Add to this a growing population of ethnically and socially diverse foreigners, and you end up with one interesting cultural experience.

The Belize people are primarily of Spanish, Mayan, Creole, Caribbean, and English descent. The growing expatriate community seems to have more than its share of eccentrics, including archaeologists, ex-hippies, writers, artists, filmmakers, holistic and spiritual healers, super-savvy international investors, and entrepreneurs. There are also increasing numbers of Americans, Canadians, Germans, and Australians who have come here to seek their fortunes or to live out their golden years.

The Culture and People of Belize

Expatriates find Belize an easy country to call home in many respects. Locals are welcoming and friendly to foreigners, and English is the official language. Culturally and ethnically, locals are from varied backgrounds, and their respect for differences makes it easier for foreigners to fit in.

Belize combines the best features of Mexico, Central America, and the Caribbean. Mayan history, clear Caribbean waters, and exotic jungle wildlife share this small sliver of land, which separates parts of Mexico and Guatemala from the Caribbean Sea.

A Brief History of Belize

1502	Christopher Columbus journeys by St. Georges Cay
1524–25	Hernando Cortés probably passes through Belize while traveling from Mexico to Honduras
1570	Pirates begin coming to the area
1582	Spanish Franciscan monks build a church at Lamanai
1629	Phillip IV of Spain creates coast guard to ward off pirate activity
1640	Indian uprising in Bacalar
1642	Pirates sack Bacalar
1670	Spain and England sign a treaty allowing England to stay in areas where it is already logging timber
1779	Spanish attack English colony

1783 Treaty of Versailles recognizes boundaries of log-wood activities in Belize

1796 England and Spain go to war; England wins

1859 Boundaries with Guatemala set

1862 Belize becomes a British crown colony

1981 Belize gains independence

1985 Government signs economic pacts with United States

RECOMMENDED LIVING AREAS

Belize City Tiny, ramshackle Belize City is the only true "city" in Belize, with a modest population of 65,000. There is a redeeming charm about this dilapidated city, desperately in need of a fresh coat of paint. The residents of Belize City are friendly and, for the most part, honest. Violent crime is virtually non-existent, but, as in most cities, you would not be wise to walk the streets alone at night.

The city is divided into 13 sections, each of which reflects a different part of Belize's history. Haulover Creek, an tributary of the Belize River, separates the city's commercial center from the northeast residential section. Albert and Queen Streets, Belize City's two main drags, constantly bustle with activity and are joined across the creek by the Swing Bridge.

The southern section is the oldest part of Belize City and forms its business district. On Regent Street is St. Johns Cathedral, the oldest Anglican church in Central America. Also on Regent Street, and overlooking the city's Central Park, is the beautiful Supreme Court building.

Along the north shore of the peninsula sit some of the many British-style colonial houses in Belize. Perched on the peninsula's eastern tip is the Fort George Lighthouse and the burial grounds of Belize's Portuguese patron, Baron Bliss.

Just 30 miles north of Belize City, and worth the extra effort, is the Community Baboon Sanctuary, where nearly 1,000 black howler monkeys are protected. Nearby Altun Ha, a Mayan ruin site spanning 2,000 years of history and once home to 10,000 Mayans, is also worth a visit. Set in the surrounding jungle, Maruba is a good resort that specializes in tours to the site. Lamanai, in northern Belize, is the oldest Mayan site in the country. Ruins of an old church and an abandoned sugar mill here are also of interest.

Real estate in and around Belize City is not nearly as romantic and picturesque as it is on the romanticized outlying cays. There are some beautiful colonial homes in the old section of the city, but most are in need of considerable renovation. Foreigners have already purchased many of these homes, intending to restore them to their original grandeur.

The majority of homes in the rest of Belize City are dilapidated and decrepit compared to U.S. standards, requiring imagination and fortitude on the part of any prospective expatriate tenants. To give you an idea of the market, recent property listings included a small two-bedroom, two-story wooden house selling for $37,500.

About 15 miles west of Belize City is a 550-site subdivision called Tropical Park, one of the many projects of local legend and land developer Emory King. A few sites remain on the market for $5,000 each. King and a local builder are beginning construction on two-bedroom, 1,000-square-foot homes that will sell for less than $40,000. Tropical Park is a nice spot, convenient to the city and offering ready access to utilities. Financing is available; with 10 percent down you could arrange monthly payments of as little as $110. For more information on the project contact Emory King, P.O. Box 107, Belize City, Belize; tel. (501) (2) 77453.

For general information on properties in the area contact Tom Giblin, tel. (501) (6) 23232, or Multi Investments Realtors, tel. (501) (2) 35151.

Corozal   Water lovers flock to the seaside town of Corozal, located just 10 minutes from the Mexican border town of Chetumal.

Accessible air travel makes it easy to reach other destinations from here, an asset that has made Corozal attractive to many retirees. Corozal is part of a designated free trade zone, which also makes it attractive for those considering business opportunities in Belize.

Just before you reach Corozal, Belize's northernmost town (ideal for swimming and boating), be sure to visit the Crooked Tree Wildlife Sanctuary, where the waterways are fantastic and offer tempting opportunities for anglers. Inside the sanctuary is Crooked Tree Village, population 800, one of the oldest inland settlements in Belize.

Corozal itself is a relatively modern little town on a protected bay, near the Mayan site of Los Cerros. Recently a new development began at Consejo Shores, landscaped with tropical plants and wired for electricity. Water must be collected in cisterns, however. Lots measuring 100 by 200 feet sell for $30,000 to $50,000. Lots measuring 80 by 200 feet at La Horizons sell for $30,000 on the water and $15,000 inland.

For more information on these and other properties, contact Tony Castillo at La Horizons Land Development, tel. (501) 42-2055, fax (501) 42-2829. Another good resource is William Wildman of Belize Land Consultant Ltd., P.O. Box 35, Corozal, Belize; tel. (501) 41-2005.

Cayo District This remote highlands district, tucked back in the jungles of Belize, is a favorite with expatriates looking for a back-to-nature experience. Activities here reflect the verdant surroundings: spelunking, canoeing, kayaking, hiking, bird-watching, and other outdoor pursuits.

Large areas of this district are unoccupied, and many of the available properties include extensive acreage. A recent listing near San Ignacio advertised 31.72 acres, two primitive concrete and wooden houses, many fruit trees, and farm equipment for $97,000. Another recent sale included a pair of two-story, treated-pine houses on two hilltop lots for $136,000. For more information contact Glenda Gwinn at Cayo Real Estate, 15 Burns Ave., San Ignacio, Cayo District, Belize; tel. (501) 92-3739, fax (501) 92-2057.

One of the more interesting places to stay in Belize lies in the middle of the jungle in the Cayo District. Rosita Arvigo and her husband, both doctors of naprapathy, settled in their current home of Ix Chel in 1983. Their 35 acres of jungle land adjoin the Macal River. Five acres are given over to their farm, where they live with their teenage daughter, Crystal.

From the farm, the two operate a research center, working with groups in Washington, D.C., to find natural treatments for both cancer and AIDS. They also organize conferences on traditional healing, present lectures on medicinal plants, and practice alternative medicine. Best of all, the farm accepts retired volunteers interested in helping with research. Retirees can sign on for three- to six-month stays. A small fee covers the cost of room and board at the farm. For more information, contact Rosita Arvigo, Ix Chel Farm, San Ignacio, Cayo, Belize.

Ambergris Cay   Most foreigners looking for a retirement home or second home in Belize gravitate to Ambergris Cay, the area of Belize that most fits people's expectations of Caribbean lifestyle. It is also the region of the country that is most appealing to the expatriate in search of convenience and comfort.

A barrier island 30 miles long and anywhere from 1,000 feet to three miles wide, it is the most developed of Belize's many outlying islands. Still, it is a relatively unspoiled place. There are just three main roads in San Pedro, the island's only town, and people get around in electric golf carts.

The barrier reef along Belize's shores is the country's most well-known feature and most popular tourist attraction. It is 200 miles long, and the opportunities for snorkeling, diving, and fishing along the reef and atolls are endless.

This cay lies a mere 15 minutes by air from Belize City and is the hottest destination in Belize, with beachfront condos, cable TV, and several restaurants. Prices are higher than in other regions, although some bargains can still be found. Those bargains generally aren't found along the beach, however.

Holiday Lands development sells 5,000-square-foot beachfront lots for $100,000. Condominium properties at Banyan Bay, with tiled kitchens and peaked hardwood ceilings, start at $212,000. Playador offers condos with palm-thatched roofs starting at $75,000.

Development on Ambergris Cay is restricted. You cannot build higher than two stories, and you may not buy up large tracts of land (say four or five acres) at one time. A typical 50-by-100-foot beachfront lot sells for $25,000 to $35,000; a 100-by-100-foot beachfront lot sells for about $65,000. In general, count on $750 to $800 per beachfront foot. Lots in the second row back from the beach sell for about half as much, and lots in the third row even less.

It costs about 20 percent more to build a home on Ambergris Cay than on the mainland because of the cost of importing materials. Expect to pay $55 to $70 a square foot. Ambergris Cay is the only place in Belize where you will find resort-style developments catering to foreign buyers.

Paradise Villas, just a few minutes outside San Pedro proper, is one of the few developments that is firmly established. Three years ago, it was the first project of its kind on this island. It offers oceanfront, two- and three-bedroom town houses, each fully and tastefully furnished and equipped. The 24 units are arranged in a semicircle so that each resident has a view of the beach from the front porch.

The private complex at Paradise Villas includes a pool, restaurants, bars, gift shops, dive shop, medical clinic, and facilities for bicycle, moped, and golf-cart rentals. There are no new homes available, but occasionally resales come on the market starting at $160,000.

Another development, called Royal Palm Villas—larger in scale and bit farther out from San Pedro—is in the beginning stages of construction. If this development lives up to expectations, it will be even more impressive than Paradise Villas. The complex includes not only a pool, dive shop, and restaurant but also its own private marina. A finished and furnished model is ready for inspection. One-bedroom units start at $99,900.

Retirees interested in proximity to conveniences with the feeling of remoteness should take a look at the other end of Ambergris Cay. The northern tip of the island remains completely undeveloped, with nary a hotel, restaurant, or dive shop in sight. And for forward-looking investors, it perhaps holds the greatest potential for appreciation.

Palm Bay Club, an ambitious project, is now nothing more than a large and fairly impressive single-family home being used as a model. The success of the project will depend on the proposed construction of a commuter airstrip nearby. The architect designing the complex and the individual homes is first rate, making this development potentially one of the best investments in the area.

If you're tempted to get in on the ground floor of this project, you can take advantage of predevelopment prices starting as low as $6,000 for a 10,000-square-foot plot. Furthermore, financing is being offered through the developer. With a 10 percent down payment, you can arrange a 10-year loan at 10 percent interest. In other words, you could buy into this project with as little as $600 cash.

For more information on real estate in Ambergris Cay, contact one of the following realty companies:

✦ Southwind Properties, P.O. Box 1, San Pedro, Ambergris Cay; tel. (501) 26-2005

✦ Triton Properties, Barrier Reef Dr., San Pedro, Ambergris Cay; tel. (501) 26-3783

✦ Tropical Land Real Estate, P.O. Box 65, San Pedro, Ambergris Cay; tel. (501) 26-2231

Punta Gorda   This quiet community is cited by those in the know as the next place to boom in Belize. The coastal town is located on a seawall, surrounded by rolling hills and fruit farms. Development is still several years away so prices remain low and amenities few.

Currently the town has about 2,800 residents, 13 restaurants, a branch bank, two pharmacies, and several grocery stores. Air service is available from Punta Gorda to Belize City several times daily.

Recent real estate listings include a 25-acre farm on the Columbian River for $45,000 and a 50-acre farm with fruit trees and two creeks for $50,000. Also for sale are a 2,000-acre farm for $61,600 and a 33-acre lot with Caribbean frontage for $143,000.

For more information, call Bonita Momme, P.O. Box 48, Punta Gorda; tel. (501) 72-2270, fax (501) 72-2449; or Harry Gomez, New City Area, Punta Gorda, tel. (501) 72-2130.

Placencia This peninsula on the southern coast is home to a small expatriate community and offers many of the comforts of home, including electricity, running water, and small hotels. Plantation at Placencia is under development, with 15,000-square-foot lots on the beach selling for $40,000 to $50,000. Lots on the lagoon side start in the teens. For more information, contact Belize Land and Development at 602/595-6458, fax 602/595-6459. Maya Beach is another property site under development, with canal lots beginning at $12,000.

RENTING IN BELIZE

Rental prices vary depending on location and amenities. The highest rental prices are found on Ambergris Cay and in Belize City. For details on current rental properties in Belize, contact Mary Hawthorne of the Cay Management Company, tel. (501) 26-2531, fax (501) 26-2831.

BUYING REAL ESTATE

Don't come to Belize looking for property that is dirt cheap. There's little of that to be had, particularly in the areas where you'll likely be interested in buying. What you will find is property that is an exceptional value and that holds the potential for considerable appreciation during the next several years.

Likewise, don't come to Belize expecting to re-create the lifestyle you had back home. You can't. Belize is a Third World country. Once you get beyond Belize City or San Pedro, for example, electricity and phone service can be sporadic, indoor plumbing a luxury, and paved roads a distant dream. Heed warnings about the need for caution when purchasing property in Belize—particularly out on the cays, where the settings are romantic and impulse buying is far too common.

Don't do anything you wouldn't do back home. Don't hand over cash to a stranger. Don't sign a contract until you've had a lawyer check it out. Don't buy into plans of future development without written guarantees. And, above all, don't purchase anything without title insurance.

The Buying Process   There are no restrictions on foreign ownership of real estate and property in Belize. The system of ownership is based on British common law. Once you've found a property you're interested in, the first step is to engage a lawyer you trust. One recommendation is W. H. Courtenay & Co., P.O. Box 214, 37 Regent Street, Belize City.

The lawyer's fee is 1 to 1.5 percent of the purchase price of the property. In exchange for this fee, the lawyer's most important role is to research the title to the property in question. The lawyer is also responsible for taking care of paperwork and all necessary registrations.

Even after your lawyer has assured you that a title is unencumbered, you still need to invest in title insurance. Only recently available in Belize, title insurance can be arranged through Belize Title & Guaranty, P.O. Box 107, Belize City, Belize; tel. (501) 27-7453.

Other fees associated with buying property include a land transfer tax of 3 percent and a stamp duty of 5 percent. Real estate agents charge 7 to 10 percent.

Some financing is available. The few banks that make loans are offering 5-, 10-, and 15-year terms with interest rates of 15 percent and down payments of 25 to 35 percent. Better terms can sometimes be arranged through the property developer. (The prime rate of interest in Belize is currently 12 percent.)

Real estate taxes are 1.5 percent of a property's current value or 4 percent of a structure's annual rental rate. Tax on a $60,000 home, for example, might be $900 a year. Before purchasing any property, you or your lawyer should check the records to make sure that the property-tax payments are up to date.

It is up to the buyer to arrange a home inspection, and this is a good idea. You should also have a surveyor check the property boundaries. If a mortgage is involved, the bank will have the property appraised.

COST OF LIVING

A couple needs about $1,100 a month to live in Belize—slightly more in the cays, where costs are higher due to transportation. Although Belize is not overly expensive, it is not cheap, and many foreigners are disappointed to find prices only slightly lower than those they were accustomed to back home.

The cost of electricity here is the third highest in the world. Gasoline is expensive, too, as is food, most of which must be imported. Costs are even higher out on the cays, where everything must be imported twice, first to Belize and then to the islands.

A good hotel can cost as much as $200 a night—but, then again, a budget hotel might be only $5. Restaurant prices can also vary widely—an expensive restaurant may run you up to $35 per person, but there are veritable feasts available in small restaurants, where lobster dinners are only $10. Sandwiches cost about $1.50, beer $1, and coffee 50 cents.

Belize City and Ambergris Cay are the most expensive cities in Belize. In general a typical couple can expect to pay the following for common goods and services:

electricity	$40/month	coffee	$7.50/pound
gasoline	$2.50–$3/gallon	milk	$4/gallon
maid service	$10/week	chicken	$1.50/pound
bananas	$.50/bunch of six	fish	$1–$3/pound
bread	$.60/loaf	video rental	$4
steak	$2/pound	compact disc	$18
head of lettuce	$1.50		

$\mathcal{D}$AY-TO-DAY $\mathcal{L}$IVING $\mathcal{C}$ONCERNS

Public utilities such as electricity and water are available in most towns but often not beyond town borders. Many residents collect rainwater in cisterns and rely on generator power.

City water typically costs about 10 cents a gallon. The water supply in Belize City is generally considered safe to drink, but stick to bottled water elsewhere.

Even those with electrical services sometimes supplement it with generator power for financial reasons—the cost of electricity in Belize is the third highest in the world. Many people also use kerosene and bottled gas for stoves and refrigerators.

Fortunately, and perhaps surprisingly, Belize is reputed to have the best mail service in Central America. A letter sent by airmail to the United States usually takes a week to arrive.

$\mathcal{T}$AXES

Belize is an excellent tax haven because of its banking secrecy laws. Investors can create an IBC (international business company), which is not subject to taxation, limits the owner's liability, and can manage portfolio assets. Belize trusts are another popular investment option. Assets generally go in the trust tax-free.

U.S. citizens are tax exempt on $600,000 of income, or $1.2 million for a married couple. Personal income tax is progressive, ranging from 15 to 45 percent. Retirement income can be tax exempt under some circumstances, and the value-added tax on goods is 15 percent.

Making the Move

To visit Belize you must have sufficient funds, a return ticket, and a passport. You can visit Belize for three months without a visa, but after one month travelers must obtain permits from the consulate.

You must live in Belize for one year to be granted permanent residency. You can enter the country on a tourist visa, apply for residency, then renew your tourist visa every 30 or 90 days until residency is granted.

To become a resident, a U.S. citizen must deposit $600 in a Belize bank; other foreigners must deposit $1,200. Retirees can take advantage of Belize's retirement residency program, available to those with at least $750 a month from Social Security, pensions, or trusts. You can apply for this residency program as soon as you arrive in Belize. Processing of residency applications usually takes six to eight weeks.

You must have a green card and be a resident of Belize for at least five years to become a citizen. If your parents are Belize citizens, you are automatically a citizen. Only citizens of Belize are allowed to vote in elections. For further details, contact the Immigration and Nationality Service, Belmopan, Belize, tel. (501) 82-2423.

A More Expensive Option   The Belize Economic Citizenship Program allows you to obtain Belize citizenship and a passport within 30 days for a cost of $75,000. With a passport, you can reside, work, and own property without restriction or a residency period.

To apply for the BECP, you need a completed application form, a negative HIV test, a police report showing a clean record, a birth certificate, a marriage certificate (if applicable), a copy of your passport, and six passport photos. The registration fee is $25,000 ($20,000 is refundable if your application is denied). You must also contribute a $25,000 investment fee to the Economic Citizenship Investment Fund. Once accepted, family members can be added for $5,000.

What to Bring, What to Leave Behind Import duties are hefty in Belize: 80 percent of value on cars, 45 percent on pickups. Some imports are subject to stamp duties of 12 to 14 percent. The best way to import goods is with the help of a customs broker.

A foreigner establishing residency in Belize is allowed a one-time duty exemption on used household goods and tools of trade. This exemption was recently expanded to include cars and boats.

Bringing pets into Belize is a simple matter. Obtain forms from Belize's immigration office. Pets need to be accompanied by a current health certificate and proof of recent shots.

MEDICAL CARE

Doctors in Belize are generally first-rate; many have been trained outside the country, often in the United States. The hospital in Belize City, on the other hand, is a disgrace. But plans for a new hospital are underway.

Health care in general is very affordable—$10 for a doctor's visit and about $15 a day for a hospital stay. Doctors and hospitals usually require immediate cash payments for health services.

The St. Francis Hospital and Diagnostic Center at 28 Albert Street is available to travelers. The Belize City Hospital on Eve Street is located in the modern part of town.

Health insurance is available at competitive rates from several local carriers. Some residents also maintain coverage with insurance companies in the United States or England.

$\mathscr{F}$INANCIAL $\mathscr{M}$ATTERS

Residents find that Belize is fast becoming known in the international banking world, much like Grand Cayman Island, thanks to banking secrecy laws that have attracted investment from around the globe. The country's four major banks are Atlantic Bank, Bank of Nova Scotia, Barclay's Bank, and the Belize Bank Ltd.

A checking account costs about $7.50 a month in Belize. Banks also offer retained mail services—holding mail or dispatching it at specific intervals for $25 a year. Foreign checks (including cashier's checks) are held by banks for six to eight weeks. The Belize dollar (equal to approximately 50 cents in U.S. currency) is the official currency of Belize.

Advice for Entrepreneurs and Investors Within the past year the government of Belize has enacted modern legislation that establishes the country, once and for all, as a competitive offshore financial center. Its new innovative programs in the areas of trusts and taxation are some of the cleanest and most user-friendly in the world.

Belize is attractive to the foreign investor for other reasons as well. Formerly under British rule, the country has a legal system based on the Westminster model. A member of the Commonwealth of Nations, Belize has recently enjoyed substantial economic growth. It is politically stable, the local language is English, and its telecommunications systems are modern and efficient.

Belize's wages are the highest in Central America, a fact that has earned Belize a growing refugee problem. People from Honduras and El Salvador migrate to Belize, where they know their labor will be better rewarded.

$\mathscr{T}$RANSPORTATION

Road conditions vary by location. Most retirees will rely on an automobile to get around, particularly a four-wheel-drive vehicle in outlying areas.

Good air service is available through Belize City. International carriers include American Airlines, Continental, and TACA. Local flights are available aboard Island Air, Maya Airways, Tropic Air, and others.

A number of bus lines serve Belize, among them Novelos, Venus, and Battys. Most routes run from Belize City to Corozol, Orange Walk, San Ignacio, and Punta Gorda.

$\mathscr{L}$EISURE $\mathscr{T}$IME

Perhaps the greatest attraction for retirees in Belize is the geography of the country itself. There is no shortage of recreational opportunities. Retirees can fill their days canoeing, white-water rafting, hiking, horseback riding, spelunking, exploring Mayan ruins, swimming, or just soaking up the sun.

The waters off the coast offer some of the best sailing and fishing in the world. Tarpon, bonefish, and snook are among the many fish that frequent these waters. Belize also offers world-class scuba diving along the longest living barrier reef on earth. Nearly every hotel has a dive shop.

The best way to see the country, especially the many Mayan ruins, is by horseback. One organization that specializes in beach trekking on horseback is Isla Equestrian on Barrier Reef Drive in San Pedro.

For help planning your travels in Belize, contact Tommy Thomson at Tropical Travel Representatives, 5 Grogans Park, Suite 102, The Woodlands, TX 77380; 281/367-3386, fax 281/298-2335. Tommy has traveled extensively throughout Belize.

$\mathcal{A}$DDITIONAL $\mathcal{R}$ESOURCES

Belize Tourist Board, 421 Seventh Ave., Suite 1110, New York, NY 10001; 800/624-0686, 212/563-6011

Discovery Tours, 800/926-6575 or 561/243-6276

Embassy of Belize, 2535 Massachusetts Ave., NW, Washington, D.C. 20008; 202/332-9636

Useful Web Sites

www.ambergriscaye.com
www.awrem-com/belize
www.belizenet.com

Canada

by PARIS PERMENTER AND JOHN BIGLEY

The majority of Americans looking for retirement havens may still head south to warmer climates, but not everyone enjoys tropical heat. If you think you'd feel more at home with polar bears than beach bunnies, try heading north to Canada. Northern Canada is frosty, but the coastal regions are temperate, perfect for year-round seaside walks and taking in a host of natural beauty.

Canada has more to offer than scenery and mild weather. It enjoys significantly less violent crime than the United States. According to the *Places Rated Almanac* (1997), Toronto averages around two homicides per 100,000 residents, compared with more than 23 per 100,000 residents in New York City.

Because of the exchange rate, the cost of living is lower in Canada than in the United States, and Canadian savings accounts often earn higher interest. Senior citizens are offered many discounts on travel, services, and entertainment. Canada's government-run health-care system is inexpensive, and patients are charged on a sliding scale. (All figures in this chapter are given in U.S. dollars.)

For the outdoor enthusiast, Canada (especially near the coast) offers excellent skiing, fishing, canoeing, sailing, hiking, mountain climbing, hunting, bird-watching, swimming, and more. For this reason and others that contribute to overall livability for retirees, Vancouver and nearby Vancouver Island in the west and Nova Scotia in the east will receive the most attention in this chapter. These regions are beautiful and unspoiled, with scenic ocean views and relaxed settings. Prices are much more reasonable in these areas than in Toronto, for example, which can be even more expensive than New York City.

THE CULTURE AND PEOPLE OF CANADA

American retirees will find Canadians very similar to Americans both in customs and traditions. Canada also offers a similar degree of personal freedoms and civil liberties. English and French are the official languages of Canada. Most Canadians speak English, except in the French-speaking Quebec province. Throughout Canada, you'll find everything posted in both English and French, which makes travel and fitting in that much easier. Even in the province of Quebec, you'll do just fine with English, a smile, and a friendly *merci*.

A Brief History of Canada   Canada's known history begins about 40,000 years ago with the arrival of nomadic tribes from Siberia across the Bering Strait. Now known as the Inuit, these first residents left their mark on Canadian culture. Since European settlement, Canada has seen many changes.

1497	John Cabot lands on Cape Breton Island and claims it for England
1498	Cabot takes another expedition to Baffin Island and Newfoundland
1534	Jacques Cartier is sent by France to explore the region
1608	Samuel de Champlain founds a settlement (today Quebec City) on the St. Lawrence River
1713	Peace Treaty of Utrecht divides land between European powers

1759   Fall of New France to Britain
1778   Captain James Cook becomes the first European to reach the Pacific coast
1812   War of 1812; Britain retains hold on Canada
1867   Confederation of Canada
1929   Great Depression in Canada
1941   Canada declares war on Japan
1959   Queen Elizabeth presides over the opening of the St. Lawrence Seaway
1967   World's Fair held in Montreal
1977   Toronto Blue Jays win their first baseball game
1988   Calgary hosts Winter Olympics

RECOMMEND LIVING AREAS

Vancouver—Mountains and Sea   If you stand in the heart of Vancouver, you'll see snowcapped mountains in all directions. To the east lie the Coast Mountains, rising 4,000 feet and flanked by superb ski slopes. To the west and across the Straits of Georgia are the mountains of Vancouver Island, which cradle many high-mountain lakes and offer canoeists pristine and quiet paddling. To the south, in Washington state, lies Mount Rainier, one of the primary links in the Cascade chain of mountains that finally peters out in California with Mount Lassen.

Skiers especially enjoy Vancouver. Snow seldom blocks the roads along the coast, but it is heavy in the nearby mountains, and skiing conditions are excellent throughout the winter and spring.

While Vancouver may be located near the ski slopes, this region also enjoys Canada's warmest winters. Wintertime temperatures range from 32 to 43 degrees Fahrenheit and seldom drop below freezing. Summers are mild, with days ranging from 54 to 74 degrees Fahrenheit.

The city of Vancouver on the mainland is not to be confused with Vancouver Island, a 280-mile strip of land across the Strait of Georgia from the city. Vancouver City is cosmopolitan and sophisticated, with fine restaurants, hotels, and museums. This city is infused with an international energy, thanks partly to strong business ties with the Pacific Rim.

You can shop for fine art on Granville Island, enjoy a panoramic view of the city with a skyride up Grouse Mountain, or meditate at the Dr. Sun Yat-Sen Classical Chinese Garden in bustling Chinatown. Just a short distance away, nature lovers find plenty of year-round fun skiing, fishing, mountain biking, scuba diving, sailing, and more.

As with most other metropolitan areas, the cost of living in Vancouver is higher than in the rural regions. Taxes and real estate prices are high in British Columbia. However, senior citizens in British Columbia receive free public transportation, a 25 percent discount on car insurance, a free newspaper called the *Elder Statesman*, and discounts at many restaurants, theaters, and shops.

Convenience is a big part of life in Vancouver. The city is home to Vancouver International Airport, located 11 miles southwest of the city with nonstop service to 32 cities.

Real estate prices have soared in recent years, spurred by investment from the Far East and the changing economy of Hong Kong. Today the average single-family home in East Vancouver sells for $218,000. In Western Vancouver prices average $505,000. Condominium prices run $94,000 on the east side of the city and $132,000 on the west side.

Recently, a one-bedroom apartment in South Granville went for $96,000. In the Fairview area, a two-bedroom townhouse, one of just five units in a large stone building, recently sold for $165,000. A three-bedroom home in the Marpole area recently sold for $303,000.

A novel way to live in Vancouver is aboard a houseboat. You can buy a houseboat in the Sea Village development for about $90,000 or in the development known as Annacis for $65,000.

The Sunshine Coast, extending from Langdale to Lund near Vancouver, is popular among retirees. A varied, scenic stretch, it contains peninsulas, lakes, islands, and fjords. One of the nicest places along this coast is the town of Gibsons, where housing is inexpensive. Waterfront lots average $15,000 to $20,000. For more information call the Gibsons Chamber of Commerce, 604/886-2325.

Richmond lies between the north and south arms of Fraser River, roughly 30 minutes from Vancouver and 30 minutes from the U.S. border. Although the town is flat, it has views of the surrounding mountains. Single-family houses start at $108,000, and townhouses range from $92,000 to $285,000. Prices in Coquitlam, within commuting distance of Vancouver, are higher. A recent three-bedroom, two-bathroom, ranch-style home with dining room and fully fenced yard was listed for $120,000.

White Rock is a prime seaside community 27 miles from Vancouver bordering the warm, shallow waters of Semiahmoo Bay in the southwest corner of the lower mainland. Retirees flock here for the town's beauty and perfect weather. Houses are relatively inexpensive, from $70,000 to $140,000. The Seapark development has luxury condominiums for $55,000 to $108,000.

Good sources for Vancouver real estate information are Mark Stark Re/Max, 604/737-8865, and Jo Carr, 800/771-9222. For communities surrounding Vancouver, call Vancouver and Lower Mainland Real Estate, 7062 Vivian Dr., Vancouver, BC V5S 2K3; 604/657-5432.

Victoria and Vancouver Island   While Vancouver City is cosmopolitan and sophisticated, Vancouver Island is peaceful and relatively unspoiled. Most of the half-million people on Vancouver Island inhabit the east coast. The west coast is rugged, cut by fjords and piled high with mountains, home to only a handful of fishing villages. The Pacific coast of Vancouver Island has a rugged beauty found nowhere else in North America. Here you can wander alone for hours along sandy beaches between surf and virgin rain forest.

The main city of Vancouver Island (and the capital of British Columbia) is Victoria, which retains its British cultural heritage amid the constant scent of flowers. This lovely city has twice the national average of retired people (about 16 percent of the population), and for good reason: Victoria enjoys Canada's nicest weather. Spring comes early and winter temperatures seldom fall below freezing. Less rain falls on this city than elsewhere along the West Coast. In Victoria, a sub-Mediterranean zone, temperatures range from an average of 40 degrees Fahrenheit in January to nearly 74 degrees Fahrenheit in July, with an eight-month frost-free season.

Outdoor activities are a big draw in this region of the country. Golfers say they never miss a day. Sailors race the wind in every season. Scuba divers claim that the waters around Vancouver Island are the clearest in the Northern Hemisphere.

The Gulf Islands, between southern Vancouver Island and the mainland, are also beautiful and peaceful. BC Ferries schedules frequent runs from Swartz Bay to all the Gulf Islands. Salt Spring Island is the largest and most populated, but it's still known for its relaxed, back-to-nature atmosphere. A popular getaway, Salt Spring attracts visitors for sea kayaking, bird-watching, and other outdoor activities.

The cost of living on these islands varies. Vancouver Island is higher priced than the mainland but less expensive than the Gulf Islands. Retirees will enjoy some perks here, including free public transportation, a 25 percent discount on car insurance, and many discounts at restaurants, theaters, and shops.

Conveniences vary from island to island. Vancouver Island is served by Victoria International Airport, located about half an hour from Victoria. Jet service isn't available out of this airport—only commuter flights into neighboring cities, where you can make easy connections. The Gulf Islands are served by BC Ferries, which dock just a short cab ride from the airport. Ferry service is also available into Vancouver.

The median price for single-family homes in Victoria is $60,000, a good deal less than in White Rock. Nanaimo, on Vancouver Island, has some of the lowest housing prices in Canada; houses in general cost less than $70,000. A three-bedroom house here rents for $320 to $400 a month. Fine homes in choice locations go for as little as $35,000. A new three-bedroom home on the waterfront can be had for $40,000.

Nanaimo sits on the spectacular Strait of Georgia and has gorgeous beaches. It also has more shopping space per capita than any other town in North America. And it has an airport, which makes it convenient for residents and visitors. For more information, contact Tourism Nanaimo, 800/663-7337.

Campbell River, also on Vancouver Island, has homes in the $45,000 to $55,000 range. The town is not far from Strathcoma Provincial Park, known for its spectacular waterfalls. Good sources for Vancouver Island and Gulf Islands real estate include Windermere Salt Spring Realty, 1101-115 Fulford Ganges Rd., Salt Spring Island, BC V8K 2T9, 250/537-5515 and Re/Max of Nanaimo, 1-5140 Metral Dr., Nanaimo, BC V9T 2K8, 800/335-3966.

Nova Scotia If you love the ocean, Nova Scotia is the place to retire. During the summer, fog rolls in off the water and shrouds the towns. The fog stems from temperature differences between the warm waters of the Gulf Stream and the cold Labrador current, which carries icebergs south even in the summer. At night you can hear the surf pounding and the foghorns blowing. This rugged province is a good place to wander along a waterfront and contemplate the lives of early seafarers. *Titanic* buffs will learn that rescue boats went out from Halifax when word first reached shore that the ship had hit an iceberg off Newfoundland. Today many ship's artifacts fill area museums.

Wildlife draws many travelers to this region as well. Wild Icelandic miniature ponies are found on some of the uninhabited islands, while whales can be seen on many guided tours. Birders can spot bald eagles or sail out to an island preserve to add species such as guillemots and razorbills to their life lists.

Nova Scotia's coast is lined with coves and small beaches carved by the sea, each a secret treasure for you to discover. The Bay of Fundy, which washes the west coast of the province (and separates the 375-mile peninsula from New Brunswick), is home to the highest tides in the world. The Northumberland Strait has the warmest saltwater north of the Carolinas.

In Nova Scotia, the weather in January is similar to that in the northeastern United States, with temperatures ranging from 15 to 32 degrees Fahrenheit. Like Vancouver, this Atlantic province has marvelously cool summers, with temperatures ranging from 54 to 74 degrees Fahrenheit.

When you step off the boat in Nova Scotia you have the uncanny feeling that you're in Scotland, not Canada. Nova Scotia means New Scotland, and much of the province was settled by Scots. It is in fact as picturesque and unassuming as any little town on the north coast of Scotland, with miles and miles of dramatic coastline lined with quaint fishing villages, bobbing boats, and centuries-old lighthouses. Woods, apple orchards, and pastures end suddenly at the edges of cliffs, which plummet into the sea.

The two main regions of the province, Nova Scotia proper and Cape Breton Island, drew boatloads of Scotsmen during a wave of immigration from the Highlands in the 1700s. On western Cape Breton Island, most adult residents have Gaelic-speaking ancestors, and you are apt to overhear conversations in Scottish Gaelic among the older residents. They'll switch to English to be polite in the company of strangers.

Fiddlers in this province retain a Scottish style abandoned by most Scottish musicians long ago. You'll find informal music sessions throughout the island at all hours—participants and dancers welcome. A stretch along the coast from the causeway at Port Hastings to Margaree Forks is known as the Ceilidh Trail; here traditional music and dance flourish.

Halifax International Airport, 26 miles northeast of Nova Scotia city, provides air service into this area via Air Canada, Air Nova, Canadian Airlines, Air Atlantic, Northwest, and other carriers. Car ferries also make the trip from Bar Harbor and Portland, Maine, and Saint John, New Brunswick.

Real estate prices vary across the island but average about $60,000 for a detached home and $45,000 for a semi-detached property. Various rental homes and apartments are also available. Recent listings in Halifax include:

* A three-bedroom home with two attic rooms for $35,700
* A two-bedroom, one-and-a-half-story home with kitchen, alarm system, and all-plaster walls for $38,500
* A four-bedroom home with wood-oil combination forced-air heating, a studio, and a private drive for $50,000

The most popular place in Nova Scotia among American retirees is the south shore around Bridgewater, Yarmouth, and Digby. Here, along Mahone Bay and in Chester, lovely homes overlook the water. A waterfront home in Crousetown recently sold for $53,500. The house, located on 2.3 acres on the banks of the Petite River, was 150 years old with a new roof. Two good sources of real estate listings in this area are Anthony Walters, Claussen-Walters Ltd., P.O. Box 428, Lunenberg, NS B0J 2C0; 902/634-4040 and Century 21 Rapid Realty, 111 Dufferin St., Bridgewater, NS; 902/543-2121.

RENTING IN CANADA

Renting is a good way to get the lay of the land in Canada before committing to buying a home, and prices are reasonable. The best sources for rental information are local newspapers. In Victoria, recent classified ads included rental houses within walking distance of downtown Victoria for $785 a month from October through March, the slow tourism season. Near Nanaimo, rental prices are lower. Recently, a waterfront condo with baseboard heaters, a dining area, and living room with wood-burning fireplace rented for $155 a week during low season and $235 a week during high season. In Vancouver, where the vacancy rate is a meager .5 percent, rentals are tough to find. Prices average $683 per month for a one-bedroom apartment and $785 for a two-bedroom unit. Rentals in Nova Scotia include properties such as a one-room schoolhouse within walking distance of the beach, refurbished with a dining room, living room, and full kitchen, for $215 a week.

$\mathcal{B}$UYING $\mathcal{R}$EAL $\mathcal{E}$STATE

As an American, you can buy property in Canada even if you are not a full-time resident. The amount of land you can purchase is limited in some provinces, but you can buy a one-acre lot anywhere.

Generally speaking, the procedure for buying a house in Canada is the much same as it is in the United States. You make the purchase through a Realtor, who must be licensed in the province. It is wise to have a lawyer review any contracts before you sign, and you must perform a title search.

Buying a property will require a down payment of at least 25 percent of the purchase price, unless you have mortgage loan insurance (in which case you must put 10 percent down). Most retirees prefer to pay cash because mortgage interest is not tax deductible in Canada.

The details of real estate transactions are governed by provincial real estate associations. For complete information, contact a real estate agent or the real estate association in the province where you wish to live. For general information on Canadian real estate, contact the Canadian Real Estate Association in Ottawa, Suite 1600, 344 Slater St., Canada Building, Ottawa, ON K1R 7Y3, 613/237-7111.

For information on property in British Columbia, contact the Provincial Real Estate Association, Suite 309, 1155 W. Pender, Vancouver, BC V6E 2P4; 604/683-7702. For information on property in Nova Scotia, contact the Provincial Real Estate Association, 5687 West St., Halifax, NS B3K 1H6; 902/423-9145.

COST OF $\mathcal{L}$IVING

Depending on the area you choose, to relocate to Canada you should have an income of at least $10,000 per person per year, before taxes. Because of the good exchange rate in Canada, you'll find the cost of living less than in the United States. Here's a rundown of some typical expenditures a retiree might make during an average month:

electricity	$68/month	head of lettuce	$.87
gasoline	$1.60/gallon	coffee	$5.50/pound
movie ticket	$6.20	milk	$3.50/gallon
white wine	$8/bottle	chicken	$1.65/pound
maid service	$9.37/hour	fish	$4.85/pound
bananas	$.60/pound	video rental	$3
bread	$1.80/loaf	compact disc	$1
steak	$3.25/pound		

Note that Canada uses the metric system. It might take a little getting used to buying groceries measured in kilograms and liters.

$\mathcal{D}$AY-TO-DAY $\mathcal{L}$IVING $\mathcal{C}$ONCERNS

Telephone and electrical service are similar to that in the United States. You'll find both 110 and 220 volt outlets, with the same configuration as for U.S. appliances. Utility costs in the coastal areas, thanks to cool summers and mild winters, are lower than in other regions of Canada.

$\mathcal{T}$AXES

Taxation can be one of the drawbacks to retirement in Canada. Upper-income residents can pay as much as 60 percent of their income in various taxes.

All residents of Canada are required to file Canadian income tax forms. The federal government charges a minimum tax of 34 percent on income of more than $38,125. Provinces add their own taxes;

amounts vary greatly. In British Columbia, combined federal and provincial taxes are 50.46 percent. Nova Scotia residents pay a total tax of 51.85 percent.

Everyone is entitled to a basic deduction of $2,064. If you receive U.S. Social Security, you can add $715 to the deduction. People born before 1915, or who are blind or disabled, can add an additional $1,292 to the deduction. The U.S. Internal Revenue Service requires U.S. citizens to file a tax return based on their world income, even citizens who are permanent residents of another country. For more information contact Department of the Treasury, Internal Revenue Service, 950 L'Enfant Plaza South SW, Washington, D.C. 20024; 202/622-2000.

A Goods and Services Tax (GST) is charged throughout Canada. This 7 percent federal tax is applied to most goods and services. In addition, individual provinces also tack on a sales tax. Goods sold in Nova Scotia are subject to the Harmonized Sales Tax, a 15 percent federal/provincial tax. British Columbia levies a 7 percent provincial sales tax. Visitors can apply for a rebate on the GST. Save all your receipts and pick up a copy of the Tax Refund Application for Visitors at customs offices, duty-free shops, and other visitor sites.

Making the Move

You can immigrate to Canada at a Canadian embassy, high commission, or consulate outside Canada. You cannot stay in Canada while applying for residency; you must apply while living abroad. The selection system separates applicants into three groups:

* Family: You have a relative living in Canada who has legally promised to give you financial assistance
* Refugee: You are escaping persecution
* Independent: You are applying on your own with or without the financial help of relatives in Canada

Most American retirees apply as independents. To immigrate as a retiree, you must be at least 55 years old and prove that you have enough money to support yourself (bank records, proof of pension, investments, property titles, or tax records may be used). The amount required varies.

Immigrants must also pass a medical examination. Because Canada has a form of socialized medicine, the government doesn't want to take on anyone who may prove an undue burden on federal programs.

Your application is most likely to be approved if you can prove some ties with Canadian relatives or friends. Owning a summer home in Canada may also help. While applications are processed as quickly as possible, thousands are received each year. First priority is given to family members and refugees. Independents must have patience.

Becoming Permanent Officials may ask for birth or baptismal certificates, separation or divorce papers, educational transcripts, technical or professional certificates, and letters of reference to go along with your application for residency. If your application is approved, you will also need these papers when you get to Canada.

Fees for permanent residence include a Right of Landing fee of $700, an application fee of $355, and a processing fee of $90 (this is not refunded if your application is denied).

If your application is denied, or if you would rather avoid all the red tape, you can stay in Canada for up to three months at a time without a visa. To extend your stay, go to an immigration office at least a week before your three months is up. Just cross the border for a day or two and then return. The fee for a visitor visa with multiple entries is $107, or $285 per family.

U.S. citizens may become Canadian citizens without forfeiting their U.S. citizenship. However, with dual citizenship you will need to file an income tax return in both countries. For more information, contact the Embassy of Canada.

What to Bring, What to Leave Behind Customs does have restrictions on what may be brought into Canada, including firearms.

Handguns are restricted weapons and can be brought into the country only for use at an approved shooting competition. For more information, ask for a copy of the brochure "Importing a Firearm or Weapon into Canada" from the Canada Customs Office.

If your application for residency is approved, you can bring with you, without paying tariffs or taxes, most household and personal goods you used before arriving in Canada. But you must keep all these goods for a least 12 months after arriving in Canada. If you don't, you'll have to pay normal duties and taxes.

Cars and trucks you owned and used before arriving in Canada can be brought into the country if they meet Canadian safety regulations. However, they can be used only for individual or family transportation.

Are you relocating with Fido? Bring a certificate issued by a vet certifying that the animal has been vaccinated against rabies during the previous 36 months.

MEDICAL CARE

Canada's provincial governments are responsible for administering health services. Each province has an insurance policy that ensures all residents receive necessary hospital care, including physicians' care, nursing care, meals, laboratory procedures, and many drugs. Out-patient and mental-health services are included in some provinces.

The cost of ambulance services and extended care must be met partially by the user. If you are over 65, hospital coverage is virtually free, as are most medical procedures, and the price of dental care is reduced.

Canadian Health Care Insurance plans offer basic medical and other health-care services; these plans are available to all Canadian residents. Payment methods vary from province to province. Some charge monthly premiums, while others pay health-care costs with provincial taxes. You can also obtain private health insurance to cover costs not covered by the provincial program. Programs such as Blue Cross offer services in Canada.

Although doctors' services are paid by government insurance plans, most doctors charge extra fees. Dental fees are higher in Canada than in the United States—$700 to install a fixed bridge, for example.

Tourists, transients, and visitors are not covered by provincial insurance policies. For a new resident, the usual waiting period before insurance begins to cover medical service is three months after residency has been established. Age, economic status, and previous medical conditions are not considered when coverage is determined. Note that your provincial health-care program doesn't provide full coverage when you travel, whether outside the country or just outside your home province.

Health care in Nova Scotia is rated among the best in Canada, aided by the presence of Dalhousie University Medical School in Halifax, which attracts top researchers and specialists. Halifax alone is home to six hospitals.

Medical care is also excellent in British Columbia. Victoria is home to two hospitals with 1,760 beds; Vancouver boasts 20 hospitals with over 9,000 beds.

$\mathscr{F}$INANCIAL $\mathscr{M}$ATTERS

Once you arrive, you'll find that the Canadian banking system is very much like that to which you're accustomed. If you are drawing U.S. Social Security, you can opt to have your Social Security check deposited directly into your bank or financial institution. Contact the Social Security Administration to set up the deposits.

Opening a checking account with a Canadian bank is a similar matter. You'll need a local address, an identification card, your passport, and funds. Most banks charge a fee for writing checks. ATM fees are $1 or more per use.

One popular investment option with retirees is the Retirement

Savings Plan (RSP). Available from trust corporations, the RSP shelters income from taxation and also earns interest.

$\mathscr{T}$RANSPORTATION

Getting around Canada is simple. With the exception of distances being marked in kilometers rather than miles, you'll find travel in this country much like travel back in the United States.

Public transportation is a good option in the larger cities. Vancouver is home to 602 city buses, 212 trolleys, and 120 light rail coaches. Victoria is served by BC Transit. Rates vary according to distance, but a typical fare on Vancouver's BC Transit is $1.10 within a zone, $1.60 for a two-zone fare. During off-peak times, riders can travel for $1.10 anywhere.

Train service throughout Canada is excellent, thanks to VIA Rail, 888/VIA-RAIL. Commuter and tourist service is available, from scenic Rockies excursions to city-to-city service. In British Columbia, train service is also available through BC Rail, 800/363-3733.

Air service is dependable and readily available. Domestic carriers include Air Canada and Canadian, as well as U.S.-based airlines. Special fares for people over age 62 are available on bus, air, and rail fares in some provinces. Carry proof of age when you purchase tickets.

Driving in Canada is simple. U.S. driver's licenses are valid when driving in Canada. Road signs and regulations are similar to those in the States (in Quebec, right turns are not allowed on red lights). Gas and oil are sold by the liter; the price of gasoline varies by location but averages $1.60 a gallon. Oil costs about $3.15 per quart.

Always carry proof of car ownership as well as proof of insurance. Also, check with your insurance company before departing to obtain a Non-Resident Inter-Provincial Motor Vehicle Liability Insurance Card. The minimum liability insurance requirement in Canada is $200,000, except in Quebec where the limit is $50,000.

$\mathcal{L}$EISURE $\mathcal{T}$IME

Aside from ice hockey (the national pastime), skiing is Canada's most popular outdoor activity. British Columbia has some of North America's best skiing. The province's sparkling, powder-covered slopes are numerous and include the Rockies, the Bugaboos, the Purcells, the Selkirks, Chilcotin, Cariboo, and the Monashees.

Mount Washington is Vancouver's biggest ski area and has lift service from 3,600 to 5,168 feet. This area enjoys one of the highest average snowfalls of any ski region in the world. A two-hour drive from the Nanaimo ferry terminal and a four-hour drive from the Victoria ferry terminal, Mount Washington offers more than 20 downhill runs serviced by two triple and two double chairs.

Whistler Mountain offers the highest serviced vertical drop in North America. It has more than 60 runs, trails for skiers of every level of experience, and the longest ski season in North America thanks to glacial skiing. Nearby are the longest fall-line runs in North America, with uninterrupted skiing for up to three miles at Blackcomb. The excursion from Vancouver to Whistler is easy either by a two-hour car trip (follow Highway 99) or by bus or train.

Gibson Pass, in the Cascade Mountains three hours from Vancouver, offers excellent cross-country skiing. The area also has two powder runs and two chairlifts for downhill skiers.

Aquatic Activities Some say Canada has the best fishing in the world. Generally, the farther north you go, the better the fishing. Salmon fishing is good in British Columbia. Rockfish, cod, flatfish, perch, and dogfish are abundant along the Pacific coast. These white-meat fish are relatively easy to catch; rocky areas, pilings, reefs, and kelp beds are likely spots.

Nova Scotia is Shangri-la for boaters. Its harbors and rolling hills make perfect refuges for Atlantic sailors. If you're looking for a place to park your yacht, consider one of the following clubs:

❦ Armdale Yacht Club, Halifax
❦ Bedford Basin Yacht Club, Halifax
❦ Brad d'Or Yacht Club, Baddeck
❦ Canadian Forces Sailing Association, Shearwater
❦ Cornwallis Sailing Club, Annapolis—French Basin
❦ Dartmouth Yacht Club, Bedford Basin
❦ Lennox Passage Yacht Club, D'Escousse
❦ Lunenburg Yacht Club, Herman's Island, Lunenburg County
❦ Royal Cape Breton Yacht Club, Sydney
❦ Royal Western Nova Scotia Yacht Club, Montague Row, Digby

Additional Resources

Canadian Customs
Atlantic Region, 1557 Hollis St., P.O. Box 3080, Station Parkland
 Centre, Halifax, NS B3J 3G6; 902/426-2911
Pacific Region, 333 Dunsmuir St., Vancouver, BC V6B 5R4;
 604/666-0545

Immigration Information
Embassy of Canada, 1746 Massachusetts Ave. NW, Washington,
 D.C. 20036, 202/682-1740

Retirement Information
Canadian Pensioners Concerned, 7001 Mumford Rd., Suite 238C,
 Halifax NS B3L 4N9; 902/455-7684

Tourism Offices
Canadian Tourism Commission: 800/577-2266
British Columbia: 800/663-6000
Halifax: 800/565-0000
Nova Scotia: 800/565-0000

Vancouver: 800/663-6000
Vancouver Island: 250/382-3551
Victoria: 250/953-2033

Useful Web Sites
http://tourism.nanaimo.bc.ca
http://travel.bc.ca
http://ttg.sba.dal.ca/nstour/halifax
http://explore.gov.ns.ca/virtual.ns
www.cdn-emb.washdc.org/
www.travelcanada.ca
www.travel.bc.ca
www.tourism-vancouver.org
www.islands.bc.ca
www.gov.nb.ca/tourism
www.mls.ca

Costa Rica

by JEFFREY LAIGN

Escape the rat race and live the good life in Costa Rica. It's become a cliché among retirees in the United States, but then don't let popularity dissuade you from thinking there are still good retirement opportunities here. There are plenty. And there are still dozens of reasons why Costa Rica has become the foreign retirement capital of the world.

For one thing, Costa Rica is the most stable, friendly, and crime-free country in Central America. It's also one of least expensive. You can live well here on less than $600 a month, which may be why many of Costa Rica's more than 30,000 U.S. retirees have nicknamed their second home "Hawaii—for half the price."

Certainly the weather in Costa Rica rivals any that Hawaii has to offer. The editors of *National Geographic*, in fact, have dubbed Costa Rica "the country with the most ideal climate in the world." With an average year-round temperature of 72 degrees Fahrenheit, it's always spring in this Central American Camelot. That means that on nearly any day of the year you can enjoy Costa Rica's palm-lined beaches, blue-green mountains, and majestic volcanoes.

But Costa Rica offers retirees much more than postcard-perfect vistas. Because the country enjoys a stable economy and government, it sees no need to maintain an army. Thus, funds that might have been channeled into military operations are spent, instead, on social services.

As a result, literacy tops 90 percent in Costa Rica, and average life expectancy is 74. In addition, Costa Rica boasts good roads, efficient transportation, impressive centers for the arts, and schools and hospitals that rival any in Latin America.

Another reason to live here is the people. Ticos, as Costa Rica's 3 million inhabitants whimsically refer to themselves, are downright friendly. Nearly everywhere you go in this country (the size of West Virginia) you'll be genuinely welcomed.

Even the government rolls out the red carpet to retirees. The country's liberal *pensionada* program was designed to attract foreign capital, and, by any standards, it's working. In the last decade, U.S. investment in Costa Rica has swelled by nearly 30 percent.

Foreign retirees are granted all rights of Costa Rican citizenship with only two exceptions: They cannot vote in elections, and they aren't permitted to earn wages from Costa Rican employers (although foreigners can own and manage their own businesses here).

When you combine the benefits of such generous provisions with the dirt-cheap property taxes levied in most locales, it's easy to understand why *Money Magazine* considers Costa Rica to be the "number-one retirement country in the world."

Of course, no country is without its problems. Petty and violent crime rates have risen over the past three years in Costa Rica—an unavoidable side effect of increased tourism and population. A U.S. Consular Service report recently warned tourists not to be complacent about traveling to Costa Rica, where two U.S. citizens were recently killed during robbery attempts.

Overall, however, compared with U.S. cities, violent crimes are rare in Costa Rica. Petty crime is more common, although still lower than in the United States, and retirees would do well to learn to live with Costa Rica's few faults as part of the trade-off for living in a country with so much to offer.

$\mathcal{T}$HE $\mathcal{C}$ULTURE AND $\mathcal{P}$EOPLE OF $\mathcal{C}$OSTA $\mathcal{R}$ICA

Learning to accept and enjoy cultural differences, which may be more annoying than problematic to retirees, is an important part of the assimilation process for recent expatriates. In Costa Rica you may be turned off by traditional machismo attitudes that prompt men to whistle at women or brag about their latest encounters. Because Ticos tend to be inordinately polite, however, machismo is far less pronounced here than in other Latin countries. More common is the "Mañana Syndrome." You ask a Costa Rican friend to meet you for lunch at noon, and she doesn't show up until one. You arrive for a business meeting promptly at three, and nobody else sits down at the table until after four. Latin Americans simply don't run on the same hustle-bustle clock as we do. This may take some getting used to, but most people learn to appreciate the upside of Costa Rica's relaxed lifestyle.

A Brief History of Costa Rica   Several Indian tribes called Costa Rica home before Columbus landed at Puerto Limon in 1502. During his first days in the region, Indian chiefs presented the explorer with gold jewelry and art, which may have prompted him to name the place Costa Rica (rich coast).

But Costa Rica's Indians had not accumulated the wealth that Spaniards had encountered among the Aztec and Inca empires. Thus, Costa Rica was left to develop its agricultural riches—and they are bountiful indeed. Green from November through May, Costa Rica has rich volcanic soil that's perfect for growing coffee, bananas, and a wide range of other fruits and vegetables.

Unlike many of its tumultuous Central American neighbors, Costa Rica has enjoyed a relatively peaceful history. In 1948 the government abolished the army. A year later, Costa Rica formally adopted the constitution that governs it today.

Today Costa Rica is a prosperous nation with a thriving culture. The country boasts two major universities, and the population as a whole is sophisticated and well educated. Costa Ricans also are avidly pro-American. Everywhere you travel in Costa Rica—from the Pacific Northwest to the glittering beaches of the Caribbean—you'll find yourself welcomed by friendly Ticos.

*R*ECOMMENDED *L*IVING *A*REAS

Covering just 19,700 square miles, Costa Rica is the second-smallest country in Central America, after El Salvador. Sandwiched between Nicaragua and Panama, Costa Rica forms a sort of "land bridge" between the Caribbean Sea and Pacific Ocean.

The Caribbean coast of Costa Rica is a 125-mile-long lowland, with few good harbors. The 600-mile-long Pacific coast has two deep bays formed by the Nicoya and Osa Peninsulas. In between, the country is bisected by a mountainous backbone interrupted by the verdant Central Valley.

Unlike expatriates in other Latin American countries, foreigners in Costa Rica don't feel the need to bunch together in walled compounds or retirement developments. Most feel comfortable living anywhere. What you may find, though, is that foreign retirees—especially North Americans—tend to congregate in the more expensive neighborhoods, simply because Costa Rica's low cost of living permits a higher standard of living.

San Jose and the Central Valley Two-thirds of Costa Rica's population lives on the great plateau of the 1,800-mile-long Central Valley, where springlike breezes waft and temperatures in the low 70s make for near-idyllic living. You'll find many retirees living on the cool hillsides that flank the region, enjoying the brisk, zestful climate that nurtures some of the finest coffee beans grown anywhere in the world.

It is in this beautiful region that Costa Ricans established their cosmopolitan capital, San Jose. Graceful and stately, San Jose perches in the shadow of two volcanoes, Irazu and Poas, which periodically flare up in a primordial display of natural fireworks. To this point the volcanoes have posed no danger to residents.

San Jose offers retirees many modern amenities. Rich in theaters, parks, bookstores, and galleries, San Jose enjoys a reputation throughout Latin America as a world-class center of culture. Life here is gracious and refined, as you'll discover if you decide to settle here. And many Americans do.

Most expatriates (including retirees and diplomats assigned to Costa Rica) choose to live in the suburbs of San Jose, an hour or two away. Communities such as Escazu, Rohrmoser, Los Yoses, and San Pedro are tree-lined enclaves offering many of the amenities you'll find in San Jose, including supermarkets, banks, sidewalk cafés, restaurants, bookstores, and art galleries.

These charming bedroom communities have witnessed a major development boom in recent years. In Escazu, clusters of modern bungalows housing retirees are scattered among the town's elegant Spanish colonial–style mansions and small peon houses.

Escazu also offers several shopping centers and supermarkets, linked to San Jose by a new highway. Housing here is also affordable. A typical two-bedroom, one-bathroom house, for example, may list for $90,000.

In San Pedro, home of Costa Rica's national university, you'll enjoy a wide array of cultural amenities, including the annual University Week celebration in April, which features colorful floats and a carnival-like atmosphere.

Other expatriates choose to live in Alajuela, 20 miles from San Jose, which has its own comprehensive infrastructure. If you like cooler, windier weather, you may want to join the hardy band of retirees in the hills around San Rafael de Heredia or in Cartago, the jewel city of the scenic Orosi Valley with its man-made Lake Cachi.

Higher in the mountains surrounding San Jose the environment is almost alpine, with towering pine trees and icy ponds on winter mornings. You can find prime real estate near Monte de la Cruz and San Jose de la Montana.

Another major residential area surrounds the huge man-made Lake Arenal, which has grown increasingly popular with retirees in recent years. This is a fishing and windsurfing paradise, with a smoldering volcano and hot springs at the nearby resort of Tabacon. A fully remodeled, three-bedroom, three-bathroom home with views of the lake and volcano list in this region for as little as $115,000.

The Pacific Coast   Just about anywhere along Costa Rica's Pacific Coast you'll run into gringos. Playa del Coco and Nosara, for instance, are long-established retirement communities.

Farther down the coast, you'll find some of the world's best fishing and surfing at Jaco Beach, a popular resort, or at the less-crowded Dominical, where expatriates have established a strong foothold. Beaches are beautiful here, and real estate prices are more than reasonable. Near Jaco Beach, for example, you can pick up a three-bedroom, two-bathroom condo for $70,000.

Dominical, on the Baru River, offers some of the best housing values in the country. One recent listing showcased a four-bedroom home with a large kitchen and fruit orchard (and even a meandering creek) for $39,000. The house has no electricity, but there's a hookup nearby.

Near Dominical is a newly renovated four-bedroom, two-bathroom home with walk-in closets, sitting on 30 acres brimming with orange, avocado, and lemon trees and with impressive ocean and mountain views, for $299,000. At Escaleras, another Pacific retreat near San Martin, $65,000 will get you an acre of land (with a river running through it), three bedrooms, one bathroom, and a large living/dining room with teak floors and bamboo ceiling.

You'll find outstanding condo buys throughout Nicoya Peninsula, a refreshingly uncrowded area known for sailing and fishing. From San Jose it's a two- to five-hour drive, partly over rutted roads, but the trip is worth making. Other developments along the Pacific Coast include Tango Mar, a private community with its own beach and riding club, and several areas of new housing around Manuel Antonio Beach and National Park.

The Caribbean Coast Not as many retirees choose to live along the Caribbean Coast. That's because this region can be hot and muggy, and the annual rainy season lasts a full six months. However, there are some appealing areas.

The seaside city of Puerto Limon, for example, has a large foreign community and a reputation for world-class reggae music. And you'll find some of the best snorkeling and surfing in the tropics at Cahuita, Puerto Viejo, and other small towns that flank the Cahuita National Park on the Atlantic Ocean.

Here's a tip if you think you might enjoy the steamy, tropical life: Spend a month or two at one of the coastal resorts before making a final decision to settle here.

*R*ENTING IN *C*OSTA *R*ICA

Renting is a good strategy for any foreign retiree during the first year or two in Costa Rica, while you're still getting used to the culture and figuring out where you want to live. Most rental properties come equipped with basic comforts like dining rooms, hot water, bathrooms, and laundry rooms.

The best way to find a good apartment is to talk to retirees who've already been through the experience. Read the local papers. There are scads of ads in the *Tico Times* and *Costa Rica Today*. You'll find even better ads in Spanish-language newspapers such as *La Nacion* and *La Republica*.

Expect to pay $300 to $500 a month to rent either a small home or a large apartment. Even in San Jose you can easily find a suitable rental home for $500. And the most lavish mansions, equipped with servants, rarely rent for more than $1,000 a month in most parts of Costa Rica.

ℬUYING ℛEAL ℰSTATE

Before you make a substantial investment in real estate, decide what sort of lifestyle you want to maintain. Throughout Costa Rica there are plenty of bargains. There are also luxurious accommodations with ocean views, landscaped gardens, swimming pools, and bungalows for servants. The questions are, how much do you want to pay each month and how big a down payment can you make?

The best way to get the best deal is to visit Costa Rica and spend time in the region you like. If you try to find an affordable home on the Internet, you may be looking in the wrong place. Bargains usually aren't listed there. What you will find are sellers who are asking too much or having a difficult time selling a property. A house or apartment that rents for $200 a month doesn't need to be advertised in cyberspace.

Talk with several Costa Rican Realtors and ask to see what they have. However, be advised that in Costa Rica real estate brokers are not regulated by the government as they are in the United States. Many are rank amateurs. That's not to say they're dishonest; they simply have no rules to follow.

One agent who does know what she's doing is Irma Morice de Petersen, who's married to an American and operates Find-A-Home at Apartado 444, Centro Colon, San Jose. Irma can locate a home or apartment in San Jose or a beach cottage on either coast. She and her husband have been in business for more than 15 years and specialize in finding solid, fairly priced real estate for Americans.

You might also want to contact Marilyn and Ginger Henderson, who own ERA-Carico Real Estate Co. Inc., Centro Commercial El

Pueblo, Suite 120, San Jose; tel. (506) 233-8057, fax (506) 255-3351. They have offices both in the Florida Keys and Costa Rica.

Since 1981, the Hendersons have helped hundreds of Americans relocate, find or sell homes, and acquire commercial or development properties. The Hendersons can assist you with establishing Costa Rican residence and setting up a bank account. They can also put you in touch with local professionals, from attorneys to physicians.

Whether you buy a townhouse in San Jose, a ranch home in the hibiscus-scented suburbs, or a beach cottage along the surf-walloped Pacific Northwest coast, one thing remains the same: Housing in Costa Rica is plentiful and affordable. Unless you settle in San Jose's ritziest neighborhood, expect to spend no more than about 60 percent of what you'd pay for similar housing in the United States.

The Buying Process Don't try to do it all yourself. Real estate is a large investment, and you're a stranger in a strange land. Hire a local attorney to help with the purchase of your real estate. Be sure the lawyer conducts a thorough title search and makes certain there are no encumbrances on your property. Then, obtain all necessary documents for purchasing property at the Registro de Propiedades in the San Jose suburb of Zapote.

Once you've bought your property, ignore the persistent rumors that squatters will take over your place unless you post an armed guard at the entrance. There *are* laws in Costa Rica upholding the principle that abandoned land can be claimed by whoever uses and improves it, but these laws apply only to agricultural acreage. The intent of the legislation is to prevent a few families from owning huge tracts of land they don't use, while peones are left with nothing. If someone tries to take over your house or lot, simply call the police, as you would back home.

Problems sometimes arise when people buy property that could be used for farming and then leave it for a long time without checking on it. If you are planning on buying land to build on in five or ten years, have a friend or an agent inspect the property every three months or so and call the police if anything's wrong.

A more frequent problem is property ownership that is in question. That is, did the owner buy the property legally, and did the seller have the legal right to sell? That's why it's essential to have a good lawyer check out real estate before you buy.

As a rule, always have your lawyer close a real estate deal. Never allow the seller's attorney to "save you money" by handling the paperwork. And, above all, never buy property that is already in dispute. Be clear with your attorney that you want a property that is clear of any ownership issues.

COST OF LIVING

A recent survey reported that the average Costa Rican family lives on 40,000 colónes (about $150) a month. If you're willing to adopt a similar lifestyle you can get by on the same amount. The good news is that you don't have to.

In general, goods and services in Costa Rica cost from two-thirds to three-fourths of what you would pay in most parts of the United States. That means you can live fairly well on less than $600 a month. Here's a sample monthly budget:

rent (three-bedroom home)	$260	cable TV	$26
housecleaning	$26	transportation	$26
food	$44	insurance	$26
water	$7	miscellaneous	$26
electricity	$26	entertainment	$104
telephone (base rate)	$13	total	$584

Here's what you'll pay to put food on the table in Costa Rica:

chicken breast	$1.76/pound	fruit cocktail	$1.99/can
beefsteak	$1.76/pound	French bread	$.50/loaf
fish (sea bass)	$3.25/pound	apples	$.50/pound
rice	$.34/pound	potatoes	$.43/pound
beans	$.45/pound	carrots	$.08/pound
sugar	$.34/pound	tomatoes	$.57/pound

DAY-TO-DAY LIVING CONCERNS

Costa Rica operates on Central Standard Time, six hours behind Greenwich Mean Time. Telephones are plentiful and convenient to use. The country code for Costa Rica is 506.

In general, most amenities you've become accustomed to in the United States are available in Costa Rica—even the Internet. At this time, the government agency Radiografica Costarricense (RACSA) is the only Internet provider. RACSA offices are in downtown San José, near the old U.S. embassy building; tel. (506) 287-6463. For $15 you get five hours of service a month, with extra time billed at $5 an hour. Hookup fees are about $40 for residents and $80 for nonresidents, which includes the first month's service. You can pay automatically by credit card and suspend service while you're out of the country by notifying RACSA a week in advance.

TAXES

Property taxes in Costa Rica are far lower than in the United States—typically no more than 1.25 percent of assessed value. And there are no capital gains taxes on real estate in Costa Rica, so you can earn a good profit by picking up properties today and selling them a few years later.

It used to be that folks who qualified for residency received a ton of tax breaks. They could import $7,000 in household goods tax free, and every few years they could import an automobile without paying duty. Same deal for refrigerators and other major appliances.

Understandably, those tax breaks for foreigners spurred a lot of resentment among Costa Rican citizens, who had to pay twice as much for an automobile as the gringo who lived next door and paid minimal property tax. Consequently, the fabulous tax breaks of yore are no more. Only those who qualified previously are grandfathered into the system and can continue to take advantage of earlier low rates.

Making the Move

Moving to Costa Rica is easy. You can live in the country simply by obtaining a six-month extension on your tourist visa. And the visa is so flexible that you can start a business or make investments while on it.

To settle in Costa Rica, you may decide to enter one of the country's permanent residency programs and become a *pensionado*. A resident pensionado must demonstrate a lifetime income of at least $600 a month earned outside the country and agree to exchange that amount each month for colónes at a government bank. In addition, you must renew your pensionado card every two years. You also mustprovide a number of documents, including an application to the director of intelligence and security, a notarized statement guaranteeing that you won't earn wages in Costa Rica, a sworn statement that you have no police record, birth and marriage certificates, a certified copy of your passport, a certificate of nonresidence, and several passport-size photos.

Sound like a lot of work? Here's a tip: Join the Costa Rican Residents Association and let them handle much of the paperwork for you. The fee is just $50, and it's a good investment, considering all the time you'll save. You can contact the organization at Apartado 700-1001, San Jose.

After living in Costa Rica as a permanent resident for five years, you'll be eligible for citizenship, which can be obtained without losing your rights as a U.S. citizen. For quick, easy answers to many of your questions, call the Costa Rican Tourism Institute's toll-free number: 800/343-6332.

Making an Application   It can take from a few months to a year before your residency is approved, depending on the thoroughness of your preparation and the efficiency of the government agent who is handling your case. In the meantime, your residency status is legal and won't be challenged.

Most people find it convenient to let an attorney or someone familiar with the application process apply for them. Of course, many people have applied on their own, but there are plenty of sad stories told by people who failed to attain residency because they didn't know what they were doing. And let's face it, few people enjoy standing in line, facing indifferent government clerks, and trying to understand questions in a foreign language.

In any event, start the process at home. It's much easier to obtain the forms in the United States than to request them by mail from Costa Rica. Your regional Costa Rican consulate will charge about $40 per document. Validation and translation of foreign documents is handled by a Costa Rican consulate and the Ministry of Foreign Affairs and Culture of Costa Rica.

You'll need 20 photographs for adults (seven profile and 13 front shots) and 16 photos for minors (seven profile and nine front shots). Several certified copies of your passport are required, and you'll fill out a questionnaire of personal information.

You may be required to take a physical exam. As a retiree, you'll have to sign a statement that you won't work for pay while in Costa Rica (without authorization) and that you'll spend at least four months a year in Costa Rica. (The months needn't be consecutive.)

What to Bring, What to Leave Behind Customs regulations have been revised recently, and there is no government brochure detailing what you can and cannot bring into the country. That, unfortunately, leaves many decisions subject to interpretation.

Basically, every six months tourists and residents can bring $500 in merchandise into the country tax-free. The disabled may bring a wheelchair. In addition, personal articles used by travelers for work or play—clothing, handbags, medicines, sports equipment, cameras, tents, musical instruments, and computers—are also allowed in tax-free. However, be prepared to argue with customs agents about what constitutes a "personal article."

Goods over the $500 limit and not considered personal articles will be retained in customs until import duties are paid. The amount of duty depends on the type of merchandise, and the categories are numerous. If the value is over $100, you'll need a customs broker to handle the paperwork. The procedure can be quite complicated.

To qualify for the $500 exemption, merchandise packed in suitcases or boxes need not enter the country at the same time you do. You have a grace period of three months before or after you arrive. But it's highly recommended that you arrange to bring merchandise with you on the same flight. If your goodies end up in a customs warehouse, you may not have to pay duty, but it could be time-consuming and expensive to sort through the red tape.

Having things shipped to you is not reliable or recommended. One couple in Costa Rica received a Christmas present of chocolates from a well-meaning friend. The box was valued at $10, but the couple was required to pay about $30 in duty.

What About Pets? You can bring your pets with you to Costa Rica, provided you're willing to spend a few bucks and put up with some paperwork (along with inevitable delays). Contact Jefe del Departamento de Zoonosis, Ministerio de Salud, Apartado 10123, San José; tel. (506) 223-0333, and request an import permit. Complete the form and send it to the ministry with the fee and documents.

You will need a health certificate signed by a registered veterinarian and certified by a Costa Rican consul. Your hometown veterinarian should be able to handle all the paperwork, which must state that the animal is parasite-free and has all current vaccinations against rabies, distemper, hepatitis, parvovirus, and leptospirosis. The animal's rabies shots must be at least three months old but less than three years old.

*M*EDICAL *C*ARE

For most retirees, medical care is of major importance. In Costa Rica there's no need to worry. The country is home to scores of medical professionals (many of whom were trained in the United States), and it enjoys what may be the most technologically advanced medical infrastructure in Central America.

Costa Rica is relatively free of diseases that plague many of its neighbors. In most areas, the level of sanitation and health management matches that of the United States. Nevertheless, it's always wise to avoid eating uncooked or undercooked foods as a precaution against intestinal disorders.

If you do get sick, you'll find that medical care in Costa Rica is of the highest quality—and usually at prices that seem too good to be true. The most expensive hospital room in the country costs about $80 a day. It doesn't matter whether you're a resident, tourist, or illegal alien—if you get to a hospital the doctors will treat you.

As a member of the country's official retirement program, any U.S. retiree can join the Costa Rican social security system, which guarantees cradle-to-grave medical coverage for only $25 a month. Costs for private health care are not much higher, and quality is outstanding.

In San Jose both the Clinica Biblica and Clinica Catolica are fully equipped to handle most complex operations, including kidney and bone-marrow transplants. The first kidney transplant in Central America took place at Catolica.

Outside the capital, 20 regional hospitals and 60 local clinics provide comprehensive health care. Costa Rica's top hospitals include Clinica Biblica, Clinica Catolica Guadelupe, Clinica Santa Rita, and Hospital San Juan de Dios.

$\mathcal{F}$INANCIAL $\mathcal{M}$ATTERS

Costa Rica has the most stable economy in Latin America. From time to time there is inflation in Costa Rica, but it has not amounted to much in recent years. At the same time, there has been an ongoing devaluation of the colón (basic unit of currency in Costa Rica) against the dollar, about a colón or two a month. That means that while prices may rise, you get more colónes to the dollar, and your actual costs stay the same or go down.

If you're traveling in Costa Rica it's best to use traveler's checks or U.S. currency. Avoid exchanging more dollars than you need or you may get stuck with unusable colónes in some regions of the country. The country's central bank, Banco Central de Costa Rica, operates a good currency exchange office at the San Jose International Airport.

Costa Rica's Banking System It used to be that checking accounts could be opened only in government-owned banks in Costa Rica, but legislative changes in 1996 permitted private banks to handle checking. Private banks in Costa Rica are generally more efficient and user-friendly than government banks, but before you invest in a private bank investigate its track record and talk to your attorney about its reliability.

Loans are extremely difficult for foreigners to obtain, and interest rates are sky high—more than 30 percent in many cases. You can use a cashier service for receiving deposits and cashing checks at most San Jose banks. The service is available Monday through Saturday from 8 a.m. to 7 p.m. All bank deposits in Costa Rica are insured by the government, and most banks maintain 24-hour ATM machines.

The most convenient way to transfer or wire funds from the United States and Canada is to use Banco Internacional de Costa Rica (BICSA), which has a branch office in Miami and operates under Florida state law.

Doing Business in Costa Rica   Costa Rica has tolerant laws for foreigners who want to open businesses here. While many countries refuse to allow foreigners to compete with local interests, Costa Rica welcomes foreign business investment with open arms. There are just two conditions: You must create jobs in Costa Rica, and your business cannot harm the fragile rain forest environment.

All you need to start a business is your tourist visa, and the government offers plenty of tax breaks to help you get going. Costa Rica's liberal laws encourage foreign investors to live here and reinvest, instead of siphoning profits into foreign bank accounts. This in turn bolsters Costa Rica's economy.

If you think you'd like to open a business in Costa Rica, here's a tip from California entrepreneur Robert Masek, who bought a nightclub between Escazu and Santa Ana with his partner, Graham Henslow, from England: "First, spend at least six months here, looking around and doing market studies. Second, either do something you really know well, or focus on something you've always wanted to do but don't need to make a living at."

Opportunities for investment abound in Costa Rica. Some investments even qualify you for immediate residency. For example, the Techos de Paz (Shelters of Peace) Investor Residency Program requires a minimum investment of $50,000, of which $10,000 is channeled to purchase housing bonds issued by the Banco Hipotecario de la Vivienda (the country's local home mortgage institution) and used to finance low-cost housing. The rest of the money can be invested in whatever endeavor you like. The problem is you'll never get the $10,000 back. In effect, it's a donation that buys residency with a minimum of red tape. An alternative to this instant-residency plan is to invest $60,000 in an approved tourism or export business, $100,000 in a reforestation project, or $200,000 in any other type of business.

Where to Turn for Business Help   Starting a business in a foreign land can be a risky and confusing. Fortunately, there are people who can help you to get started in Costa Rica. These organizations provide aid for entrepreneurs:

❧ Oficina de Turismo (tourist office), P.O. Box 777, 1000 San Jose; tel. (506) 223-1733, fax (506) 225-1452
❧ Association of Residents of Costa Rica, Apartado 700-1011Y, San Jose; tel. (506) 233-8068, fax (506) 233-7862
❧Costa Rican Coalition for Development Initiatives (CINDE), Apartado 7170 1000, San Jose; tel. (506) 220-0366, fax (506) 220-4750

$\mathcal{T}$RANSPORTATION

It's easy, convenient, safe, and cheap to get around in Costa Rica. Expect to pay 45 cents per liter for regular gas. Taxis cost 71 cents for the first kilometer (about two-thirds of a mile), 32 cents per additional kilometer. City bus fare is 21 to 43 cents.

If you choose to live in a city like San Jose, you may be better off using public transportation and avoiding the expense of maintaining an automobile. Auto insurance is a government monopoly, so you can't save by shopping around.

If you do decide to own and operate a car, be aware that some Costa Rican drivers are daring and aggressive. For this reason, accident rates in Costa Rica are unusually high. Obey the posted speed limits on highways; Costa Rican police love to set up radar traps.

Be sure to carry your passport when driving; there's a fine for not having it. Police will sometimes accept a photocopy of your passport, provided you have a copy of the page showing the date you entered the country. But your original passport is preferred. Photocopies of your driver's license are not acceptable.

$\mathcal{L}$EISURE $\mathcal{T}$IME

From deep-sea fishing to limbo dancing, there's plenty in Costa Rica to occupy your leisure time. In lively San Jose you'll find open-air restaurants, bars, and nightclubs on every corner. Costa Ricans, as you'll discover, love to party. And they sure know how to dance. Catch the action at famed clubs like El Gran Parqueo and Higuerones, both in the suburb of San Rafael de Desamparados. For quieter fun, try sipping a tall fruit drink on the patio of the Hotel Grano do Oro or taking in some cool jazz at the Shakespeare Bar.

If you're a risk taker, you can try your luck at the craps and roulette tables in the two dozen gambling casinos throughout Costa Rica. Or, if you'd rather cool down with a flick, you'll have plenty of opportunities. For some reason, Costa Rica boasts more movie houses per capita than any nation on earth. Entertainment prices in Costa Rica tend to be far lower than in the United States. Expect to pay $5 for dinner in a restaurant, $3.25 for a movie, $5 to go dancing, and $13 for a live concert.

If reading is more your speed, you'll have three libraries from which to choose in San Jose alone. Plus, there are daily arrivals of the *Miami Herald*, *New York Times*, and other American newspapers, along with two English-language papers published in San Jose (the *Tico Times* is the largest newspaper published in Central America).

$\mathcal{A}$DDITIONAL $\mathcal{R}$ESOURCES

Costa Rica Embassy
2114 S St. NW, Washington, D.C. 20008; 202/328-6628

Costa Rica Consulates General

185 N. Wabash Ave., Suite 1123, Chicago, IL 60601; 312/263-2772

4532 W. Napolean Ave., Metairie, LA 70001; 504/581-6800

1732 Yenisey St., Rio Piedras, San Juan, PR 00927; 787/282-6747

1600 Northwest Le Jeune Rd., Suite 102, Miami, FL 33126;
   305/871-7485

1870 The Exchange, Suite 100, Atlanta, GA 30339; 770/951-7025

80 Wall St., #718, New York, NY 10005; 212/425-2620

870 Market St., Suite 647, San Francisco, CA 94102; 415/392-8488

1605 W. Olympic Blvd. Suite 400, San Diego, CA 90015, 213/380-
   7915.

Useful Web Site

www.wtgonline.com/country/cr/gen.html

Czech Republic

by JOHN LYONS-GOULD

For those who want to enjoy traditional European city life at a fraction of the cost of Paris, world-class skiing, and a beautiful countryside dotted with grand spas, the Czech Republic is hard to beat. Rich food, some of the best beer in the world, good transportation and medical facilities, low crime rates, and an exciting cultural life round out the list of reasons people give for retiring here.

The Czech Republic, the homeland of Franz Kafka and the stomping grounds of Ernest Hemingway, is once again attracting a world-class literary community. Publications, artists, and entrepreneurs are flourishing here in a new-found freedom left by the fall of communism six years ago. And an emerging free-market economy offers tremendous opportunities and incentives for foreign investors.

At the Rudolfinum Concert Hall in Prague, retirees can absorb every note of Dvořák's *New World Symphony*, performed by the Czech Philharmonic in its native city. Or retirees can leave the medieval streets of Prague for the ancient lands of Bohemia and Moravia, stopping along the way to admire Gothic and Baroque churches and Renaissance castles.

There are, however, some caveats for potential retirees, especially those who choose the country's capital and largest city, Prague.

Although housing and living costs are cheaper in Prague than in other major European cities, finding an affordable place to live here is a lesson in patience and fortitude. Competition is stiff, terms can be confusing, and frustrations can run high. Once you find a place, you're ready for round two—becoming a resident—which has come to resemble something of an endurance event on paper. And while the Czech Republic is in many respects artful and naturally beautiful, Prague has the worst air pollution in Europe, especially in winter, when people with respiratory problems are urged to leave the city. Finally, while Czech winters are mild in comparison to those in many European countries, winter is a definite season to contend with for five months of the year here.

As the so-called "Roof of Europe," the Czech Republic gets its water from only rain and snowfall; all rivers that begin here drain into neighboring countries. The Danube and the Moldava flow to the Black Sea, and the Elbe ("Labe" to the Czechs) flows to the Baltic Sea.

Prague is the seat of power—and most everything else in the Czech Republic. The city is at its best during the Prague Spring Music Festival. It's not bad in summer either, when people take to the outdoors, lingering at sidewalk cafés, especially along the Vaclavske namesti.

Prague is made for walking, and visitors should take time to tromp its seven romantic hills on both sides of the River Vlatva. The most famous bridge across the river is the Baroque Karluv Most (Charles Bridge), a fourteenth-century landmark with rows of Baroque statues on either side and two watchtowers. The Old Town Hall clock features fifteenth-century mechanical figures of Christ, the apostles, and the Angel of Death (who tolls the hour). Nearby are the famous Carolinium (Charles University, established in 1371), the Tyl Theater, and the Powder Tower, part of the gate to the new town.

Other popular travel destinations in the Czech Republic include the cities of Brno, Spindleruv, and Mlyn in the Krkonose Mountains, Strbske Pleo in the High Tatras, and Karlovy Vary (formerly Karlsbad) and Marianske Lazne (formerly Marienbad), two of the country's most famous spas.

$\mathcal{T}$HE $\mathcal{C}$ULTURE AND $\mathcal{P}$EOPLE OF THE $\mathcal{C}$ZECH $\mathcal{R}$EPUBLIC

Czech home life is a relatively private affair. Visitors—even relatives and close friends—usually call ahead before dropping in and observe fairly formal etiquette. Friends usually socialize in pubs or coffeehouses and consider an invitation to a home-cooked dinner a real honor.

Domestic roles are very traditional: women cook and men start what little conversation takes place at meals. Showing respect is foremost among Czechs. People address one another by title and last name in public. There is a genuine warmth behind all this formality, though, and most expatriates have wonderful things to say about the country's citizens.

One would think, with all the churches gracing the city's skyline, that the people of the Czech Republic are mostly religious. In reality, almost half of the country's residents consider themselves atheist.

Learn the Language Although the Czech language is Slavic— related to Ukrainian and Russian—its alphabet is Western. So you will be able to read signs and addresses. Keep in mind that the letters *l* and *r* are vowels (which explains why the language looks unpronounceable). *H* is pronounced like the *ch* in *loch*. *C* is pronounced like *ts*.

Many people in the Czech Republic speak English. However, nothing gets a smile faster than a foreigner in Prague who can utter at least a few well-timed Czech words or phrases—because most Czechs understand how difficult their language can be for Westerners. Take time to learn the basics like *prosim* (please), *dekuji* (thank you), *dobry den* (hello), and, of course, *jedno pivo* (one beer).

There are a number of schools in Prague where English is the language of instruction and retirees can begin to wrestle with the formidable opponent that is the Czech language. These include the International School of Prague, the English College in Prague, and the English International School.

A Brief History of the Czech Republic   Dig in and enjoy one of Europe's most historic destinations, originally settled by the Celts around the fourth century B.C. The region saw the arrival of slaves and Christian missionaries before the peak of the Kingdom of Bohemia in the fourteenth century.

The year 1918 marked the formation of the independent state of Czechs and Slovaks, which gave way to German occupation from 1939 to 1945 and a communist takeover in 1948. The Communist Party's promise to build "socialism with a human face" was abandoned in 1968 when the Soviet Union led an invasion of Czechoslovakia.

The fall of the communist regime sparked new growth and economic changes in the region. The split of Czechoslovakia in 1993 created the Czech Republic and Slovakia and gave the Czech people a promising, if somewhat challenging, future.

Enjoy New Traditions   The cuisine of the Czech Republic is an important part of the culture and is influenced by neighboring peoples. You'll find roast goose, sauerkraut, and dumplings from Germany; schnitzels from Vienna; goulash from Hungary; and sour cream, vinegar, and pickles from the East.

Notice something missing? That would be fresh vegetables, grains, and other members of the cholesterol-free family. A typical Czech dish like *Veprovas Knedlikem a se zelim*—roast pork served with sauerkraut and dumplings—is usually followed by a cousin of strudel or fruit-filled dumplings.

If you're looking for the best of what the Czech Republic has to offer the world, you need look no farther than the closest pub in Prague. Two of the most famous and celebrated beers in the world, Pilsner Urquell and Budwieser Budvar, are brewed in the Czech

Republic. Lager was invented here, and the local brews are considered national treasures.

A good way to jump in and get your palate wet (so to speak) is to spend time in one of many cafés and tearooms in and around Prague. Try Cafe Milena, run by the Franz Kafka Society; enjoy the smoke-free Kavarna ve Sternberskem palaci after viewing the old masters at the National Gallery; or try Hemingway's purported favorite drink (rum *moqito*) at La Cubana Cafe Bar.

To help lighten up the winter months, Czechs hold numerous balls—from informal dances to black-tie affairs. They celebrate Christmas on December 24 with carp and potato salad. St. Nick brings toys to children on December 6, while the parents go out and party.

Spring brings the renowned Prague Spring Music Festival (one of many classical music festivals) and the pagan-based Burning of Witches, celebrated with backyard bonfires. Summer is the time for international film festivals in Karlovy Vary and Prague and folk festivals in many towns. Fall is a time to celebrate the harvest of grapes and the young wine called Burcak, along with medieval and Renaissance festivals in North Bohemia towns.

Develop Your Own Cultural Identity   Some 30,000 American expatriates and retirees live and work in Prague. While you'll want to get to know other Americans, don't ignore the reason you came to the Czech Republic in the first place. Meet the challenges of assimilating into a new culture head-on, with patience and a willingness to try new things.

When you do crave the comforts of home, spend some time at the Globe Bookstore for new and used English-language books, housing resources, and a popular café frequented by writers and travelers. Zahranicni Literatura on Gorkeho namesti 6 also offers a good selection of English and American paperbacks. Finally, check out the U.S. Embassy's Cultural Centre and Library at Hybernská 7, complete with American books, magazines, newspapers, cultural programs, and occasional exhibits.

ℛECOMMENDED ℒIVING 𝒜REAS

Since Prague is the cultural and economic heart of the Czech Republic, most expatriates and retirees live in this capital city of just over 1.2 million people (approximately one-tenth of the country's population). The city is divided into 10 districts (similar to the *arrondissements* in Paris). The smallest districts—Prague 1, 2, and 3—lie at the center of the city, with the highest real estate prices and tourist traffic in Prague 1, the city's cultural core. The four outlying districts offer the best and most affordable living arrangements for expatriates.

Prague 1 includes Old Town, Malá Strana (the Little Quarter), and the Castle District. These neighborhoods are historic and extremely beautiful, but also plagued by the worst air pollution in the city, parking difficulties, and noisy nights.

The residential neighborhoods of Vinohrady and New Town in Prague 2 offer views of the river, nearby entertainment and shopping, and convenient transportation, which is why housing is particularly hard to find here. Zizkov, an historically working-class area, constitutes the majority of Prague 3, which is also central to most shopping, entertainment, and transportation.

There are pleasant villas in the further reaches of Prague 4 and good deals on apartment buildings near the border of Prague 2 in this sector. However, transportation is not as accessible in Prague 4, and the area contains tracts of *panelák* (government housing), which can be dreary to look at.

Prague 5 boasts nice parks and relatively clean air in a good transportation corridor. Housing here ranges from sketchy in areas of Smíchov near the river to grand on the hillsides of Barrandov.

Next to Prague 1, Prague 6 is considered the most desirable living area. The sector has good housing and good airport access. It is home to many foreign businesspeople, as well as embassies, parks, and international schools—which is why many families choose to live here and why housing prices are so high.

The mixed commercial and residential areas of Holsovice and Letná hug the River Vltava in Prague 7, where large impressive parks and a zoo dominate the environment. North and northeast of center, Prague 8 and 9 are significantly removed from the heart of Prague and thus seem unattractive to many home buyers and renters. But you can find better real estate deals here than any other place in the city. Finally, Prague 10 seems to spread east and southeast forever and gets increasingly industrial as it goes. However, the inner parts of Prague 10 contain nice apartment buildings, detached homes, and row houses similar to those in Vinohrady.

Renting in the Czech Republic

Finding a place to live is a prerequisite to applying for residency in the Czech Republic. And aside from establishing residency, finding housing in Prague is one of the most frustrating experiences you will have here.

Properties range from one-room efficiencies to countryside castles. Communist-era pre-fab housing can be less than satisfactory, fixtures won't always work, and prices may be higher than you anticipated. The upside to the housing search is that everyone faces the same challenges, and the shared frustration actually fosters a sense of community among residents.

Work with a translator if you are not fluent in the language and expect to see listings like these:

- Prague 2: 134-square-meter, three-bedroom flat, terrace, very nice. $2,100.
- Prague 6: Two- and three-bedroom apartments. Recently reconstructed to high standard. Garage parking. $960 and $1,500.
- Mala Stana: Riverfront. Seven flats available in Prague's newest high-end development. Beautiful views, open plans, landscaped interior courtyard, garage, concierge simply outstanding. Prices start at $1,500.

In addition to rent, expect to pay about $30 to $60 per month for gas, oil, water, sewage, and trash collection. You can pay cash at the local post office for these services, or you can make arrangements with your landlord to have the charges included in your monthly rent payment.

As in most places, one of the best ways to find housing in Prague is by word of mouth, even from strangers you ask on the street. If you have a job, ask your coworkers if they know about any apartments. If you have a job pending, ask your employer to help you find housing as part of your work agreement.

Instead of looking for rental ads, put your own "Flat Wanted" notice on bulletin boards in places frequented by foreigners, including the Globe Bookstore and Coffeehouse, Radost FX, the British Council, and Meduza Cafe. Don't forget full-service Laundromats like Laundryland, Vinohrdaska, and Prague Laundromat in Prague 2 and Laundry Kings in Prague 6.

You may also want to advertise for housing in the Czech-language *Announce B-Edition*, a newspaper published three times a week. Be sure to hire a good Czech translator before placing your ad. You can also advertise in English in the *Prague Post*, but then your price quotes will come in dollars—you'll get a better deal if you agree on rent in Czech currency.

If money is a limiting factor, consider renting a room in a Czech family flat. You'll give up some freedom and privacy, but the positives of living with an extended family can be tremendous—and rent can be significantly cheaper.

If you have the money, hire a real estate agent who finds flats and arranges leases. Rent will be higher and you will pay a commission, but having a middleperson working out details with a landlord can save you a lot of time and frustration. Real estate firms specializing in renting to foreigners in Prague include Tide Reality sro, Realit Konzult, Shell Realty Corporation, City of Prague Accommodation Service, Nest Realty, Lexxus People and Places, and Sorent Reality.

BUYING REAL ESTATE

You can't buy real estate in the Czech Republic until your residence visa comes through. When you are ready to buy, several real estate agencies handle home sales and employ English-speaking staff members. These include Rossignol Partners Ltd., Starometske nam. 17, 102 00 Prague 1; tel. (42) (02) 2421-3077; fax (42) (02) 2422-1838; and Nexus Europe, Belgicka 36, 120 00, Prague 2; tel. (42) (02) 254-704; fax (42) (02) 253-471.

For an extensive listing of properties in the Prague area, you can subscribe to the monthly *Prague Realty Guide*. A one-year subscription is $70. Expect to see listings similar to the following:

* Row houses: Two large three-bedroom homes with a great location. Two-car garage. Easy access to the center of Prague. $168,000.
* Duplex in Prague 8: Garden, 300 square meters. Three bedrooms, one bathroom. $114,000.
* House in Prague 4: House with two bedrooms. To this house belongs a barn. $78,000.

Should you decide to buy property in the Czech Republic, be careful. Currently, title insurance does not exist here, nor do deeds. Ownership of property is transferred through contractual listings in the National Register. Ownership disputes are not uncommon, partially due to poor record keeping and a confusing system of marking property boundaries. However, buying quality real estate in the Czech Republic at reasonable rates is not impossible. It just takes time, careful research, and the help of people who can guide you to informed decisions.

COST OF LIVING

Retirees report being able to live in Prague for under $1,500 a month per couple. Prices outside the capital are 10 to 20 percent lower.

When it comes to consumer goods, quality and supply may fall short. Fresh fruits and vegetables, often imported, are limited in Prague and are available only in season. Supplies of perishables are sporadic, and the quality of both meat and vegetables varies greatly. Local dairy products are good, although milk may spoil quickly since it is not refrigerated during distribution.

If you are looking for foreign foods, Little Caesar's Pizza, or other tastes of home, the best place to shop is probably Tesco in Prague 1, which serves as a combination department and grocery store. Kotva in Prague 1 is another good market/department store.

The government store, Tuzex, maintains outlets in major cities and sells a limited variety of imported goods, including food, liquor, cigarettes, and clothing. Local products are substantially cheaper through Tuzex than through other sources.

Here's what you can expect to pay for some everyday items in the Czech Republic:

gasoline	$3.20/gallon	coffee	$6.30/pound
movie ticket	$2	milk	$2/pound
bottle of beer	$.50	chicken	$1.15/pound
maid service	$3.50/hour	eggs	$1.20/dozen
bananas	$.36/pound	video rental	$7
loaf of bread	$1.20	compact disc	$21
steak	$3.20/pound	woman's haircut	$16
tomatoes	$.60/pound		

$\mathcal{D}$AY-TO-DAY $\mathcal{L}$IVING $\mathcal{C}$ONCERNS

Although violent crime and car theft have risen in the past few years, Prague is relatively safe, particularly in comparison to the United States. Pickpockets are the most common threat. Don't carry your wallet in your back pocket, do keep money and identification in separate places, and do keep photocopies of passports and other documents at home or at your hotel.

After more than 40 years of censorship, the press in the Czech Republic is now ranked as one of the best in the world, with more than 90 national and regional daily periodicals. The dual state and private broadcasting system continues to grow as investors and advertising dollars increase.

There are a few coin-operated pay phones in Prague, which require phone cards for operation. Around 45 percent of homes in the republic currently have phone service.

$\mathcal{T}$AXES

The Czech government ushered in a new tax system in 1996, based on the tax principles of the European Community. Income taxation is simple. If you stay in the republic for less than 183 days, you'll pay personal income tax only on income earned in the country. If you stay longer, you'll pay tax on your entire income for the year. Income is taxed on a sliding scale, from 15 to 40 percent.

The basic value-added tax (VAT) rate of 22 percent applies to all goods ordered in the republic, but not to exported goods. Most food, fuels, pharmaceuticals, and services are taxed at 5 percent. Other taxes include road, property, gift, and inheritance taxes. The 39 percent corporate income tax rate is expected to fall.

Contact the American Center for Culture and Commerce or the British and American Chambers of Commerce for updated information on taxes in the Czech Republic.

$\mathcal{M}$AKING THE $\mathcal{M}$OVE

You must have a valid passport to enter the Czech Republic. You don't need a visa if you're staying less than 30 days. With a visa, your stay cannot exceed 180 days (a rule that prompts many foreigners to leave the country briefly every three months to get their passports stamped).

Currently, you must find a place to live before you can apply for permanent residence, and your local address must be indicated on the application. (Those lucky enough to have relatives in the Czech Republic can qualify if relatives agree to house them for a time.)

The Czech Ministry has set up an automated, multilingual help line, (42) (02) 6144-1119, to get you started on your residency application. You will still need to complete the application form in Czech and submit the following:

* Documentation of reason for stay (offer of work, marriage license, etc.)
* Proof of monthly income or bank account balance
* Notarized affidavit from a landlord or other proof of housing
* Certification of a clean criminal record
* Translated birth certificate

You might also need a doctor's statement showing you to be free of certain infectious diseases.

Be aware that the application, if approved, gives you residency for only one year or less, depending on your visa. If you want to establish permanent residency or Czech citizenship, your application will have to be based on family reunion, marriage, asylum, or support of the international political interests of the republic.

What to Bring When you enter the Czech Republic, you may import 250 cigarettes or the equivalent in tobacco, one liter of wine, one liter of spirits, and up to 1,000 kilograms of gifts duty-free. If you bring valuables, such as a camera, be sure to carry your receipt—or you may have to pay duty on the items when you leave.

Be sure to bring important personal items that may not be readily available in a foreign country. In the Czech Republic especially, you'll want a six-month supply of medications you take regularly, eyewear and contact-lens solution, and copies of prescriptions and medical and dental records.

What About Pets? As crazy as it may sound, your pet will need its own animal passport with photo, as well as a certificate of health from your veterinarian. Veterinarians are good and inexpensive in Prague, and Czechs, for the most part, are great dog lovers.

MEDICAL CARE

Routine and emergency medical care is adequate in Prague, but a shortage of hospital beds, lack of organization, and the language barrier may pose problems for you. On the positive side, costs for care and medicines are much lower than those in the United States. If you need emergency medical attention, dial 155 (toll free) on any phone for an ambulance, or take a taxi to Na Homolce Hospital in Prague 5.

Government-sponsored medical care for Czechs and for residents with Czech health insurance is free, but funding for facilities is low and physicians are generally underpaid. Many physicians leave after their required government service and look for work in the private sector.

Private clinics, aimed at foreigners with private insurance, are now common in Prague—with English-speaking staff, Western-style care, and higher fees. The Charles University Faculty Polyclinic has a foreigners' section, staffed by an English-speaking general practitioner, pediatrician, and dentist. A doctor is on call at all times. Other clinics that cater to foreigners include the American Medical Center in Prague 7, First Medical Clinic of Prague in Prague 2, Polyclinic at Narodni in Prague 1, and the Canadian Medical Center in Prague 6. There are also some Western-trained doctors with private practices in Prague, but they are hard to find and may not accept insurance or credit cards.

Health Insurance   Your residency permit in the Czech Republic entitles you to state health insurance that is adequate for most foreign residents. Doctor visits are free when you show your insurance card, and prescriptions are significantly discounted.

If you do not qualify for Czech insurance, make sure you obtain an international insurance policy. Your current carrier should be able to help with the process.

Medications   Since the Czech equivalents of American medications are hard to identify and locate, bring a good supply of necessary medicines with you, or plan to order via mail. The U.S. Army Hospital Pharmacy in Nuremburg, Germany, is a good source for medications.

Look in the front of the yellow pages to find a list of *lekarnas* (pharmacies) in Prague that are open 24 hours. The pharmacy at Ma prikope 7 is one of them. Pharmacies take turns staying open late in Slovakia. Look for a list posted on each front door. For after-hours service, ring the bell.

$\mathcal{F}$INANCIAL $\mathcal{M}$ATTERS

Upon arriving, you'll convert your dollars to Czech crowns. Keep the original exchange receipts so that when you leave, bankers won't think you changed money on the black market (if you are caught using the black market, you could be deported). It is illegal to buy crowns abroad and bring them into the country.

When exchanging money, stick with major banks. They charge about 2 percent commission, provided you meet the minimum transaction amount. Steer clear of exchange outlets around Prague that might seem convenient but have higher commissions and hidden fees. Remember that changing money on the streets is illegal.

Most tourist-oriented businesses accept credit cards, although grocery stores, pharmacies, and gas stations do not. Most businesses do not accept personal checks. Traveler's checks are usually accepted only by banks and exchange offices. You can exchange American Express traveler's checks at the Amex office without paying a commission. Many banks offer access to international Cirrus and Plus networks, but ask your bank in the United States about finance charges first.

Banking Banks are open Monday through Friday 7:30 to 3:30, with an hour off for lunch. At present, the largest and most stable Czech banks include Komercni banka, Ceska sporitelna, Ceskoslovenska obchodni banka, and Zivnostenska banka.

You can open an account at Zivnostenska banka—all it takes is a passport and some patience. Many banks will require you to change your dollars into Tuzex bonds or Czech currency before opening an account.

Advice for Foreign Entrepreneurs Since 1989 and the fall of communism, the Czech Republic has implemented an aggressive program to reintroduce a market economy, including liberalization of trade policies, internal convertibility of currency, privatization programs, and tax reform. Most indicators say that these measures are working and that the Czech economic transformation is nearly complete. Encouraging signs include a prevailing private sector, a stabilized exchange rate, controlled inflation, and increasing market demand.

Liberal economic policies, a highly skilled labor force, wage controls, low production costs, and an exchange rate favorable for export businesses have attracted many foreign investors to the Czech Republic in the past 10 years. Multinational corporations such as Coca-Cola, Proctor and Gamble, and Volkswagen have opened production plants in the area. Careful research of emerging markets can lead to strong investment opportunities for retirees as well.

TRANSPORTATION

Prague's only airport is just three miles from the city center, at the end of the A bus line. Cedaz express airport buses, Belinda shuttle company (look for the line of white cars), and taxis will take you anywhere you want to go in Prague for reasonable rates.

The best way to get around Prague is by tram and metro line. You can purchase tickets at automats, metro stations, and local Trafika shops. "Season tickets" are good for 3, 7, and 15 days. The Karlovo Namesti, Muzeum, Mustek, and Nadrazi Holesovice metro stations provide maps and information in English. Payment is based on the honor system, but plainclothes ticket checkers routinely stop commuters to verify payment.

Taxi drivers can charge any fare they please in Prague, as long as their rates are posted. Call for a cab in advance when possible and arrange a price over the phone. For usually reliable service with English-speaking dispatchers, use AAA Taxi or ProfiTaxi.

To drive in the Czech Republic you must have liability insurance, available from from the Czechoslovakian Insurance Company at reasonable rates. The insurance is valid throughout Europe. A valid U.S. driver's license enables you to drive legally in the Czech Republic, but an international license is required in some neighboring countries and is recommended. It is available from the AAA.

For a nominal fee and with a valid foreign license, you can get a Czech driver's license (which also serves as an international license and is valid indefinitely) from the embassy. Without a valid license, you'll need to take a lengthy and expensive driver's training course and a thorough exam.

Once you're on the road, local maps and street signs use Czech spellings that aren't always easily associated with the English spellings used in guidebooks. Take your time and learn the basic Czech spellings of things like Old Town (Stare Mesto), Main Station (Hlavni nadrazi), and Prague Castle (Hradcany).

$\mathcal{L}$EISURE $\mathcal{T}$IME

Lakes and rivers are everywhere in the Czech Republic and Slovakia, but it's difficult to rent a boat. However, tour companies will take you for rides on the Vltava, Luznice, and Sazava Rivers. The Lipenska and Orlicka Dams in Southern Bohemia and Vranovska Dam in Southern Moravia boast ideal conditions for sailing and windsurfing.

There are good golf courses near Prague and horseback riding in the countryside. The Slovak mountains offer great kayaking and fishing. For river fishing, you'll need a license, valid for a year, as well as a permit, valid for a day, week, month, or year. You can get a fishing license at the local office of the Czech National Tourist Organization.

Czech and Slovakia are also perfect for hikers. Paths lead you through beautiful countryside and into lovely little towns. Main paths are marked red, and the less-traveled ones are marked yellow.

Spas in the Czech Republic and Slovakia are world-renowned for the beauty of their surroundings. They are free with a physician's prescription. Without one, they are still very cheap. Most are located in lovely old manor houses and offer concerts, horseback riding, tennis, fishing, swimming, hunting, and skiing. Medical care at spas is excellent. Packages range from $40 to $70 per day.

Marianske Lazne (Marienbad) in western Bohemia is the most beautiful spa in central Europe. Lovely parks, gardens, and forests surround the facility. Karlovy Vary, also in Bohemia and once known as Karlsbad, is the most famous Czech spa. Peter the Great, Beethoven, Goethe, Liszt, and Karl Marx are among those who have taken its waters. The two spas also have the best golf courses in the country.

Outstanding downhill and cross-country skiing await you in the Krkonose ski areas of Pec pod Snezkou, Spindleruv, Mlyn, and Harachov, as well as in the Sumava, Jizera, Jeseniky, and Krusne Mountains. You can rent skis through hotels and a few recreational organizations.

For spectators and players alike, football (soccer) is by far the most popular sport in the country. Historically, Czechoslovakia's national ice-hockey teams have ranked among the top teams in the world. But Czech hockey has lost a number of its best players recently to the NHL and other foreign leagues. Another popular sport, kickball, originated here. It is similar to volleyball but requires players to kick the ball over a low net.

Shopping   Prague is by no means a mecca for shoppers, but more and more street markets and boutiques are opening up to serve the tourist industry. High-quality Bohemian crystal is available most everywhere throughout the country, and antiques dealers in Old Town and the Lesser Quarter offer some valuable and interesting pieces. But beware of fakes and inquire about pieces needing an export license.

ADDITIONAL RESOURCES

General Information
Czech Embassy, 3900 Linnean Ave. NW, Washington, D.C.,
   202/274-9100

Directories and Newspapers
Czech Yellow Pages: cross-referenced in English and German to
   help you find just about anything in Prague; delivered free to all
   homes
Prague Naturally: An English guide to health services, nutrition, and
   recreation in the Czech Republic; sold for $4 in travel agencies
   and bookstores
Prague Post: one of the best English-language resources in the Czech
   Republic, offering everything from news to property listings to
   personal ads
Resources: a directory of names and numbers that is updated quarterly.
   Expatriates doing business in Prague rely on it for well-organized,

easy-to-find information on everything from foreign companies to lawyers to fine dining.

Useful Web sites
www.radio.cz
www.czechsite.com/index.shtml
www.timeout.com/prague/
www.czech.cz/washington/

Ecuador

by JEFFREY LAIGN

If Ecuador isn't on your list of retirement options, it should be. Sandwiched between Colombia and Peru on the Pacific coast of South America, this small but magnificently diverse South American country offers everything you're looking for in a retirement haven—and much more.

The first thing you'll notice about Ecuador is its breathtaking scenery and amazingly varied terrain. It's hard to imagine that in a single destination you can enjoy lush tropical rain forests, stark deserts, sparkling beaches, and snowcapped Andean peaks. When the grand-children come to visit, you're only a few hours away from a skiing adventure or a jungle trek.

And, of course, there are the Galapagos. Upon these desolate lava piles in the Pacific, Darwin confirmed his theory of natural selection. If you retire in Ecuador you can spend countless hours logging the evolution of mammoth tortoises, flightless cormorants, marine iguanas, and other wild anomalies.

Despite its topographical extremes, Ecuador, for the most part, enjoys springlike weather year-round. The highest recorded temperature in Quito, the nation's capital, is 86 degrees Fahrenheit; the lowest, 32 degrees.

Seasonal weather here is determined not by a calendar but by altitude. The higher you go, the cooler it gets. Travel down to the eastern jungles and the temperature climbs with the humidity level.

Picture-perfect scenery and near-perfect weather are not the only reasons to consider Ecuador as a retirement home. Compared with neighboring countries, Ecuador is politically and economically stable.

What's more, you'll discover prices here that you haven't seen since the 1950s. That means your cost of living in Ecuador will be less than half of what it is in the United States. Many of the 10,000 or so foreigners who have chosen to make Ecuador their second home, in fact, live well for under $12,000 a year.

There are disadvantages to living anywhere, but in Ecuador the drawbacks are relatively minor. Occasionally a volcano flares up, or the country may revisit a long-standing border dispute with Peru. And, as everywhere, Ecuador has its crime problem, although it's not serious. Quito is quite safe unless you're walking around in the Old City at night. Be aware that pickpockets sometimes prowl the streets here, as they do in Guayaquil. Crime in suburbs and outlying areas is rare, and violent crime anywhere in Ecuador is practically unheard of.

The Lay of the Land   Ecuador's name derives from the Spanish word for equator, the invisible line that divides the Earth horizontally into northern and southern hemispheres and runs across Ecuador. The Andes Mountains, which cross Ecuador from north to south, divide the country into four distinct regions, each with its own climate and environment.

In the Costa (lowlands) region of Ecuador, the climate is warm, with average temperatures ranging from 76 to 90 degrees Fahrenheit. During the rainy season, from December to May, the region is warm and very humid.

In the Sierra (highlands), temperatures are determined by the altitude. A subtropical climate prevails in the Andean valleys; at higher altitudes, the weather is more springlike, although nights can be chilly.

The Andes feature lofty volcanic peaks such as Chimborazo (at 20,696 feet, nearly as high as Mount Everest) and Cotopaxi (at 19,614 feet, the highest active volcano in the world).

The Oriente (Amazon) region normally has a warm, humid, rainy climate. The average temperature here ranges from 72 to 80 degrees.

The Galapagos Islands make up the fourth region. Here the weather is warm and dry, with an average yearly temperature of 85 degrees.

Flora and Fauna As you might expect with such climate variations, Ecuador has a vast and extremely diverse number of plants and animals. Although it's only the size of Nevada, Ecuador is one of the world's most biodiverse countries.

More than 25,000 species of vascular plants are found here— more than in all of North America and 10 percent of the species known in the world. The Andes region alone supports more than 1,000 species, and 800 species have been collected in the Amazon basin and along the coast.

Ecuador also is home to 320 species of mammals, 350 species of reptiles, 375 species of amphibians, 700 freshwater fish species, and 450 species of marine fish. About 18 percent of all known bird species call Ecuador home, giving it the densest bird population in the world.

THE CULTURE AND PEOPLE OF ECUADOR

Politically and socially, Ecuador has much to offer foreign retirees. A presidential republic, Ecuador enjoys a stable democracy based on the Roman-French tradition of civil law. Congress is empowered to pass laws, and courts must uphold them.

The country's population numbers approximately 12 million, about half of whom are mestizo, descended from Europeans and Indians. The other half are of unmixed Indian, Spanish, and African descent.

Ecuador maintains no official religion, but 95 percent of Ecuadorians are Roman Catholic. Spanish is the official language, but you'll frequently hear a number of native languages, including Quechua and Shuar. About 88 percent of the population is literate.

A Brief History of Ecuador   The original inhabitants of Ecuador were the Incas, who built one of the world's great empires. A vast asphalt-covered road linked Quito, the northern capital of the empire, with Cuzco, the southern capital, in Peru.

You can see remnants of that mighty empire at Ingapirca, the only major Incan ruin left in Ecuador. Once the residence of Incan emperor Huayna Capac, Ingapirca was built during the fifteenth century and is believed to have been a religious center as well as a fortress.

Long before the arrival of the Incas, the Canari tribe worshipped the moon at this location. Later, Incan sun worshippers took full advantage of Ingapirca's topography, which permits precise observation of the stars.

The glory that was the Inca empire came to an end in 1532, when Spanish conquistadors subdued the Indians. For the next three centuries, Ecuador remained under colonial rule.

In 1822 Ecuadorians won their independence from Spain with the help of Venezuelan general Simon Bolivar, South America's great liberator. Ecuador then became part of the Republic of Greater Columbia. In 1830 Ecuador seceded and became a separate republic.

Modern Ecuador   Today Ecuador offers a fascinating mix of old and new. Quito is a lively city full of restaurants, bars, and nightclubs. But in and around the city you'll see Indians dressed much as they were when the Spanish arrived here.

The first thing you'll notice about the Indians is that many sport skillfully woven Panama hats, which remain miraculously free of wrinkles whether rolled in a ball or squashed by a truck. The world-famous hats originated not in Panama but in the Ecuadorian coastal town of Montecristi. At the turn of the century, Ecuador shipped thousands of the sun-blocking hats to workers on the Panama Canal, hence the name.

Learn the Language Although you'll encounter many Ecuadorians who speak, or at least understand, English, you'll fare much better in this country if you brush up on your Spanish. Before leaving home, consider enrolling in a language school such as Berlitz, which maintains offices in major cities throughout the United States.

RECOMMENDED LIVING AREAS

Quito In the wake of the Spanish conquest, Quito's inherent beauty attracted a wealth of European artists, painters, and architects, who set about building the colonial city that stands today. The Indians they hired as apprentices soon began to display their own unique talents, and in less than 15 years the Indians supplanted their Spanish instructors as Ecuador's master craftsmen. Today you can see classic examples of Indian art adorning the city's 87 churches, monasteries, and other buildings dating from the colonial era.

Quito is an eclectic city of 1.1 million. Around the kaleidoscopic Plaza de Independencia you can spend hours people-watching, as Indian women in colorful shawls lug bundles on their backs, artisans display their crafts, and businessmen hurry off to work. In city parks, old men relax on benches and smoke cigarettes, as children play nearby amid many flowering trees.

Quito is a cosmopolitan city with excellent restaurants representative of many cultures—from Italian, Spanish, and French to typical Ecuadorian. The city's many shops, boutiques, bookstores, and other urban amenities make it an interesting and desirable place to relocate.

Guayaquil With a population of 1.8 million, Guayaquil is Ecuador's largest city. This coastal town also is the country's industrial and commercial metropolis, as well as the traditional home of most of the country's economic institutions.

Guayaquil may not be the world's greatest tourist destination, but it's considered Ecuador's most "Western" city in temperament and style, which is why some U.S. retirees—especially those wishing to operate businesses—choose to settle here.

On the western side of the Rio Guyas, along the innermost reaches of the gulf, Guayaquil is conveniently located en route from Peru to the mountains, or as a point of departure for the Galapagos. Two hundred years ago Guayaquil was an arena of political conflict during the country's struggle for independence. Today Guayaquil is a thriving metropolis offering a wide range of hotels and excellent restaurants.

The Malecon, a promenade along the waterfront, bustles with pedestrians and cars on one side and a procession of boats on the other. This is where you'll find most of the government and municipal buildings. At sunset, many locals take their evening constitutionals along the Malecon, ending at the clock tower on Avenida 10 de Agosto.

Guayaquil is busy 24 hours a day. And its status as Ecuador's most active city finds expression in its exciting nightlife. You won't find as much folkloric dancing here as in other Ecuadorian towns, but there's plenty of Western-style entertainment including discos, movie theaters, and nightclubs. The city's main square is Plaza Centennario, where a monument to the heroes of national independence has stood since 1920.

Cuenca Cuenca, Ecuador's third-largest city (population 275,000), has the feel of Old Spain with its narrow, winding, shop-filled streets. The Tomebamba River skirts the old section of this colonial city. Ancient, ochre-colored wooden buildings cling precariously to a towering bluff, while clusters of women wash their clothes on mounds on emerald-green grass below.

Because many Ecuadorians consider it remote, Cuenca is over-looked by the average tourist, making it all the more attractive as a retirement home. The city's skyline is not cluttered with high-rise towers or condominiums. Instead, it gleams with church domes. Cobblestone streets lined with red-tiled adobe buildings lead to flower-filled plazas.

The Cathedral Nueva dominates Calderon Park in the heart of the city. Construction began on the building in 1880, but it remains unfinished because of architectural miscalculations. Bells imported from Germany still stand at the entrance to the nave.

Renting in Ecuador

Quito offers a number of good rental prospects. At Post Avenida Gonzalo Suarez near the Intercontinental Quito Hotel, for example, you can rent a new, beautifully furnished two-bedroom, two-bathroom apartment with fantastic views of surrounding mountains for $500 to $800 a month.

In other, less-trendy areas, the same type of apartment will rent for as little as $300. You may not have the location, but the views are generally just as pleasant. In Cuenca, costs are even lower. A Spanish-style house with red-tiled roof, patio, and garden might set you back a mere $250 a month.

Buying Real Estate

Location will play a large role in determining the price you pay for a home in Ecuador. In the center of cosmopolitan Quito, home prices can rival those of many cities in California. But just 20 minutes away you can buy an unfurnished two-bedroom, two-bathroom apartment with kitchen, living room, dining room, and servants' quarters for about $30,000. Good places to look are in the Valley of Chillos and in Conocoto. In San Rafael, 30 minutes from Quito, you can buy a large home for less than $80,000. And in Vilcabamba, a similar home might start at $75,000.

How to Find Your Dream Home Here's a tip some retirees have found helpful: Look for properties that are classified as semi-commercial. They offer the best market value. And who knows? You may eventually want to start up a business from your home. If so, you'll be zoned for it.

It's also useful when seeking a home to peruse the classified section of local newspapers such as *El Comerico, El Universo, Mercurio,* and *Telegrafo.* You may or may not need a translator, depending on your familiarity with the language.

Remember that few Realtors here are likely to speak English. You'll need to speak Spanish or hire a translator. One agency that does have an English-speaking staff is Cooper y Asociados at Avenida Almagro, 1923 El Whimpeer St., Quito, tel. (593) (2) 527-272. Also try Cobira, at Avenida Republica 189 y Almagro, tel. (593) (2) 551-232.

The Buying Process Don't buy a home without the help of local experts. Hire an Ecuadorian attorney, who will conduct a thorough title search and make certain there are no encumbrances on your property. The attorney will also handle all the paperwork involved in your real estate purchase.

COST OF LIVING

You can buy almost anything in Ecuador that you currently use in the United States—from computers to cereal. Quito offers every facility you'll need, including several large shopping malls where you can find clothing, books, toys, and jewelry.

In the town of Guayaquil, major supermarkets Supermaxi and Mi Comisariato carry abundant fresh fruits, vegetables, seafood, fresh milk, and European-style yogurt. To shop at either of the two supermarket chains you must become a member. When you join, you will receive a coupon card that entitles you to a 10 percent discount on groceries.

Prices in general are far lower in Ecuador than anywhere in the United States. You can live like royalty here for $12,000 a year—far less if you watch your pennies. How much would you pay for dinner for two at a good restaurant in San Francisco? In Ecuador the bill may come to a whopping $7. Electric bills for a five- to seven-room house with full appliances often total less than $10 a month. Even a double room in a deluxe hotel is only about $65.

With prices like these, many U.S. retirees can afford to hire servants (a common practice in Ecuador): one to clean, one to drive, and another to cook. Domestic help will expect to take home about $40 a month. For more information on hiring help, contact an organization such as Agencia de Empleos San Cayetano, Sucre 544, or Agencia Comerical de Colocaciones, Benalcazar, 419, Bolivar.

Grocery prices are much lower in Ecuador than in the United States. Here's what you can expect to pay for some common grocery items:

bread	$.71/loaf	chicken	$.58/pound
sugar	$.16/pound	apples	$.37/pound
rice	$.16/pound	oranges	$.40/pound
canned soup	$1.15	bananas	$.07/pound
frozen peas	$.46	onions	$.20/pound
milk	$.88/gallon	potatoes	$.12/pound
eggs	$.53/dozen	tomatoes	$.28/pound
beefsteak	$1.07/pound		

$\mathcal{D}$AY-TO-DAY $\mathcal{L}$IVING $\mathcal{C}$ONCERNS

You'll find that living in Ecuador is not all that different from living in the United States. One cultural difference you'll enjoy once you get used to it is the observance of mid-afternoon siestas. As in most Latin American countries, shops, banks, and other places of business generally close from noon to three. That may be annoying at first, but once you settle into the more leisurely pace of Ecuadorian life you'll appreciate this time to "stop and smell the roses."

You'll also have to acquaint yourself with the metric system. Continental Ecuador is on Eastern Standard Time, and the Galapagos Islands are on Central Standard Time. There is no Daylight Savings Time in Ecuador.

Ecuador's electrical power is generated and administered by a company called INECEL, as well as private operators. Electricity is produced mainly by hydroelectric plants and a few thermoelectric plants. Current is generally 110 volts, 60 cycles, just as it is in the United States.

To call Ecuador you must dial the international access code (011 in the United States), followed by the country code (593) and the code for the city (Quito is 02, Guayaquil is 04, Cuenca is 07). When calling from abroad, dial the last digit of the city code only. Do not dial 0.

$\mathcal{T}$AXES

Under Ecuador's republican system of government, all taxes and tax exceptions must be authorized by congress. In addition, the country operates a tax-collecting agency similar to the U.S. Internal Revenue Service. Personal income tax is paid progressively on income higher than $3,800 at rates of 10 percent, 15 percent, 20 percent, and 25 percent. Capital gains tax in Ecuador is 8 percent. Value-added tax is assessed at 10 percent.

$\mathcal{M}$AKING THE $\mathcal{M}$OVE

Tourists visiting Ecuador must have a valid passport and a round-trip ticket. No visa is required if you're staying 90 days or less. To stay longer you must obtain a visa from immigration authorities before you enter the country.

If you are planning to live in Ecuador long-term, request a visa from the Ecuadorian consulate nearest you or from the Ecuadorian Embassy in Washington, D.C. Six types of visas are available. As a retiree, you'll likely be interested in Visas I, II, or III.

Applying for a Visa   Visa I is for immigrants who can support themselves on income from bonds, stocks, or other permanent overseas income. Applicants must demonstrate a monthly income of $1,000 (plus $350 per dependent over 18). To obtain this visa, you must present an original, permanent copy of your U.S. federal income tax return, which must be notarized, legalized, and authenticated by an Ecuadorian consul and the Ministry of Foreign Relations. Or you must submit an original bank-deposit record demonstrating that you have $5,000 deposited at the Central Bank of Ecuador.

Visa II is for investors in Ecuadorian real estate, money certificates, stocks, or security bonds (from state or national credit institutions) worth at least $50,000. To obtain the visa, you must show copies of property deeds and registered stocks, bonds, or trusts.

Visa III is for those people who invest at least $75,000 in industry, agriculture, cattle farming, or export businesses. Visa IV is for those who wish to perform administrative or technical functions in general or specialized industries or institutions. Visa V is for people employed in various technical professions and those working in

Ecuador under international contracts. Visa VI is for dependents of residents of Ecuador.

When applying for any of the visas, you will need to present a passport valid for at least six months from the date the visa is issued and a copy of your police record. An individual visa also covers your husband or wife, father, mother, children, brothers, sisters, and grandchildren. Brothers and male grandchildren may live as dependents until they are 18; sisters and granddaughters may live as dependents until they marry.

As for what you should bring when you relocate to Ecuador, a foreign retiree can import household goods and personal items duty-free once every three years.

MEDICAL CARE

As in many foreign countries, you should take health precautions if you plan to live in Ecuador. Most doctors recommend that you receive inoculations against typhoid, polio, tetanus, and hepatitis before you make the trip. Malaria suppressant and yellow fever inoculations are recommended if you intend to travel in the lowlands. The high altitudes of the Sierra might cause health problems for some people, especially the elderly and those with heart conditions. Also be careful about food and water. In most areas of Ecuador tap water is not fit to drink.

If you do get sick, you'll be glad to know that good health care is available in Ecuadorian cities. Most doctors in Quito, in fact, were trained in the United States or Germany. Ecuador also maintains good hospitals, but check with your American insurance company to make sure they will cover you in Ecuador.

Your best medical contact in Ecuador is Dr. Alavaro Davalos. Davalos is the attending physician for the U.S. embassy in Quito and was appointed by Queen Elizabeth II to fill the same position at the

British embassy. He holds a Ph.D. in tropical medicine and speaks excellent English. He will be happy to refer you to other qualified physicians. You can reach him at, La Colina 202 y San Ignacio; tel. (593) (2) 500-268.

$\mathscr{F}$INANCIAL $\mathscr{M}$ATTERS

Ecuador enjoys a relatively stable economy, with low labor costs and a hospitable environment for foreign investment. The government places no restrictions on foreign currency in Ecuador. Local banks offer savings accounts with interest rates that are currently as high as 25 percent for local currency.

Currency may be freely converted in Ecuador. The country has an "exchange band" system that allows Banco Central (Central Bank) to intervene in the market to adjust liquidity conditions whenever supply and demand for foreign currency are incompatible with the government's economic goals. The Financial Law of 1994 regulates all private-sector financial institutions, including banks, finance companies, and savings and loan cooperatives.

The Capital Markets law of 1993 spurred activity in the equity and bond markets. The law transformed stock exchanges from for-profit private corporations into nonprofit private corporations. Profits must be reinvested in the exchanges, thereby strengthening the institutions. The law also abolished all discriminatory taxes on foreign investment and created tax incentives aimed at fostering growth in the equity market.

In 1993 the government took measures to spur direct foreign investment in Ecuador. Among other things, it eliminated the 49 percent ceiling on foreign ownership of banks and insurance companies, lifted restrictions on repatriation of profits, and simplified registration procedures. Today foreign investors enjoy "national treatment" in all regards in Ecuador and benefit from bilateral treaties to prevent double taxation.

TRANSPORTATION

There are the inevitable pros and cons of getting around in Ecuador. Gas is cheap—as low as 40 cents a gallon. But cars carry a 40 percent import duty.

The government has invested $338 million to develop and improve roads, but you may not want to use them. Driving can be hazardous in Ecuador, and many expatriates hire a chauffeur.

Taxis are plentiful and cheap in cities. Not all taxis have meters, but drivers are usually honest and rarely overcharge. A taxi ride from the airport to downtown Quito costs about $1. A bus ride almost anywhere in Quito amounts to pennies.

The Trolebus (trolley bus) is a system of electric buses in Quito. The buses run the length of the city and make only scheduled stops. Affiliated buses extend the system's range from the farthest northern neighborhoods to those in the extreme south. Best of all, one low fare grants you access to the entire system. In recent years, fares have been as low 25 cents.

LEISURE TIME

Ecuadorians, especially in Quito, love to go out in the evening to dine and dance. As in Spain, it is fashionable to dine around 9, and you can usually find one restaurant in every deluxe or first-class hotel that stays open 24 hours.

Quito boasts a number of fine restaurants, including Reina Victoria Pub (Reina Victoria 530 y Roca), Old El Paso (Reina Victoria y Pinto 305), and Cevicheria Brisas del Pacifico (Reina Victoria 918 y Pinto). Quito is also honeycombed with hole-in-the-wall cafés and street vendors selling foods of all different descriptions. Restaurants, bars, and hotels automatically add a 10 percent service charge to your bill, and an additional moderate gratuity is expected if service is good.

Hotels throughout the country offer casinos, shows, and orchestras. By all means, visit one of the *pena folkloricas*, nightclubs featuring folk music and dancing. Audience participation is encouraged at these colorful clubs. One of Quito's most popular is the Pacha Mama.

Another of Quito's popular meeting places is the Ben Bar in the Hotel Alameda Real on Avenida Amazonas. But if you drink, do so with caution. High altitudes magnify the effects of alcohol.

Futbol (American soccer) is a national passion. Most towns have teams, which play on weekends in Quito and Otavalo. Also popular are bullfights, marlin fishing, and *pelota de guante* (glove ball), a peculiar Ecuadorian game played with a leather glove and ball.

Travel is a popular pastime. Expatriates enjoy visiting nature preserves and Incan ruins. Until 1966, when a dirt road was laid, the ruins at Ingapirca were isolated from the rest of Ecuador, accessible only by foot. Today Ingapirca is a two-hour drive from Cuenca through velvety green countryside flanked by snow-capped Andean mountains.

Visiting the Galapagos Islands A great advantage to living in Ecuador is that you can visit Galapagos National Park for far less than what tourists pay. A thousand kilometers off the west coast, this archipelago is home to dozens of unique plant and animal species, including the giant sea turtles that gave the islands their name.

It's not hard to understand why Darwin journeyed here to develop his theory of evolution. About half of the plants and nearly all of the reptiles in the Galapagos exist nowhere else on earth. Besides sea turtles, you're likely to encounter sea lions, penguins, birds by the tens of thousands, and giant marine iguanas that resemble prehistoric dinosaurs.

Species also abound on San Cristobal Island, the region's administrative center. Santa Cruz is home to the Darwin Center for Galapagos Island Research, which amazes tourists with fascinating wildlife exhibits.

Espaniola, one of the most beautiful islands, is a favorite playground of sea lions and birds, including albatrosses and boobies. Isabella, the largest island, also is populated by great numbers of birds, as well as colonies of iguanas. And volcanic Mount Alcedo offers unparalleled views of the region.

Santiago is a gorgeous island with thousands of iguanas, birds, and sea lions, which will gladly join you in a swim along Espumuilla Beach. Seymore is a nesting ground for frigate birds. During mating season it's fascinating to observe the breast of the male frigate, which inflates like a big red sack as the male attempts to court the female.

The islands' human inhabitants are no less colorful. In 1932, sexy baroness Eloisa de Wagner Weherborn arrived on Floreana with three lovers in tow. The quirky iconoclasts proceeded to shed their clothes and lead a rather uninhibited existence until, one by one, they mysteriously vanished. More than 5,000 people still live in the Galapagos, including a fair share of eccentric expatriates.

Shopping Unique to Ecuadorian shopping malls are *artesinas* (Indian markets), shops that sell Indian handicrafts made locally and in other Latin American countries. There are, in fact, more Indian markets in Ecuador than in any other South American country. You can find great bargains on shawls, ponchos, blankets, scarves, wood carvings, hangings, jungle fruits, and such culinary oddities as *cuy* (roast guinea pig), a delicacy enjoyed by Indians since the days of the Incas.

One of the best markets in the country is in Otavalo, a two-hour drive from Quito. On Saturday morning, Otavalo Indians set up stalls in the public square and sell handicrafts, pottery, and hand-loomed woolens ranging from ties to ponchos. All items are made using ancient methods, and they rank among the finest such products in the world. Best of all are the prices. A sweater that might cost $150 in New York can be bought here for $20. A rug that would cost $600 in Los Angeles carries a $50 price tag here. Authentic Panama hats range from $15 to $30, and intricately designed Inca wall hangings are a steal at $14.

For leather goods, stop at Cotacachi, near Quito, where every store in town sells expertly tooled handbags, luggage, shoes, and hats. A leather coat may cost as little as $50, and a purse can be had for $10.

$\mathcal{A}$DDITIONAL $\mathcal{R}$ESOURCES

Central Bank of Ecuador, Avenida 10 de Agosto y Briceño, Quito, Ecuador; tel. (593) (2) 583-083, fax (593) (2) 571-807

Chamber of Commerce of Guayaquil, Avenida Olmedo 414, Guayaquil, Ecuador; tel. (593) (4) 323-130/534-411, fax (593) (4) 323-478

Chamber of Commerce of Quito, Avenidas Amazonas y República, Edif. Las Cámaras, piso 6, Quito, Ecuador; tel. (593) (2) 443-787, fax: (593) (2) 435-862

Ministry of Education and Culture, Mejía 321, Quito, Ecuador; tel. (593) (2) 216-224, fax (593) (2) 580-174

Ministry of Finance, Avenida 10 de Agosto 1661 y Jorge Washington, Quito, Ecuador; tel. (593) (2) 503-328, fax (593) (2) 500-702

Ministry of Labor and Human Resources, Luis Felipe Borja y C. Ponce, Quito, Ecuador; tel. (593) (2) 526-666, fax (593) (2) 503-122

Ministry of Public Health, Juan Larrea 445, Quito, Ecuador; tel. (593) (2) 521-733, fax (593) (2) 569-786

Ministry of Public Works and Communications, Avenida 6 de Diciembre 1184, Quito, Ecuador; tel. (593) (2) 222-749, fax (593) (2) 223-077

Ministry of Tourism, Reina Victoria 514 y Roca, Edificio CETUR, Quito, Ecuador; tel. (593) (2) 522-387, fax (593) (2) 228-301

Useful Web Site:
www.ecuador.orgecuador/

HECTOR BERLIOZ

France

by ROSANNE KNORR

France is the world's number-one tourist destination, which is not surprising since it's jam-packed with scenic beauty, culture, history, fabulous cuisine, and wine. But one can't ever cover the possibilities in a two-week vacation. Retiring here provides you the leisure to explore more fully and to sample the good life France has to offer.

Many of the pleasures found in France are small and subtle: a perfectly browned baguette, a bike ride beside a ripening vineyard, a restful chat over a glass of wine in a sidewalk café. The French know how to squeeze pleasure from every moment of life, and retirees in particular have plenty of moments to fill.

From sophisticated Paris to restful country villages, from the jet-setting beaches of the French Riviera to the sky-high ski havens in the Alps, from the rustic Pyrenees to Normandy's historic cliffs backed by verdant hills dotted with cows, France offers something for every lifestyle and taste.

For years the French have been castigated by tourists for their so-called arrogance. In reality, away from Paris and tourist traps, the average French person is delightful and welcoming to those who take the time to get to know them. The French are normally courteous and appreciate this quality in others.

117

The Culture and People of France

It's been said that the French spend a third of their time planning a meal, another third eating it, and the last third discussing it. This is not far from the truth. Long lunches are the norm, with most people taking two hours to relax and enjoy the meal. In the countryside, most businesses close for two to two-and-a-half hours at midday. In large cities, big shops may stay open through the lunch hour.

Parlez-Vous Français? If you plan to live in France, attempt to learn the language. The French are proud of their native tongue and have not accepted the dominance of English as an international language. You'll find people much friendlier and easier to get to know if you at least try to use their language, rather than expecting them to use yours. It will also make life in general more enjoyable, and you can participate more fully in local activities if you have a grasp of French.

If you live in Paris, the Alliance Française, the Institut Catholique, and the Sorbonne offer French classes for foreigners, as do numerous private language schools. You'll find schools in other major cities throughout France as well. Plus, many French people are delighted to exchange French lessons for English lessons. Find a partner by talking to your neighbors or placing advertisements on bulletin boards in local schools.

A Brief History of France With its long line of conquerors and kings, France can keep even the most avid history buff busy and happy. Discover interesting facts for yourself as you visit battlefields and churches, museums and châteaus throughout your new home. These are a few historical highpoints:

450 B.C.   The Gauls begin settling the country
121–58 B.C.   Rome expands its influence, contributing roads, architecture, and cultural history

A.D. 200–500   Franks, Burgundians, Goths, Vandals, and Britons emigrate, diversifying the names and heritage of various regions of the country

800   Charlemagne creates the Holy Roman Empire

1152   Henry II of England marries Eleanor of Aquitaine, making a large region of France part of Britain

1337–1453   The Hundred Years War aims at removing English influence in France

1789   The French Revolution begins with the storming of the Bastille prison, symbol of royal power, on July 14

1799   Corsican Napoleon Bonaparte takes power and creates the Code Napoleon, which remains the basis for French civil legislation

1812   Napoleon's war with Russia, which eventually ends with his exile to Elba, begins; after his escape, he was defeated definitively at Waterloo

1914   World War I begins in France, with German invasion

1940   World War II begins; France is occupied by Germany in the north, with the Vichy regime managing the south

1944   D day assault of Normandy begins the liberation of France, culminating on August 25, 1944, in Paris

1968   Student demonstrations in the Latin Quarter spread across the country, leading DeGaulle to relinquish power; Gaullist and socialists shift the political power back and forth for decades

Recommended Living Areas

Each region of France has its own personality. If you don't like crowds, avoid Paris, Lyons, Marseilles, the Alps in winter, and the South in summer. If you don't want to hear English spoken, restrict your visits to the Aquitaine, especially the Dordogne, to the off-season. Central France is committed to the agrarian way of life, though it has urban centers. Here you'll find the least diluted French experience.

You'll probably want to settle in a place that's convenient for travel in Europe and for family and friends who visit from the United States. In general, the areas around Paris and the Loire Valley—Toulouse in the southwest, Montpellier in the center, Lyons in the Rhone Valley, and Aix-en-Provence—are all within easy proximity to the city centers by fast train or plane.

In reviewing some of the best areas in France for foreign retirees, the City of Light is the obvious place to start.

Paris   Vibrant, culturally rich, historic, and a hub for travel throughout France and Europe, Paris is magnificent. It's a bit overpowering at its tourist-packed busiest, but it's still livable. Many neighborhoods feel like small towns, where you know the butcher and the breadmaker and can pop down to the local bistro for a meal.

In Paris everything is at your doorstep—from haute cuisine to high fashion. Parks are everywhere and offer swimming, tennis, and racquetball. Paris is where the world comes to appreciate the arts, including concerts, opera, and museums without equal.

Yes, Paris has it all—for a price. Housing here is among the most expensive per square foot in all of France (not to mention the rest of the world). The average apartment is teeny-tiny by U.S. standards, but then, with all that Paris offers, you don't have to stay home much. A small two-bedroom apartment with living room, galley kitchen, and one bath sells for about $130,000.

Provence and the Côte d'Azur   With orchards of olive, orange, and lemon trees, and acres of lavender and poppies, Provence and the Côte d'Azur have been the objects of travelers' romantic visions for a long time. In the French countryside, this is the most developed and most expensive region. Although far from Paris, it's well-served by the Nice and Marseille airports, as well as train service.

In the Côte d'Azur, the greatest number of expatriates live along the eastern part of the coast, from Marseille to Menton in the Maritime Alps and inland about 20 miles. The area from St. Tropez eastward (including Cannes and Nice) is the most developed and most expensive. Finding reasonably priced property here is next to impossible.

Due to the large concentration of wealthy foreign property owners, real estate values here do not bear much relation to those in the rest of the country. In general, a studio apartment in the best part of Cannes costs as much as a five-bedroom house in Languedoc-Roussillon.

Inland from the Côte d'Azur prices are also creeping up in sleepy farming villages, as the "simple life" and Provençal farmhouses have become trendy. During summer the area is crowded and culturally active, with concerts, theater, and lectures. Bouche de Rhone and Var are set in an agricultural wine-growing region, with lovely villages where you can buy a vineyard or an old farmhouse for restoration. Development reaches only about 10 miles inland. In summer the area is quiet, slow, and hot. In winter the mistral blows, and the area becomes quiet, slow, and cold.

Some of the most charming houses in southern France are in the region's hill towns, where houses are built onto each other; your terrace may be your neighbor's roof. But don't worry about disturbing your neighbors—walls may be as much as a yard thick. The tiled roofs often have fine chestnut beams. Some of these houses have small walled gardens once used to grow the family vegetables. Today they're perfect places to relax and enjoy the views of the valley below.

Most villages also have outlying hamlets where you might find a house for sale. The valleys hold sprawling farmhouses ready to be renovated. On the edge of a medieval village, a three-bedroom villa with guest annex goes for about $264,000.

Burgundy Burgundy is a region of vineyards, dense forests, and rolling hills, yet it's only two hours to Paris on a good auto route. It's also only a day's drive to Switzerland, Italy, or the Mediterranean.

Gardening is a local obsession in Burgundy, offering the promise of such favorites as fresh raspberries, walnuts, and herbs. Many people bicycle through the country along its network of canals and often stumble upon wild strawberries along the way. Ballooning over the vineyards is popular in fall when vines are ripe. You can also hike, go horseback riding, or just relax and watch the daffodils grow.

You'll find centuries-old châteaus, Celtic and Roman ruins, and an amazing number of Romanesque sites in Burgundy. This is a stable region—financially, culturally, and agriculturally—and still authentically French. There are many fascinating towns, easily accessible on well-maintained roads. Auxerre has an inner city that is a national treasure, including a Gothic cathedral with exquisite stained glass and a rare eleventh-century crypt painting. The central shopping district features a well-maintained, sixteenth-century clock tower and half-timbered buildings.

In the villages of Burgundy you can find cottages for as little as $40,000, though some renovation will be required. Honey-colored stone farmhouses in the southwest corner go for about $42,000.

Perigord The southwest of France is known for its spas (it has about 30 major ones) and the rough shores of the Atlantic. The old *département* of Perigord encompasses the modern départements of Dordogne, Gironde, Lot, Lot-et-Garonne, Tarn, and Gers. Perigord is a weather-beaten, rocky area similar to New England, but it also has verdant farms, historic chateaus, quaint old villages, and scrumptious truffle-topped gourmet delicacies. The principal towns are Bordeaux, Périgueux, Cahors, and Toulouse.

This section of France is renowned for cuisine, wine, and history. Prehistoric artists painted caves in Les Eyzies. Sarlat retains its medieval layout and houses, and Rocamadour was the center of twelfth-century pilgrimages to see the Black Virgin. The southwestern valley of the Dordogne has prehistoric grottoes and charming hill towns—not to mention truffles and foie gras.

Perigord is also dotted with thirteenth- and fourteenth-century châteaus and fortified villages. Prices are reasonable here. A restored farmhouse with five acres of gardens, four bedrooms, and two baths goes for about $160,000. An ancient farmhouse with spacious ceilings and wine cellars, set on seven acres with views, goes for about $67,000.

And Everywhere Else The Languedoc-Roussillon region along the Mediterranean from Perpignon to Nimes is beautiful and undeveloped. You can find massive old farmhouses here for rock-bottom prices. However, the houses generally don't have insulation or central heating and have only rudimentary plumbing. This area is also plagued by the frigid mistral from November through March.

If you want a truly quiet village, investigate Brittany or Normandy. These picturesque coastal areas offer peace and natural beauty for those who don't mind the rain. They are a few hours from Paris by train and very affordable. A classic Breton stone-and-slate cottage can be found for $18,000. New homes in a southern Brittany development with a swimming pool range from $54,000 to $167,000.

Many buildings in Normandy are made of stone and *colombage*, the decorative half-timber style that is typically Norman. In the Saint-Lo area, a three-bedroom house with timberwork facings goes for about $34,000. About $130,000 buys a *maison de maitre*, or gentleman's residence, with stables and outbuildings. Since Normandy is famed for cider and calvados, here's where you'll find your house with the apple orchard.

For sunshine, scenery, and cheap prices, head west of the Rhone Valley to the Massif Central, which has national parks, excellent terrain for cross-country skiing, and low prices on property. Sharing the same summer climate as the Côte d'Azur, this region covers three departments (Ardeche, Lozere, and Haute-Loire), and prices are as low as $8,000 for a tiny, tumbledown cottage needing complete renovation. Completely restored farmhouses cost $45,000 to $60,000. Any property in the Massif region is within a three-hour drive of the

Mediterranean at the most, and in winter the area is a popular center of *ski du fond*, or ski-trekking.

In the Loire Valley, where châteaus are as common as schools, prices can be high in the more popular areas, especially the nearer you get to Paris. But the soil is fertile and the scenery is beautiful.

The people and architecture in the villages of Alsace-Lorraine, the department bordering Germany, have a dominant Germanic flavor. Compared with the cost of property across the border, real estate here is a bargain.

The Alps may seem like paradise to skiers, hikers, and those who enjoy incredible vistas and the pure Alpine air. However, property here is incredibly expensive. The Pyrenees are lower in altitude, but still ruggedly beautiful and much more affordable.

Renting in France

Rentals in France range from pocket-punishing Paris high-rises in the high four figures to country farmhouses for $400 a month.

Finding rentals in Paris takes time and hard work. If you elect to find your own apartment, set your alarm for the crack of dawn. You'll need to see the listings in the daily papers before others beat you to it. *Le Figaro* is a good place to start.

Several other publications might help. *De Particulier á Particulier* is a weekly real estate ad sheet for housing rentals and sales that covers all regions of the country. It's available on newsstands and costs about $2.50 a copy. *Le Journal des Particuliers* also provides rental and sale listings for $2. *FUSAC* is a monthly publication distributed free throughout Paris. It has a good classified housing section.

The American Church in Paris publishes the *Paris Free Voice*, an arts, entertainment, and community newspaper that often includes ads for housing and holiday rentals. Pick it up free at the American Church at 65 Quay d"Orsay. (The church is also a good place to meet fellow expatriates.) Also check the classifieds in the *International Herald Tribune.*

The Women's Institute for Continuing Education, part of the American University in Paris, has a bulletin board with postings for apartments to rent or sublet. The American Cathedral also has a bulletin board with postings for rentals and shared housing.

If your time is limited, you may want to enlist the services of an international rental agency. Families Abroad, 194 Riverside Drive, Apt. 6D, New York, NY 10025, 212/787-2434, specializes in short-term rentals (three months to a year) and deals primarily with the owners of apartments or houses. Relocation Services, 57 rue Pierre Charron, 75008; tel. (33) (1) 4289-0915, fax (33) (1) 4225-3592, works directly with companies that are transferring families for longer stays. They will help explain the nitty-gritty aspects of moving, find a garage for your car, and locate insurance for your new quarters. The fee for these services ranges from $1,660 to $2,500.

Rents and Fees How much will you pay for a rental? In Paris, it all depends on location, with the quieter and more scenic neighborhoods obviously more costly. A small, furnished, two-room (*deux pieces*) studio on the sixth floor with a balcony and elevator, near the Arc de Triomphe, may go for $960 month. A spacious, furnished, sixth-floor, one-bedroom apartment with an elevator and view of the Eiffel Tower in the posh St. Cloud suburb or trendy St. Germain de Prés could rent for double or triple that price.

An unfurnished, two-bedroom Paris apartment in the third *arrondissement* costs about $850 month. For the same amount, you could get a two-room apartment in the 10th arrondissement. The least you can expect to pay for a three-bedroom house in the fashionable western suburbs of Paris is $1,800 a month. Prices are about the same for a two-bedroom apartment in the chic 16th arrondissement.

Be prepared to pay three months' rent up front. You'll also have to pay service charges (central heating, hot water, and so on), which can run as high as 10 to 20 percent of a month's rent.

If you elect to rent through a real estate agent, you'll have to pay a finder's fee. You may also be asked to pay key money, or compensation to the previous tenant for any improvements he or she made to the apartment.

Lease Agreements   Once you've found a Paris rental that interests you, you'll be asked to prove that your monthly income is four times the basic rent in French francs. If you are unemployed, you'll have to produce a bank guarantee (it can be from a foreign bank with a branch in Paris) that states the bank will pay your rent in case of default. Alternatively, you can get a guarantee from a reputable French citizen (although you'll have a difficult time finding someone who'll stand up to a French landlord's inspection).

All leases must be made in writing. Oral agreements, as someone once said, aren't worth the paper they're not printed on. You don't need a notary to witness the signing of a lease.

Buying Real Estate

Although it is difficult to find affordable housing in Paris or the Côte d'Azur, good buys exist throughout the rest of France. About 85 percent of all foreign residents live in the south of France. A British colony has formed in the northwest and in the area from Bordeaux to the Spanish border. The Dordogne is also popular among foreigners.

Finding Your Property   Take time to explore on your own or with a local Realtor or notary. Keep in mind that if you buy through an agency, the seller pays the fee but jacks up the price of the house accordingly. It's cheaper to deal directly with the seller. Keep in mind that the asking price is not the final price. Offer at least 5 or 10 percent less, depending on the situation.

You can find properties directly through *De Particulier á Particulier* or *Le Journal des Particuliers*, available on newsstands. *French Property News* is a British-based paper with lots of real estate ads and some listings by private sellers (info@french-property-news.com), tel. (44) (181) 947-1834. Also look for classified ads in local newspapers from the specific area in which you are interested.

When you find a property you like, have it inspected. Most homes are old and may need extensive repairs. Water is an important element to consider when purchasing in the south of France. If you choose a house in a village, make sure it has water piped in from a nearby reservoir or lake. Otherwise your water may be rationed during summer. If you purchase a farm, make sure it has a well, spring, or cistern, and find out if it can be connected to a water network.

Strange-to-you rules may apply, so don't assume anything. For example, find out if your access road is private or belongs to the community. In the countryside, find out if there is a legal right of passage that allows sheep or goats to cut across your land, which is the case in many rural areas.

The Buying Process No restrictions are placed on foreign purchase of real estate in France. However, funds used to purchase property must come from abroad, dollars must be converted to francs, and all payments must be accompanied by a certificate from a French bank assuring that the money came from non-French resources. If this is not done, you may not be able to deport the proceeds if and when you eventually sell the property.

When buying property, you must use a *notaire* (notary), who will act as both a government official and a legal advisor to both parties. The notaire is responsible for making sure the vendor has full and clear title, that the vendor is paid, and that stamp duties and registration fees are paid. The notaire also collects the purchase tax and the capital gains tax.

You can find a notaire in the yellow pages or by the official signs they hang outside their offices in almost every good-sized town. You may want one who speaks a little English or has experience with foreign owners. For recommendations ask the local consulate, bank, or other expatriates in the area.

Your notaire and real estate agent will help you obtain a mortgage. You do not have to have a bank account in France to purchase property, but if you want a mortgage, you'll need one. Don't leave loan details until the last moment. And don't allow property developers, sellers, or their agents to negotiate a loan for you. Get advice from your bank.

When applying for a mortgage, the process is basically the same as in the United States. You'll need to provide information on your personal financial history, such as pay stubs, personal income tax returns, and corporate returns (if you own your own business). The longest mortgage term available is 15 years. Rates vary based on term and type of mortgage.

You'll finalize the deal with the *procuration* (final commitment), which must be signed in France or at a French embassy or consulate. When all documentation is signed, your notary will hold a meeting with the buyer and seller. If you cannot travel to France for this meeting, make sure the notary has your signed procuration with the seal of the French embassy or consulate.

Apartments are purchased *en copropriété* (with joint ownership), which means you and other apartment dwellers must contribute to the costs of building maintenance. Find out what the service charge will be; a concierge or shared heating system can raise the costs considerably. If buying from an existing owner, ask to see records of the service charges he or she has paid.

Taxes and Fees   Upon purchase of a property in France, you must pay a tax on its value. If the property was built within the previous five years and is being sold by the builder or first buyer, the tax is about 2.5 percent of the purchase price. If the property is more than five years old or has already been sold once, the tax will be between 6.5 and 11.5 percent of the purchase price, depending on the region.

You must also pay notaire fees, stamp duty, and land registration fees. As a rough guide, fees will be about 20 percent of the purchase price for new houses and 10 percent of the purchase price for older houses. Consult a lawyer or tax expert to be sure you don't pay more stamp duty than necessary.

Land tax, or *taxe foncière*, is quite low in France. The annual rate is equal to the estimate of the local rental value of the property. You do not have to pay this tax the first two years following the completion of a new building or restoration of an old building.

Buying a Paris Apartment The most expensive areas in Paris are the fashionable fifth, sixth, seventh, and sixteenth arrondissements. Rents in the 17th arrondissement, once inexpensive, are inching upward as the area becomes more trendy and popular among artists. Lower prices can be found in the 10th, 11th, 12th, 13th, 18th, 19th, and 20th arrondissements. These guidelines are just that—guidelines. Prices in any section of town can vary 30 to 50 percent from one street to another, from one side of a street to the other, and from one floor to another in the same building.

Most of the properties available in Paris are six- and seven-story structures erected after the reconstruction of the city under Napoleon II in 1850. The typical building is dressed up with balconies and cornices rimmed with wrought-iron railings and ornamental stonework. Inside, apartments usually have high ceilings, small rooms, and long hallways.

Renovating an Old House Many houses in the French countryside need extensive repair and renovation. You can buy a fine ruin with everything but the walls to redo, a recently inhabited farmhouse with primitive lighting and plumbing, a house that's renovated (but not to your taste), or a place you can move into right away. Before buying, have the house checked by an architect or construction specialist.

Price varies according to the amount of work needed. The general rule for a ruin is that restoration costs at least as much as the purchase price of the house. Ask your real estate agent to help you locate qualified but affordable local craftsmen, architects, and builders.

In addition to being costly, property renovation can be time-consuming. Most people who have renovated a ruin will tell you that they had no idea what they were getting into. Projects can drag on for three, five, even ten years, and can cost much more than originally planned. Before beginning your project, get a free estimate, called a *devis*, from at least two masons or construction firms.

Beware la Viagère   In a few instances, you may find a property with a *rente viagère* attached. This is a system of low down payment in which you promise to pay the former owner (usually elderly) the balance, as long as he or she lives. Fortunately for them, unfortunately for you, such owners tend to be long-lived. One woman became the oldest woman in France at 121, while the person who bought her house died and his estate continued to pay la viagére.

Cost of Living

Living in Paris is slightly more expensive than living in Washington, D.C., but the rest of France is a bit cheaper than comparable spots in the United States. A couple generally needs from $25,000 to $35,000 annually to live moderately well in France. A single person needs $12,000 to $26,000.

The best deals on food are local, fresh-from-the-farmer produce. Here's an idea of what you will pay for food and other everyday items and services in France:

electricity	$50–$100/ month	steak	$7.50/pound
		lettuce	$.51/head
gasoline	$4.50/gallon	coffee	$5.50/pound
movie ticket	$7	milk	$4/gallon
bottle of wine	$4	chicken	$3/pound
maid service	$10/hour	fish	$6/pound
bananas	$1/pound	video rental	$5
baguette	$.65	compact disc	$15-$20

Food in restaurants is well priced, especially if one avoids the tourist haunts and sticks to local spots. If you dine at lunchtime you can enjoy *le menu*, which is the best value in any restaurant and includes appetizer, main dish, and dessert for about $10. Ordering à la carte or in the evening will make your meal about 20 to 30 percent higher.

Big-ticket items, such as cars, sofas, and appliances, are more expensive in France than in the United States. By far the most shocking expense is gasoline, which runs about $4.50 a gallon due to hefty French taxes. Electricity is also expensive, so the French are careful to conserve it. The electric company has a system by which you can limit major appliance use to less costly days or hours.

Retirees in France can travel comfortably by train at a discount. The Carte Senior (senior-citizen card) provides 25 to 50 percent off travel on most trains. Men over 62 and women over 60 can buy the pass for about $50. The card is valid for one year with proof of age. Ask for it at any French train station. Many movie theaters, museums, and other attractions also offer senior discounts ranging from 20 to 30 percent. Air France and Air Inter offer discounts for seniors that range from 25 to 50 percent on domestic flights.

$\mathcal{D}$AY-TO-DAY $\mathcal{L}$IVING $\mathcal{C}$ONCERNS

France offers an amazing quality of life for the money. Life is pleasant, with most of the modern conveniences you enjoy in the United States. Tap water is purified and safe to drink in France, although spring water is for sale should you so desire.

Telephone service is high-tech, offering countless options. Base monthly service is inexpensive, but each call, including local ones, is billed. A consultant with France Telecom will help you pick the most economical plan based on your calling patterns.

The electrical current is different from that in the United States. France uses 220 volts, 50 cycles (versus 110 volts, 60 cycles in the

United States). You can purchase adapters for electrical plugs or transformers to use with American appliances. However, converters and transformers change only the current, not cycles, so American computers and printers—or anything with a motor for that matter—will not run properly in France.

Televisions run on the French PAL/SECAM system, as opposed to our NTSC system, so your American television won't work here either. Your American VCR will not play European videocassettes. However, you can buy a VCR in France that plays both types.

Taxes

Taxes are high in France. Management Center Europe, a business research center, estimates that a married couple in France with two children and an income of $100,000 is left with $64,000 after taxes and social security deductions. Foreigners not spending more than 183 days a year in France are taxed only on their incomes from French sources, or on three times the rental value of their residence in France, whichever is greater. If you live in France year-round and your residence is considered your fiscal domicile, you must pay tax to the French government on worldwide income.

If you are an American citizen domiciled in France with a worldwide total income of more than $70,000, you will have to pay U.S. as well as French taxes. But a double-taxation treaty between the United States and France allows you to deduct the taxes you pay to one country from your tax payment to the other.

French tax returns are simple; the government works out your tax for you. Local tax offices can be helpful, but you should obtain the services of a good accountant or one of the large international accounting firms, such as Price Waterhouse.

One French tax Americans aren't familiar with is the one on televisions. The fee is $125 a year for a color set. When you buy your TV, you will fill out a form. You'll receive a bill every year, and your payment will help support the television broadcasting system in France.

$\mathcal{M}$AKING THE $\mathcal{M}$OVE

To live in France for more than three months, you must apply for a long-stay visa before you leave the United States. Contact the nearest French embassy or consulate for information.

You will have to fill out an application form, provide passport photos, and provide proof of sufficient financial resources to live in France without working. You must also provide proof of medical insurance, proof of French residence, and a statement from the local police that you do not have a criminal record.

Once you get to France you will take the approved paperwork to the local prefecture, where you will apply for the *carte de visite*, a one-year residence permit. If your application is accepted, you will pay $181 for a physical exam. The liaison for all this will be the local mayor's office, unless you live in the town where the prefecture is located.

For more information, contact the Embassy of France, 4101 Reservoir Rd. NW, Washington DC 20007, 202/944-6000; or the French consulate closest to you.

What to Bring, What to Leave Behind In general, you may bring into France all the contents of your home or apartment (that you have owned for at least six months) free of import duty. Select your moving company with care, and distrust any firm that claims it can void customs formalities.

When moving to France, you can bring anything intended for personal use and not for resale. Americans may bring 400 cigarettes, 100 cigars, or 500 grams of pipe tobacco duty-free. Also allowed are two used cameras with 10 rolls of film and a movie camera with 10 reels of film. You can bring in as many French francs and foreign bills as you wish.

When leaving the country, you can take with you up to 500 French francs without making a declaration. No restrictions are placed on traveler's checks or letters of credit obtained outside France. All currency declared upon arrival can be taken out with you when you leave.

What About Pets?   Animals less than three months old are not allowed into France. For other pets you'll need a certificate from your veterinarian stating that your animal is free from disease. Your pet will also need a certificate of vaccination for the usual diseases, including rabies, feline distemper, and leukemia. Some shots must have been given more than a month but less than a year before travel. Double check the regulations, which change often. Contact your closest French embassy or consulate for more information.

MEDICAL CARE

French medical care is of high quality and offers distinct savings (approximately two-thirds less) over care provided in the United States. A visit to a generalist costs about $27, slightly more for house calls.

You won't have trouble locating English-speaking doctors in Paris or the larger towns. Contact the American embassy or consulate for referrals. If you need a continuous supply of any drug, ask your doctor or an international pharmacy where and under what name it is available in France. Have the dosage translated into the metric system.

At the American Hospital on Boulevard Victor Hugo in a suburb of Paris, you'll find friendly English-speaking doctors and nurses. Health care here is covered by Blue Cross/Blue Shield and Aetna insurance. Paris also has the British Hospital, 48 rue de Villiers, 92 Levallois-Perret.

Health Insurance Be aware that Medicare doesn't cover Americans overseas. To maintain the residence card required for living here, you must show proof of private insurance coverage. You may be able to use your U.S.-based coverage, or you can buy insurance from a private French carrier.

Expatriate policies are offered by several insurance companies, many based in Britain. These policies are much less expensive than comparable American policies. The premium is about $110 a month, depending on your age and health. Hospitalization is fully covered, and there is no deductible.

ℱINANCIAL ℳATTERS

The exchange rate between the United States and France has improved in recent years. For the best rates, change your currency at a bank or use an automatic teller machine to withdraw the cash you want in France from your U.S. bank account. ATMs are located throughout France in banks, railroad stations, airports, and often in big malls and supermarkets. Avoid changing money at hotels, restaurants, or shops, which overcharge.

The Banking System In general, French banking hours are Monday through Friday from 9 to noon and 1:30 or 2:00 to 4:30. Banks close at noon the day before official holidays.

Prélèvement is an automatic direct-debit system that is highly popular in France. With this system your checking account can be debited for most monthly bills, including mortgage, utilities, phone, real estate taxes, insurance, and cable TV.

Opening a Bank Account If you're going to live in France, especially if you're going to do business or make investments, you'll need a French bank account. Americans can keep up to $5,000 in a foreign account or financial instrument without having to make a declaration to the Internal Revenue Service.

However, France does not have attractive banking laws, so it's a good idea to keep only the necessary minimum in a French account. There are additional reasons you should not do your banking in France:

- France has no bank privacy laws. The opening of every account is reported to the government.
- The clearing system for checks can be slow, and bank statements are not always accurate. It takes longer to order a checkbook in France than in the United States, and interest is never paid on checking accounts.
- You cannot endorse a check, except to a bank or similar institution.
- A *chèque sans provision* (bounced check) can bring sanctions much more serious than in the United States. This is especially true with a non-resident account.

On the other hand, checks are accepted virtually everywhere in France, whether they are drawn on a resident or non-resident account. Cash withdrawal Visa cards also can be used throughout the country.

To deposit more than $850 in a non-resident bank account, you must show that the money was imported from outside France. The bank will handle the paperwork for a fee of about $12. For large amounts, have money wired from your U.S. account in French francs. Otherwise, the ATM is the cheapest way to handle infusions of cash for daily expenses.

TRANSPORTATION

If you live in a city or even a town, you can get by in France without a car. In Paris you probably wouldn't want one, since garaging it is exorbitantly expensive, and traffic jams make it easier and faster to take the Metro. A package of 10 tickets or a monthly pass called the *carte orange* (you'll need a passport-size photo to purchase the pass) are your best Metro ticket deals.

Known as the SNCF, the French railroad covers 22,000 miles. All lines radiate from Paris, where there are six train stations. The French railroad offers several economy-priced options for seniors, couples, children, and anyone purchasing tickets 8 or 30 days in advance.

Driving in France   The French countryside offers so many marvels, from wine routes to off-the-beaten-track villages, that if you live outside Paris you'll want a car. (If you live in Paris, you can always rent one for countryside visits.)

You can drive in France on your U.S. driver's license until you become a resident. Then you should have a French driver's license. This license requires a test and usually driver's lessons, which are costly. Certain U.S. states have reciprocal privileges with France (South Carolina is one), in which you can trade your U.S. license for a French one.

For French rules of the road, purchase the *Livret de Conduire* from a bookstore or driving school. Keep in mind as you taste the delights of French vineyards that the *alcooltest de dépistage* (Breathalyzer test) is used freely throughout the country.

LEISURE TIME

France is jam-packed with cultural and historic attractions—so many that one person cannot cover them all in a lifetime. For starters, visit the World War II beaches and museum in Normandy, stop at Mont St. Michel on the way, and enjoy dinner overlooking the craggy clefts of Brittany.

Tour the Loire Valley and see how many of the countless châteaus you can visit before your feet give out. Do the same with Paris museums. The Louvre and Musée d'Orsay alone could keep you busy for years of return visits, and there are countless other museums and small galleries to explore. One additional piece of advice: Get a good guidebook.

Shopping Paris offers the ultimate shopping experience, from haute couture down to bargain-basement specials. Have fun browsing the *brocantes* (antiques stores) or the outdoor markets and searching for treasures. English-language books are available in specialty bookstores in Paris and large cities. Large French bookstores often have English-language sections.

In France, grocery shopping is an experience rather than a chore. Visit outdoor markets or individual specialty stores offering colorful fruits, vegetables, meats, fish, cheeses, and breads.

Sports and Hobbies *Le foot* (soccer), biking, and tennis are among the most popular sports in France. *Pétanque*, played with steel balls that are thrown at a smaller wooden ball, is played in parks throughout the country.

If you're a movie buff, large cities often have theaters showing films in the original language. Look for the initials V.O. for *version original*. V.F. means the film is dubbed into French.

Additional Resources

French Embassy, 4101 Reservoir Rd. NW, Washington, D.C.
   20007-2185; 202/944-6000, fax 202/944-6212 (visa section)
French Government Tourist Offices
   444 Madison Ave., 16th floor, New York, NY 10022-6903;
   212/838-7800, fax 212/838-7855
   676 N. Michigan Ave. Chicago, IL 60611-2819; 312/751-7800,
   fax 312/337-6339
   9454 Wilshire Blvd., Ste. 715, Beverly Hills, CA 90212-2967;
   310/271-6665, fax 310/276-2835

Useful Web Sites

French Government Tourist Office: www.fgtousa.org
French language information: www.pratique.fr/sommaire.html
French regions, history, culture and activities: www.france.com
General information: www.info-france.usa-org/

Great Britain

by PARIS PERMENTER AND JOHN BIGLEY

A surprising number of Yanks dream of retiring to Great Britain, the land of their ancestors. They aren't drawn by visions of sunshine and warm weather. Nor are they tempted by low prices. Perhaps it is a yearning for the old ways, for civilized ideas like afternoon tea, for history and culture. Or perhaps they are attracted by the desolate beauty of the moors, the poetry of the Lake Country, or the tranquillity of the English countryside.

The British Isles are a land rich in history, where castles are as common as schoolyards. The British countryside still recalls the "mother country" for many travelers, while the capital city of London offers fine theater, famous museums, lively nightlife, and restaurants by the thousands.

Of course, weather is not one of Great Britain's assets. However, it does make for convenient conversation (it's the favorite British topic) because it is so variable. Any time you venture out for the day in Britain, you must be prepared for rain or a change in temperature.

The greatest extremes of weather are in the mountains of Scotland, Wales, and northern England. The western areas of Great Britain are wet, but the temperatures are moderate. The eastern plains are windy and relatively dry, with more extreme temperatures. The south is the sunniest area; Torquay, England's southernmost mainland city, even has palm trees.

THE CULTURE AND PEOPLE OF GREAT BRITAIN

Many retirees find life in Britain pleasant and simple. People speak English. Customs are not as unfamiliar as in other countries. Health care is good and inexpensive. And there is always plenty to do. About 13,000 American retirees currently live in the British Isles, and those numbers are increasing.

For those who do decide to live here, it is important to remember that the British often consider Americans to be brash, materialistic, and uncultured. Britons are generally more reserved than Americans and slower to develop friendships. Services are also slower and less efficient in Britain than in the United States. Take your own bag to the grocery store and be ready to pack it yourself. Twenty-four-hour service is unheard of here, and repairs can take forever.

But perhaps this slower pace and emphasis on how people conduct themselves is one of the things that attracts retirees to Britain in the first place. Once you get used to the cultural changes, it can be hard to leave.

A Brief History of Britain   The rich history of the British Isles is a book in itself, but just take note of the high points to get a head start as you explore the country:

A.D. 43   Roman Emperor Claudius invades Britain and develops a deepwater port called Londinium

1042   Edward the Confessor becomes king and makes London the capital of England

1066   William the Conqueror is victorious at the Battle of Hastings and begins building the Tower of London

1485   Tudor rule begins

1533   Henry VIII marries Anne Boleyn and starts the Church of England

1694   Bank of England founded to fund William and Mary's war with France

1802   London is the world's largest port

1837   Queen Victoria begins her reign

1863   First underground train in the world opens in London

1939   London bombed in "the Blitz"

1981   London Docklands Development Corporation begins to refurbish the docklands area

1994   Train service between London and Paris begins via the "Chunnel"

Develop Your Own Cultural Identity A good way to meet fellow expatriates as well as locals is through volunteering. You will find great opportunities in Britain. For instance, the Council for British Archeology, Bowse Morrell House, 111 Walmgate, York Y01 2UA, has information on archaeological projects in England that accept volunteers. The Scottish Conservation Project, tel. (44) (178) 647-9697, uses volunteers for conservation work throughout Scotland. Activities range from tree planting to footpath reconstruction. The following voluntary service organizations work with the poor and handicapped in Great Britain:

✦ Royal Society for Mentally Handicapped Children and Adults, 123 Golden Lane, London EC1Y ORT; tel. (44) (171) 454-0454

✦ Merton Volunteer Bureau, the Vestry Hall, London Rd., Mitcham, Surrey CR4 3UD; tel. (44) (181) 640-7355

Ready to step back into the classroom for a while? Everything from weeklong classes at Oxford to Elderhostel sessions are available on a range of subjects. For information on higher education in Great

Britain, including a directory of where you can study specific subjects, consult *Higher Education in the United Kingdom: A Handbook for Students from Overseas and Their Advisors*. It is published by the British Council and the Association of Commonwealth Universities and is available from Pearson Education, 10 Bank St., White Plains, NY 10606, 914/993-5000, or from Longman Group Longman House, Burnt Mill, Harlow, Essex CM20 2JE.

For information on retirement communities in Great Britain, contact the Retirement Home Association, 47 Albermarle St., London W1X 3FE.

RECOMMENDED LIVING AREAS

The question is not *why* to retire in Great Britain, but *where*. Many retirees are attracted to London because of its cultural opportunities. But London is expensive. Other retirees prefer a more tranquil, less expensive retirement in the countryside. The British themselves tend to retire to seacoast towns, especially in the south and west of England where the climate is milder.

Overall, the most popular places to retire in Great Britain are Sussex, the Isle of Wight, Devon, Dorset, Cornwall, the Scilly Isles, Cumbria, Somerset, Norfolk, Kent, and Hampshire.

The south coast has the warmest temperatures and the least fog; South Devon and Cornwall are remote, but warm. The most exclusive retirement areas are Budleigh, Salterton, Sidmouth, and Seaton on the south Devon coast. In Sussex, most retirees prefer Eastbourne and Bexhill. The east coast, from Lincolnshire to the Scottish border, can also be charming, but cold winds are common.

Wales is less expensive and less developed than England, although it is rainier and cooler. To retire here, you'll want to know a bit of Welsh. The most popular places to retire in Wales are Caernarvonshire, Merionethshire, Radnorshire, Cardiganshire,

Denbigshire, Montgomeryshire, Caermartenshire, Breconshire, Flintshire, and Anglesey.

If you're interested in Scotland, Edinburgh is a delightful city. Another popular choice is Inverness (on Loch Ness)—although the winters are cold and dark.

Remember, the more rural the area, the more difficult it is for foreigners to fit in and feel part of the community. It will help if you like horseback riding, gardening, and fishing—the primary pastimes in the countryside.

London—Exciting City Living It's difficult to be bored in London, whether fun for you means exploring Egyptology exhibits at the British Museum, sampling the city's many pubs, enjoying a world-class theater production, or just strolling through Hyde Park.

All this fun does come at a cost, however. Americans who move to London and try to continue to live like Americans discover that life can be very expensive. Part of the reason you came here is to experience another culture, so dig in. Use public transportation, shop in small markets, and dine in quaint pubs and local hangouts. You and your budget will be better off for it.

London is the most expensive place to live in Britain. Even homes in the countryside outside London can be pricey. One-bedroom apartments start at $105,000; houses range from $200,000 to $1 million. In just one quarter of 1997 prices rose 12.4 percent, and predictions are for prices to keep going up for the next several years.

Desirability and price vary in different sections of London. Belgravia and Mayfair are the most expensive and fashionable areas. Lower priced property with good potential for appreciation is available in Clapham, Kensington, Stockwell, Wandsworth, and Camberwell.

More established but still available to bargain hunters are Battersea and Richmond. Shepherd's Bush and Acton have particularly good appreciation potential. Hackney is also considered up-and-coming, but it may take longer before the properties there appreciate.

Certain parts of Hackney, such as Victoria Park and London

Fields, have lovely period houses and high appreciation values. However, other sections of Hackney are dominated by less-attractive council flats. Houses range from $240,000 to $400,000.

The Riverside area of London is also an increasingly popular place to live. Apartments with views of the Thames and Tower Bridge range from $350,000 to $1.2 million. Dunbar Wharf on the Limehouse Reach section of the Thames is also attracting investment; apartments there range from $410,000 to $655,000. Near the St. Katharine Dock, apartments start at $320,000.

Chelsea is another option. The recent Chelsea Village development added 46 one- and two-bedroom apartments near the Chelsea Football Club and the Fulham Broadway underground station. Prices range from $270,000 to $330,000.

For more information on properties in and around London, check with the following agents:

＊ Hamptons International, 4 Royal Court, Royal Exchange, London EC3 3LN; tel. (44) (171) 283-2111

＊ SPD Savills, 80 Wapping High St., London E 14; tel. (44) (171) 456-6800

＊ Hamptons International Head Office, 7 Lower Sloane St., Sloane Square, London SW1 W8AH; tel. (44) (171) 824-8822

Cotswolds—Old World Villages The Cotswolds—with rural farmland, country lanes, and old churches just an hour and a half northwest of London—are an ideal setting for many. A softly rolling ribbon of hills enfolds rustic villages of another, more romantic age. As you drive, you can glimpse an occasional flock of sheep meandering near the road.

The area includes the major towns of Gloucestershire, Worcestershire, and Hertfordshire. All the towns and villages nestled in these hills possess a charming uniformity. Every structure is built of the local stone—an indigenous limestone—and topped with a steep slate roof. The Cotswold economy originally was based on wool, and it is still predominately agricultural.

Real estate prices are still reasonable throughout this region. In

Bourne, a semi-detached 1930s house with three bedrooms, dining room, lounge, gas heating, and gardens was recently listed for $121,000. In Cranham, a three-bedroom detached bungalow with oil central heating, a brook, parking for up to six cars, and an acre of gardens listed for $264,000.

More economical properties are often found in Stroud, where a three-bedroom detached house with river views, dining room, kitchen with built-in appliances, cloakroom, gas central heat, and gardens was recently listed for $152,000. A house under construction with three bedrooms, full gas central heating, garage, and gardens was listed at $137,000. For information, contact Cotswold Properties, tel. (44) (145) 375-1647.

The Southwest Peninsula—Seaside Excitement The southwest peninsula, including Devon and Cornwall, is for people who enjoy smelling sea breezes, visiting fishing villages, walking harbor walls, swimming in the sea, and exploring England's maritime history. The southern coast of the peninsula faces the English Channel and has a mild climate. Gentle waves lap the secluded bays and ancient smugglers' coves. The northern coast faces the full force of the Atlantic. King Arthur, according to legend, lived at Tintagel on the north coast, where a ruined Norman castle (circa 1145) still clings to the slate cliffs.

Inland, among granite moors, Dartmoor, Exmoor, and Bodmin are designated National Trust areas. Protected from development, they remain unspoiled, with narrow country lanes that twist through the region. A two-bedroom flat in Bodmin was recently listed for $54,000. In Helston, a two-bedroom, two-story property near the harbor was listed for $81,000, while a new house with three bedrooms and a garage on a corner lot sold for $136,000. For information, call UK Property Gold, tel. (44) (124) 222-8322.

The North Country Traveling north you will discover East Anglia, comprised of Essex (the East Saxons), Suffolk ("the south folk"),

Norfolk ("the north folk"), and Cambridgeshire. The Norfolk Broads, 200 miles of navigable waterways, were dug by hand in the eleventh century to provide peat for the nearby city of Norwich. The coastline has miles of unspoiled sandy beaches.

In East Anglia, property prices are high. A restored period cottage near Saffron Walden was advertised for $296,000. It offers lovely views across the hills, a fine beamed drawing room with inglenook, three bedrooms, and four bathrooms. However, it is still possible, particularly in North Suffolk and Norfolk, to buy small cottages in the North Country for $95,000.

Because of their proximity to London, houses in Essex are more expensive. Recently, a semi-detached three-bedroom home was advertised for $184,000. A two-bedroom bungalow with gas central heat and double-glazed windows was listed for $195,000. Contact UK Property Gold, tel. (44) (124) 222-8322.

Wales North Wales is beautiful and also relatively inexpensive (South Wales is more industrial), with cottages selling for $50,000 to $60,000. A five-bedroom period house in Wales costs one-third the price of a comparable home in Chester, just across the English border. However, the high cost of property in southern England is pushing many people north, and costs will probably rise over the next few years.

If you are considering settling in Wales, learn a bit of Welsh. More than 40,000 inhabitants of the area speak this Celtic language; one-fourth of the inhabitants speak Welsh and English. Learning the language will make your life easier and charm your neighbors.

Scotland The least expensive country properties in Britain are in the Scottish Highlands, where cottages go for $50,000. Also affordable are Edinburgh and Glasgow, where three-bedroom cottages sell for $65,000.

As the fortunes of the landed gentry in this area decline, their manors and estates enter the market at relatively low prices. For example, a Scottish castle with 79 acres near Glasgow and Edinburgh was advertised recently for $208,000. A three-bedroom, two-bathroom home, built as the first school in Mey in 1875, was listed at $92,000. It is heated with radiators and is within sight of the Orkney Islands and the Castle of Mey.

In Lybster, a seven-bedroom, fully modernized home with ocean view and walled gardens was listed for $224,000. In Dunbeath Village, a traditional three-bedroom stone cottage with slate roof, oil-fired central heating, double-glazed windows, and gardens listed for $83,000. For information, contact D. W. George and Son, tel. (44) (195) 560-6060 or (44) (184) 789-2225.

$\mathcal{R}$ENTING IN $\mathcal{G}$REAT $\mathcal{B}$RITAIN

Renting can be a good option in Great Britain. Whether you are considering the fast-paced life of London or the bucolic Cotswolds, renting can be a good way to test the waters, learn more about the neighborhood, and check out the properties before you actually commit to a purchase.

How to Find Good Rental Properties Classified ads in local newspapers are an excellent way of finding rental properties. If you'd like to do some research before you head to Great Britain, check out Internet sites maintained by the many realty companies throughout the British Isles. A search containing the words *real estate*, *rental*, and the region you would like to explore will bring up a wealth of sites, complete with photos, property descriptions, and prices.

Average Rental Costs and Listings Rents vary depending on location, size, and amenities. Rents are highest in London, where flats go very quickly on and off the market. Short-term rentals start at $900 per week for a one-bedroom flat, $1,200 for two bedrooms, and $1,416 for three bedrooms.

Some sources for short-term rentals in Great Britain include:

❖ In the English Manner, 515 S. Figueroa St., Suite 1000, Los Angeles, CA; 800/422-0799

❖ The Apartment Service, c/o Keith Prowse, 234 W. 44th St., Suite 1000, New York, NY 10036, 800/669-8687, or in London, 5-6 Francis Grove, Wimbledon SW19 4DT; tel. (44) (181) 944-1444

❖ Barclay International Group, 150 E. 52nd St., New York, NY 10022, 800/223-1012, or 45 Albermarle St., Suite 4, London, tel. (44) (171) 495-2986

Londoners may also opt to rent a bedsit, the British equivalent of an efficiency. The bathroom is often down the hall, and the cooking facilities may be minimal. However, the better bedsits have private showers. Single bedsits start at about $64 a week; doubles are $80 to $135 per week. Or you can buy a bedsit starting at $80,000. One local agent that deals in bedsits is Anscombe and Ringland, tel. (44) (1) 340-2600.

The best resources for finding a bedsit or a flat are the *Evening Standard* and the *Hampstead and Highgate Express*. To find an apartment to share, look in either *Time Out* or *City Limit*, two London weekly magazines.

*B*uying *R*eal *E*state

☞

Buying property in England or Wales (Scotland is a different matter; it is discussed later) is a considerably different process than in the United States. To begin, you need a brief language lesson. A Realtor in Britain is called an *estate agent*. A lawyer is a *solicitor*. If you are obtaining a mortgage in Great Britain, you will deal with a *building society*.

Property in London is sold as *leasehold* or *freehold*. Freehold means you own the building and land outright (this is rare in London);

leasehold means you have use of the land and building for the period of the lease, which can run from 999 years on down.

By American standards, British estate agents are paid a tiny commission (2 to 3 percent). That's good news for your pocketbook, but it means the agents have little incentive to sell you anything.

In addition, estate agents are often uninformed about areas outside their locale. Take time to do your own research. Explore the area you are interested in. Find out as much as you can from longtime residents, the local papers, the town library, and historic records.

The Buying Process   Once you have chosen a property, make an offer directly or through an agent. Offers are commonly subject to survey and contract, which means you may be able to back out—with penalty.

The transactions following the initial deposit are usually handled by solicitors (both the buyer and the seller must engage solicitors). Your estate agent can recommend one. A solicitor's fees are about 1 percent of the purchase price. Stay in touch and push the process along—or settlement could take 10 months.

After you make a deposit, the seller's solicitor draws up a draft contract that describes the property in detail. Your solicitor reviews the draft and tries to dig up any additional information that might influence the future value of the property.

If a property has been registered, a single Land Certificate is all that you need to complete a purchase. If the property is mortgaged, a Charge Certificate is required. The draft contract is then returned to the seller's solicitor after amendments or approval. When it is approved by both parties, a small down payment is required.

The lender has the property surveyed, but you should have your own surveyor check as well. As the buyer, you will pay for both surveys. If the surveyors find a fault in the house, you can withdraw from the contract and collect your deposit and down payment.

To minimize the foreign-exchange risk, hedge your currency position on the currency forward market. For example, if you are buying a property for £250,000, and you think the pound might go up, buy a futures contract of £250,000.

Assuming you are not *gazumped* (a uniquely British way of saying another buyer has made a higher bid than yours during the buying process), the title of the property is transferred after the final payment has been made. Your solicitor then investigates the title and draws up the transfer document for the seller's solicitor to approve. When the document has been signed by both parties, you are the proud owner of a piece of British real estate.

The entire process, from the submission of the first draft contract to the securing of a mortgage and the receipt of your transfer document, can take several months.

Funding In England and Wales, a mortgage is not transferable as it is in the United States. Properties are always sold unencumbered by any mortgages, legal charges, or liens. Be prepared to pay a 2 percent stamp duty on properties costing more than $64,000. In addition, you may have to pay a land registry fee of about $330.

If you are a non-resident, it isn't easy to borrow money in England. You'll have better luck if you already have a bank or building society account that has been open for a year or so.

It's Easier in Scotland Buying a house in Scotland is a breeze compared with the convoluted tangle of paperwork involved with property purchases in England and Wales. The same title search and investigations occur after an exchange of contracts, which can be completed in a matter of hours or days after an offer has been made. The seller's solicitor processes much of the paperwork, so you may not even need the services of an estate agent.

Solicitors know the property markets in Scotland and can market the houses themselves. They can also arrange the survey, determine a reasonable bidding price, and make contacts for you with building societies.

Because bids can be made before the contract work is undertaken, either party may back out at any time without penalty. Once a bid has been accepted, of course, both parties are legally bound.

COST OF LIVING

The average retired couple in Great Britain needs an income of about $15,000 a year; an individual needs about $11,500 a year. You'll find that some items, such as entertainment, are a bargain. A good orchestra seat at a West End theater in London costs only $11 (a comparable seat costs $25 to $50 in New York). Groceries and restaurants are also reasonably priced. However, bus and subway fares can be high. Here's what you can expect to pay for some everyday expenses in Great Britain:

electricity	$70/month	lettuce	$.90/head
gasoline	$1.70/gallon	coffee	$5/pound
movie ticket	$7	milk	$3/gallon
maid service	$10–$12/hour	chicken	$1.50/pound
bananas	$.65/pound	fish	$4/pound
bread	$1.50/loaf	video rental	$3.50
steak	$3.50/pound	compact disc	$16

DAY-TO-DAY LIVING CONCERNS

Unlike many other retirement destinations, in Great Britain you will not have to do without the technological conveniences on which you have learned to rely. For the most part, telephone service is excellent. Internet service is also efficient and inexpensive. Electrical service is readily available and dependable in most areas. For economic reasons, many residents heat their homes with oil or gas.

$\mathcal{T}$AXES

Whether you consider Britain's taxes high or moderate depends on your income level. Expatriates from the United States may be disappointed by the lack of deductions, write-offs, and tax breaks. The basic income-tax rate in great Britain is 25 percent on taxable income up to $19,300. Beyond that amount, the flat rate is 40 percent.

Allowable write-offs are basically limited to interest payments on mortgages on primary residences up to $30,000 and investments in some companies whose shares are not listed on the stock exchange. Some good news for retirees: Britain has a double-taxation agreement with the United States—U.S. expatriates are not taxed twice for the same income.

Great Britain has no wealth tax. Capital gains of more than $8,000 per person are taxed at 25 percent (capital gains from the sale of your residence are exempt from this tax).

A 15 percent value-added tax (VAT) is assessed on most goods and services sold in Great Britain. However, this VAT is not charged on accommodations, goods, and services on the Channel Islands.

$\mathcal{M}$AKING THE $\mathcal{M}$OVE

Step one of relocating to Great Britain is obtaining permission to become a permanent resident, which may be the biggest hurdle you'll face. It can be difficult to obtain permission unless you can prove that you are a "Person of Independent Means" or that you have a British relative. (Your best bet is to prove both.)

Because jobs are scarce in Britain, authorities are especially cautious about admitting anyone who might try to take one. And because medical care is socialized and more or less free, authorities hesitate to admit anyone who might be a burden on the state medical system.

Anyone planning to stay in Great Britain more than six months must be examined by a medical inspector at the border. Admission to the country can be refused on medical grounds.

Becoming a Temporary or Permanent Resident   To enter Britain as a Person of Independent Means, you must show that you have a foreign income of not less than £25,000 a year that is transferable to Britain. You must also prove that you can maintain and accommodate yourself and your dependents without working and without relying on public funds. In addition, you must demonstrate either a close connection with Britain (close relatives or periods of previous residence, for example) or proof that your admission would be in the general interest of the country.

An extended visit to Great Britain requires a visa. To apply for one, or to apply as a Person of Independent Means, check with www.visitbritain.com on-line or the British consulate general closest to you. The application form can be hand-delivered or mailed, along with your passport, two recent passport-sized photos, and fees (a check or money order if done through the mail). You may have to go through an interview, and you may be asked for additional documents. The fee for a settlement visa is $420.

Applications take several months to process. Initially, you will be admitted for one year (you are prohibited from working in Britain during that time). You can apply for a year's extension at the end of the one-year period. You may also be required to register with the police and have an endorsement stamped in your passport.

After you have live in Britain for five years, you can apply to the Home Office for naturalization as a British subject. However, if you do, you may risk losing your American citizenship.

For more information, contact the British consulate nearest you or the Embassy of Great Britain, 3100 Massachusetts Ave. NW, Washington, D.C. 20008; 202/462-1340. Ask for the booklets "Residence in Britain—Notes for People From Overseas" and "Immigration into Britain—Notes on the Regulations and Procedures."

What to Bring, What to Leave Behind   You'll find that many flats and houses, whether for rent or sale, come fully furnished. So you need not bring many household goods with you. One thing you will definitely want to bring is a supply of any prescription drugs you will need. Be sure to carry all medicines in their prescription bottles, along with a letter from your doctor. Also, when your prescription runs out you will need to obtain a new prescription from a British doctor, so bring along a list of generic names for your medications as well. Some pharmaceutical drugs can be brought into the country only in limited amounts. For details, contact Home Office, Room 239, Drugs Branch, Licensing Section, Queen Anne's Gate, London SW1H 9AT; tel. (44) (171) 273-3806; fax (171) (44) 273-2157. For more information on importing personal effects, write HM Customs and Excise, Dorset House, Stamford Street, London SE1 9PY.

What About Pets?   To import animals into Great Britain, you must obtain an import license six to eight weeks before your scheduled departure. A health certificate accompanies the application. Do not have your pet vaccinated for rabies before departure because that shot must be administered within 24 hours of arrival in Britain.

All dogs and cats also undergo a six-month quarantine upon arrival in Britain. Before you arrive, you must reserve quarantine accommodations. A complete list of kennels and catteries licensed for quarantine purposes is available from British Information Services, 212/752-5747. All of these kennels are privately owned and vary in services and comfort level. You should also make arrangements for the pet to be transported from the port of arrival to the kennel.

ℳEDICAL 𝒞ARE

Good medical care is inexpensive—and in many cases free—in Britain. Emergency medical treatment is free for U.S. citizens, but subsequent care is not. Residents are not charged for treatment in case of emergency or for the diagnosis and treatment of certain communicable diseases.

Short-term visitors and newcomers (those who have lived in Britain for less than a year) must pay the full costs of any hospital treatment. Even so, you will find that the costs are generally lower than in the United States.

To find out if you are eligible for coverage under the National Health Service in Britain, contact the Department of Health, 3B Hannibal House, London SE1 6TE; tel. (44) (171) 972-2000.

Health Insurance One of the downsides of Britain's National Health Service is that it can take up to two years to get a non-emergency operation. For this reason we recommend private hospital insurance for retirees, which costs between $30 and $500 a year per person.

Your U.S. health insurance may cover you overseas. If it does, you may want to continue with your U.S. company for the first year or two that you live in Britain (until you are firmly established as a resident). If you decide to go with a private British company, consider one of the three largest private health insurance companies in the country:

- British United Provident Association, Provident House, Essex St., London WC2R 3AX; tel. (44) (171) 345-5531. Coverage is available to British residents up to age 74. A special SeniorCare plan offers extensive coverage for those over age 60.
- Private Patients Plan, PPP House, Upperton Rd., Eastbourne, East Sussex BN21 1LH; tel. (44) (171) 388-2468. Family insurance ranges from $800 to $1,760 per year. A special retirement health plan costs less than $32 per month. It works in conjunction with the National Health Service plan.
- Western Provident Association, Rivergate House, 70 Radcliff St., Bristol BS1 6LS; tel. (44) (182) 362-3000. Family insurance, if the oldest member is under age 60, costs around $2,880 in London and $1,920 outside London. It costs approximately $1,520 in the rest of the country.

For a full list of private health-care providers, contact Independent Healthcare Association, 22 Little Russell St., London WC1A 2HT; tel. (44) (171) 430-0537.

British life insurance (called *assurance*) companies offer some of the lowest rates in the world. English companies are among the oldest and most experienced and are free from government investment restrictions. They are able to pass on greater returns to their customers. In addition, British insurers tend to pay lower commissions to their sales staffs, which further reduces costs.

$\mathcal{F}$INANCIAL $\mathcal{M}$ATTERS

The British financial system is one of the most stable in the world. London itself has more foreign banks per square mile than any other city in the world. If you are looking for a well-respected place to keep your money, this is it.

Banking Great Britain's banking system is an account-holder's cafeteria; whatever banking services you're looking for, you should be able to find them here. More importantly, British banks have a well-deserved reputation for soundness and experience. In fact, they weathered the worldwide banking crisis of the 1930s without any major shutdowns.

British banks also offer privacy. This tradition is rooted in English common law and widely respected. Under British law, a banker has a contract of privacy with each client. An English banker will not give out information about your account to anyone without your permission or a court order.

England has none of the automatic reporting requirements that regulate the U.S. banking system. English banks don't keep used checks or microfilms of checks. Once your checks are returned, only you know what the checks were issued for and in what amounts.

Check around to see which banks offer the most comprehensive services. National Girobank, which operates through the mail and at post offices, offers free checking with no service charge, no charge for checks, and no minimum balance. National Girobank also sells foreign currency at a better rate than the major banks. You can also obtain checks that can be cashed abroad.

The four major English banks are National Westminster, Barclays, Lloyds, and Midland. English banking in general is inexpensive, but banking at Lloyds is free provided your account does not fall below $16 at any time during a quarter.

If you establish a good rapport with your English banker, he or she will usually negotiate checks for you. If, for example, you deposit a check from the United States, you will get immediate credit, even though it will take up to four weeks before the check clears.

What Should Retirees Do with Their Money? Britain is home to about 40 percent of the investment money in Europe, as well as to more than 5,000 U.S. companies. Investment possibilities are endless.

The Channel Islands are home to a booming offshore investment business. Many financial service companies and offshore banks operate in St. Helier, the capital of Jersey.

For information on investing in Britain, contact the Invest in Britain Bureau, British Consulate General, 845 Third Ave., New York, NY 10022; 212/745 0418, fax 212/745-0456.

$\mathcal{T}$RANSPORTATION

Traveling around the British Isles is much like traveling around the United States, only in a more compact format. Numerous airlines connect the country with the United States and Europe. The British Isles are also crisscrossed with well-maintained roads and served by excellent public transportation.

Mass Transit Even if you wouldn't dream of living without a car in the United States, try it in London. Public transportation there is excellent and fairly cheap. The city has good subway (called the Underground or the Tube) and bus systems, as well as good train connections for travel around the country. Travel on the Underground is much cheaper if you buy a round-trip ticket after 10 a.m., and train travel is cheaper if you purchase a round-trip ticket after 9:30 a.m. To save the most money, purchase weekly tickets for unlimited travel.

BritRail offers the Gatwick Express, 24-hour service from central London to Gatwick Airport, for $23 in first class or $17 in coach. For more information, contract BritRail at 800/677-8585 or www.raileurope.com.

Automobile Travel For many new residents, especially those choosing to live outside of London, the best way to get around is by automobile. Remember, of course, that the British drive on the left side of the road. Many Americans prefer to use a right-drive car.

You can temporarily import a motor vehicle to Britain for a six-month period. During this time you can keep the registration from your home state as well as foreign license plates, but you'll need a British certificate of insurance. The vehicle cannot be sold or rented in Great Britain and must be exported. Permanent importation makes the car subject to customs duty (10 percent) and value-added tax (17.5 percent). These charges may be waived in certain circumstances.

Once you've cleared customs, you'll need to register the car with the vehicle registration officer (VRO). For information on registration, insurance, excise duties, and use of foreign plates, contact the Driver and Vehicle Licensing Agency, Longview Rd., Swansea SA6 7JL, Wales, tel. (44) (1792) 772-134.

You can use your U.S. driver's license for up to 12 months upon arriving in Great Britain. After that you'll need to get a British license, which can be obtained only by passing a British driving test.

LEISURE TIME

Even if you are on a budget, you will still be able to afford high-quality entertainment in Britain. The British equivalent of Time Square's TKTS half-price ticket booth is in Leicester Square in London. Many theaters offer reduced prices for matinee or Monday-night performances. During summer you can listen to the best symphony orchestras in the world at the Royal Albert Hall for $3.20, and local film societies show movies for about the same price. Check local papers or libraries for listings.

Sports and Hobbies If you enjoy playing sports, you can join a club offering everything from tennis to soccer for as little as $35. Avid soccer fans can save money at matches by doing what the British do—standing.

Britain is a land of gardeners. The climate, with its plentiful rain, mild winters, and warm summers, provides a congenial environment for trees and plants, particularly in the south. The British have created a rich national heritage of parks, arboreta, herb farms, plant nurseries, and cottage gardens.

Gardening is a good way to meet the British, especially the country folk (as is horseback riding). If you have a green thumb, consider cultivating your hobby and a few new friends through an English garden society. As a member of the Hardy Plant Society, 214 Ruxely Lane, West Ewell, Surrey, for instance, you'll have a chance to learn about plants through garden visits, meetings, and free bulletins.

The Royal Horticultural Society, 80 Vincent Square, London SW1 2PE, tel. (44) (171) 834-4333, runs the famous Chelsea Flower Show as well as the largest and finest garden in England. Members receive free admission to both, a monthly newsletter, advice on gardening, and admission to England's finest garden library.

ADDITIONAL RESOURCES

British Consulate General, 845 Third Ave., New York, NY 10022; 212/745-0200, fax 212/754-3062

British Embassy, 202/462-1340

British Information Services, 212/752-5747

British Tourist Authority, 800/462-2748 or 212/986-2200

Cornwall Tourist Board, tel. (44) (1872) 274-057

Immigration Advisory Service, County House, 190 Great Dover St., London SE1 4YB; tel. (44) (171) 357 6917; Duty Office (24 hours): tel. (44) (181) 814-1559, fax (44) (171) 378-0665

Scottish Highlands & Islands, tel. (44) (349) 63434

Townsend Thoresen Cross Channel Ferry, tel. (44) (171) 583-9330

U.S. Embassy in London, tel. (44) (171) 499-9000 (24-hour number)

Wales Tourist Board, 2 Maddox St., London W1, tel. (44) (171) 808-3838

Useful Web Sites

www.visitbritain.com/

www.londonindex.co.uk/tourist.htm

www.scot-highlands.com

www.tourism.wales/gov.uk

www.ukpg.co.uk

www.barclayweb.com

www.britain-info.org/

Greece

by LESLIE DORAN

Remember high school history? Remember learning about the first Olympic Games, the Acropolis, and the birthplace of democracy? All that history is still there to absorb and enjoy for those who retire in Greece.

The people of Greece are warm and friendly. The physical beauty of Greece—from the great mountains in Metéora to idyllic island beaches—also lures visitors. The climate in Greece is moderate, virtually year-round. The exception is in the mountains, where avid skiers can take to the snow-covered slopes in winter.

Greece, with a population of 12 million, is roughly the size of Alabama. It has 9,000 miles of coastline with 2,000 islands inside its borders (fewer than 200 are populated). Athens in central Greece, Thessaloniki in the north, and Patras on the Peloponnese peninsula are the largest cities.

Athens is a modern capital city, with many of the attractions and problems of any metropolis. Water pollution is a problem that has been largely resolved, and it is now safe to frolic at the city's beaches. Air pollution is another periodic concern. The completion of the Metro, an underground subway system, will cut down on auto exhaust and help relieve pollution levels. The crime rate is much lower in Athens than in cities in the United States. Pickpockets are the main concern.

You can travel through Greece by trains (reliable), buses (more of a challenge), and automobiles (sometimes dangerous). The winding Greek roads can be treacherous for drivers unfamiliar with their twists and turns. In fact, Greece has the highest accident rate in Europe. If you plan on renting, leasing, or buying a car, make sure you bring an International Driving Permit, available through AAA in the United States, and comprehensive travel insurance.

To embrace the Greek way of life is to embrace good food, sunny days, olive oil, and wine. Daily routines will challenge you, however. You will have to convert dollars to drachmas, pounds to kilos, and gallons to liters. But the exciting cultural and historical surroundings will offset these small adaptations.

Retiring to Greece can make economic sense. The islands offer bargains in real estate, and their idyllic scenery and weather make them even more attractive. Compared to its neighbors, Greece enjoys a stable government, a developing economy, and a growing population of emigrants. In fact, it has the world's seventh largest American population receiving Social Security benefits.

THE CULTURE AND PEOPLE OF GREECE

Greek civilization emerged around 3000 B.C. The ancient Greeks were a seafaring people who not only had culture thrust upon them by invaders but also imported the best art and technology from lands they visited. The influence of many cultures can be seen in Greece's art, architecture, attire, food, and customs. Ancient Greece was itself the birthplace of much of Western culture. Important works in philosophy, art, theater, and literature emerged here.

A Brief History of Greece Greek history comes alive as you explore the country's ancient ruins. The following are but a few highlights from Greece's rich heritage:

1600 B.C.	Minoan culture is at its peak, the labyrinth is built in Crete
1225 B.C.	Trojan War
776 B.C.	The Olympic Games are established. The 200-meter dash is the first event.
750 B.C.	The city-states are created
336 B.C.	Alexander the Great comes to power
168–146 B.C.	Greece comes under control of the Roman Empire
A.D. 95	St. John writes the Revelation on the Isle of Patmos
1821–29	The Greek war of independence is fought against Turkey
1834	Athens is named the capital of Greece
1893	The Corinth Canal opens, joining the Aegean and Ionian Seas
1940	Italy invades Greece and rules for four years
1946–49	Communists are overthrown with help from the United States
1974	Greece is reaffirmed as a republic by popular vote
1981	Greece becomes part of the European Economic Community
1991	The 2,500th anniversary of democracy is celebrated in Greece

Learn the Language Since all secondary students learn English in school, it is easy to communicate in English here, especially in the cities and with younger people. But if you travel to rural areas, a basic knowledge of Greek is beneficial. Learning a few phrases will help you feel more comfortable and independent, and the attempt will endear you to the Greek people.

One way to learn the language is through an audio course before you leave your American home. Helen Dumas offers a good course, Speak Greek in Two Months, that costs only $39 and comes with a workbook and two cassettes. For more information, call 310/373-0808 or e-mail Dumas at LSAMC@earthlink.net.

For a little amusement, pick up Howard Tomb's *Wicked Greek for the Traveler*. This little book is full of snappy Greek phrases fitting almost every occasion (available from Workman Publishing, 708 Broadway, New York, NY 10003).

Enjoy New Traditions   Greece enjoys a rich cultural heritage. During the tourist season and national holidays, festivals and performances abound. The two most important state holidays are Independence Day on March 25, celebrating the defeat of the Ottoman Empire, and Ochi! Day on October 28, commemorating the defeat of Mussolini's army.

Most islands have their own festivals. In August on the island of Náxas, everyone turns out to celebrate the Dionysís Festival. Natives and guests alike enjoy folk dancing, traditional costumes, and plenty of free food and wine.

Religion is an important part of Greek life; the Greek Orthodox Church enjoys the protection of the state. When visiting religious sites such as monasteries and churches, be sure to respect dress codes. Men must wear trousers. Women must wear skirts and cover their arms. Overall, dress in Greece tends to be more formal than in the United States, except at beaches.

Develop Your Own Cultural Identity   With over 87,000 Americans living in Greece (20,000 of them receiving Social Security benefits), you will not feel isolated here. Several organizations are dedicated to making Americans feel connected, especially in the Athens area.

The American Women's Organization of Greece has 400 members and monthly meetings every third Thursday. The group is involved in environmental and philanthropic activities. Greek-English newspapers also provide information on groups for specialized interests such as hiking, skiing, gardening, bridge playing, and others.

ℛECOMMENDED ℒIVING 𝒜REAS

It is hard to name the best places to live in Greece—the choices are vast. If you like the countryside, the rural north or on one of the islands could be for you. If you prefer the arts and big-city hustle and bustle, then Athens, Thessaloniki, or their suburbs might be good choices. Cities boast international airports, efficient mass transit, good medical facilities, and many other retirees and expatriates. Read further to discover which locations suit your dreams of ideal retirement living.

Athens—City Living Athens has the all the advantages of big-city life, with a large number of foreigners already in residence. There are several American associations in Athens, and access to the U.S. embassy is convenient. The disadvantage to Athens is the cost of living—the highest in the country.

Living anywhere in or near Athens assures you a life filled with cultural feasts: great restaurants, orchestras, opera, ballet, folk dances, theater, parks, zoos, public gardens, and planetariums. There are also educational, sporting, and archaeological possibilities. The heart of Athens is the Plaka, a small island under the view of the Acropolis.

Rental houses and flats in the city vary widely in cost, from $500 a month to $2,500 a month or more. For help, contact the Joan Rothou Real Estate Agency, 90 Athinas Ave., Vouliagmeni 16671; tel. (30) (1) 896-3030, fax (30) (1) 896-3741, or Alfa-Omega Real Estate Investments, 121 Ethn. Makariou-Agia Triada Sq., Agiatriada Square, Argiroupolis; tel. (30) (1) 992-2292.

Suburbs north of Athens include Glyfada (a 20-minute drive from downtown), Vouliagmeni (a 45-minute drive from downtown), and Rafina, a fishing and port city on the Aegean (about one hour from Athens). These towns offer proximity to big-city amenities but don't suffer from Athens's air and noise pollution. Each of these communities has its own charm. Vouliagmeni boasts a spa with a reputation for treating arthritis and rheumatism. Glyfada offers great sandy beaches and a wide variety of water sports. Rafina is a charming sea-side town with ferry connections to all Greek ports.

Thessaloniki—Favorite Northern Town   Greece's second major city, Thessaloniki, was founded in 315 B.C. It has a considerable population of Americans. The busiest port on the Thermaic Gulf, Thessaloniki is more modern than Athens. It is a trade-fair center that boasts international-class exhibition facilities. It is also rich in archaeological sites, such as the famous White Tower. Built as part of a city-wall system to protect the town center during the reign of the Turks, the White Tower now houses Byzantine works of art and historical collections.

Thessaloniki was named the 1997 Cultural Capital of Europe, reflecting residents' high quality of life. The people there are warm and welcoming. Thessaloniki's climate is cooler and the weather is more moderate than Athens's, making it a great place to live.

Some sample residences for sale include a fifth-floor flat with two bedrooms, living room, bath, garage, and view for $103,000 and a first-floor flat with two bedrooms, bath, and large balconies for only $86,000. There are many rental properties, and price varies depending on amenities. For more information, contact Mpasiakoulis Realty, Gr. Lampraki 38, Thessaloniki 54638; tel. (30) (31) 218-241; e-mail mpasiakoulis@axiom.gr.

Skiáthos—Favorite Island   Skiáthos is northeast of Rafina in the Sporades Isles and has a large British expatriate community. The facilities here are close to U.S. standards, and the island enjoys good transportation and communication systems.

The small green island also has over 60 beautiful sandy beaches, as well as pine woods and olive trees. The church of St. John the Baptist and several monasteries are on the island. It has its own airport near Skiáthos Town, which is perched on two hills with a view of the harbor below.

Skiáthos Town hosts an Aegean festival of music, dance, and theater every summer, and there are other celebrations throughout the year here. There are many cottages, townhouses, and villas for sale and rent on the island. Prices range from $25,000 for a small house to $100,000 for a larger, more comfortable one. The key is to shop around. For more information, contact Constantin Moscholios, Alexandrou Moratidou 28, Skiathos Island 37002, tel. (30) 427-2-1457, or George Pipinos, 38 Kennedy St., Rhodes, tel. (30) 241-23895, fax (30) 241-20883.

Corfu Corfu, the northernmost Ionion island, is one of the most popular and often-visited Greek islands. The island has a royal history—Prince Philip, husband of Queen Elizabeth, was born here— and a palace to prove it.

The terrain is lush and mountainous, with citrus, olive, and fig trees. Traveling around, you can see the architectural influence of the Italians (Venetians) and British. The island has a British expatriate colony, which means English is widely spoken here. It attracts many artists and writers, who are drawn by its beauty.

Corfu can be expensive, but if you are willing to shop around, bargains can be found. While furnished seaside properties might rent for $250 a week, you can also get a beautiful villa for the bargain price of only $491 a month during the low season. Contact the Corfu Property Agency for more information at Kapodistriou 36, Corfu 49100, tel. (30) 661-28141, fax (30) 661-46663.

$\mathcal{R}$ENTING IN $\mathcal{G}$REECE

Renting is a good way to check out the neighbors and get to know an area before buying. Most people who live in Greece agree that word of mouth and newspapers hot off the press are your best bets for finding rental bargains. The *Athens News*, an English daily, and *Athens Today*, an English weekly, are good sources for the mainland. On the islands, customers at the local café might have the best information. You can also drive around and look for rental signs.

Renting in Athens   In Athens, rent will vary according to location and time of year. It is still possible to find bargain apartments for $500 a month in Athens. During the summer high season, unless you have a yearly lease, rents will soar. Recent examples include:

❧ A flat near the Olympic stadium on the fourth floor with a view, verandah, three bedrooms, and parking for $1,450 a month

❧ A second-floor apartment with three bedrooms, a nice balcony, and two parking spaces at $1,150 a month

❧ A luxury apartment with underfloor heat at $3,900 a month

Things to Keep in Mind   When it comes time to sign a lease, make sure the rent is in drachmas. This will work to your advantage, since the dollar is the more stable currency. It is okay to try and bargain on rent with the property owner. Check to see what utilities are included and who is responsible for paying for repairs. If the heating system is shared, you will have to pay year-round, whether you are in residence or not. Make sure that phone service is available.

Buying Real Estate

Before buying property in Greece, you should visit, then rent in the area that most appeals to you. Should you decide to buy, look for property with the help of a trusted local real estate agent. Make sure you deal with an agent who comes highly recommended from satisfied customers.

Buying a home in any foreign country is a serious step. In Greece there are some additional considerations. There are restrictions on foreigners buying property in certain border areas, including some of the islands. In addition, Greek law is currently being revised in preparation for compliance with European Union membership.

Therefore, it is best to either limit real estate purchases to undisputed areas or to consult a Greek lawyer well versed in international ownership of Greek land. You might also consult the U.S. embassy and the American Chamber of Commerce before buying Greek property. The U.S. embassy provides a list of approved lawyers.

Cost of Living

A retired couple with American dollars to spend in Greece may find the cost of living up to 30 percent lower than that of the United States. A pleasant dinner in a moderately priced restaurant starts around $15 per couple. Here are some examples of staple expenses that are regularly purchased by retirees:

electricity	$60/month	head of lettuce	$.25
gasoline	$2.50/gallon	tomatoes	$.40/pound
movie ticket	$6	coffee	$4.50/pound
six-pack of beer	$4	milk	$4.18/gallon
bottle of wine	$3	chicken	$1.02/pound
maid service	$20/day	video rental	$.50
bananas	$.84/pound	compact disc	$20
bread	$.35/pound	haircut	$10
steak	$3.18/pound		

Day-to-day Living Concerns

The amenities of life vary depending on where you choose to live in Greece. Urban areas have most of the comforts of home, including the modern conveniences you've grown to love and expect. Small electrical appliances brought from the United States will need a transformer and adapter to work in Greece. American television sets won't operate in Greece; the European system is incompatible with ours.

Greece's water meets Western standards and is safe to drink. Some may prefer bottled water, available throughout Greece, because of the heavy chlorination of tap water. In some rural areas, water can be scarce and of poorer quality. The foods of Greece are fresh and healthy—be adventurous and try local favorites.

The newly digitized national phone system is operated by OTE (Organismós Tilepikoinonión Elládos). There are direct lines to major countries, including the United States. Public pay phones operate with phone cards, obtained either at kiosks or OTE offices.

Greece doesn't have a 911 emergency service. However, you can call the Tourist Police at 171 in Athens or 922-7777 outside of Athens. You can reach the U.S. embassy in Athens at (30) (1) 721-2951 during normal business hours.

$\mathscr{T}$AXES

If you decide to retire in Greece, you will be happy to know that the Greek government will not tax your retirement income. However, if you earn money in Greece, you will pay Greek income tax regardless of your citizenship. You will, of course, have to pay your U.S. income tax as well. If you become a Greek citizen, you will be subject to more taxes.

The bad news is that Greece has a value-added tax (VAT), known as sales tax in the United States, of 18 percent on most services and goods. However, the VAT is only 8 percent on basic consumer goods.

$\mathscr{M}$AKING THE $\mathscr{M}$OVE

When traveling to Greece, you will need a current U.S. passport. It is wise to carry extra passport photos in case of emergency. Remember, your passport is valuable and should be guarded at all times. It is also wise to photocopy the information in the passport to make replacement easier.

Becoming a Temporary or Permanent Resident   As a U.S. citizen, you may enter and remain in Greece for up to three months without a visa. It is recommended that you register with the U.S. embassy, in case of emergency, when you arrive in the country.

If your visit will exceed three months, you must request a residence permit from the Aliens Bureau at Leofóros Alexándras 173, Athens (30) (1) 770-5711 at least 20 days before the expiration of the original three-month period. You must prove you have means to support yourself financially for the extended stay. Failure to follow procedures could result in fines and expulsion. Be sure you understand the conditions on which your stay is based.

What to Bring, What to Leave Behind   The Greek government has strict rules about imported vehicles. Therefore, it's easier to lease or buy a car after you arrive in Greece than to bring your car from the United States. Furniture and other large items will be cheaper to buy in Greece than to ship from home. As an alternative to buying furniture, you might want to look for a furnished house or apartment. Remember that anything brought to Greece for personal use cannot be sold or transferred to another person for at least one year

Retirees contemplating a move to Greece will be happy to know that Spot and Kit are welcome to come with you. To enter the country, you must have documentation showing that your pet is current on all immunizations and has a record of good health.

ℳEDICAL ℭARE

Greece is consistently one of *International Living's* top-ten healthiest countries, rated by the magazine's "Quality of Life Index." But, that said, you should still take a couple of preventive and prudent steps before leaving for Greece. Get a complete physical exam to assure your good health. Make sure that your immunizations are current. If you will be traveling in remote areas of Greece and its islands, a hepatitis A vaccination is wise.

Next, get extra supplies of all medication that you take regularly and get prescriptions from your physician for refills. Make sure your doctor uses the generic name for every prescription. Always carry medication in the original, labeled containers. If you have a chronic medical condition, wear a MedicAlert ID bracelet or necklace. Also, note that medicines containing codeine are illegal in Greece.

Greece spends a lower percentage of its gross domestic product on health care than any other member of the European Union. Medical care is satisfactory, but not necessarily up to U.S. standards. Services in Athens and Thessaloniki are very good, but in more remote areas practical medical help is limited. On the other hand, Greek pharmacists are highly trained and can be consulted for minor complaints.

Emergency care in Athens is rotated between hospitals on a weekly basis. Call the Tourist Police, 171, to find out which hospital is covering emergency service and to get the address. On a more comforting note, Greece has SOS doctors who make house calls 24 hours a day. All the doctors speak English; payment is expected at time of service.

Medical Insurance   Medicare and Medicaid are not available to Americans living abroad. So as part of your pre-trip list of things to do, locate a private insurance plan and get covered. There are many insurance companies to choose from; several specialize in coverage for travelers. The key is to shop around, well in advance of your departure. Be sure the policy you purchase has emergency medical evacuation coverage. This coverage will pay to transport you from a rural area to a major health-care center, including emergency return to the United States.

Universal Travel Protection Insurance (UTPI) includes more than health coverage. It compensates for trip delays, loss of baggage, and trip cancellation. For more complete information on this coverage, call 800/826-7488.

Expat Exchange, in collaboration with Columbus Insurance Group, offers special Expat Health and Travel Coverage. The plan is comprehensive and covers long-term residency overseas. For rates, contact the group by e-mail at expatseurope@columbusdirect.com.

$\mathcal{F}$INANCIAL $\mathcal{M}$ATTERS

Greece once had the worst inflation rate in Europe, up into the double digits. However, with Greece's renewed efforts to come up to the standards of the European Union, the inflation rate dropped to 4.3 percent in February 1998. The economy is still one of the weaker ones in Europe, with a per capita income of $12,000 per year (1996) and relatively high unemployment (9.8 percent in 1996).

Greece's Banking System You will be happy to know that banking in Greece is similar to that in the United States. To open an account, just bring your passport and another form of identification. You can open both checking and saving accounts, with the latter paying 3 to 3.5 percent interest. You can have two accounts, one in dollars and the other in drachmas. There are no limits on moving personal money in or out of the country.

Many banks in Greece are private, but the largest, the National Bank of Greece, is state-run. The largest private bank is Alpha Credit Bank. Most banks are open 8 to 2 during the work week. Some branches stay open later in the afternoon and on Saturday.

Several large American banks have branches in Athens, Thessaloniki, and other large cities. Examples are Citibank, American Express, and Bank of America. One of these banks would be a good place for automatic deposit of your retirement income. For daily transactions, however, consider establishing an account in a local Greek bank.

Advice for Entrepreneurs Before starting up an enterprise, establish a circle of Greek businesspeople to advise you on how to do business in Greece. You should have a trustworthy, well-established, and reliable Greek lawyer and business accountant. It could be financial suicide to start a business without these valuable services.

$\mathcal{T}$RANSPORTATION

Greece has no less than 18 international and 17 domestic airports. Major international airlines operating direct scheduled flights to Greece include Delta, TWA, Olympic Airways, British Airways, Virgin Airways, Quantas, Singapore Airline, KLM, and Gulf Air.

The Greek railway system is available on the mainland only. Trains are run by the state-owned OSE and are efficient, clean, and, most importantly, air-conditioned. First- and second-class train accommodations are almost half the price of comparable bus trips—and much more comfortable. Ticket and schedule information is available in Athens at (30) (1) 362-4402 or call the government tourist board at 212/421-5777 before you leave the States.

The privately owned bus system KTEL is extensive and serves the most remote locations in Greece. Tickets are computerized for the major routes, and seats are reserved on modern, air-conditioned coaches.

Don't forget the ferry system, hydrofoils, and catamarans for island transportation. Weekly schedules and fee charts are available from the Greek Tourist Office and local travel agencies.

Should you rent or buy a car in Greece, drive very defensively. In fact, watch out for reckless drivers no matter how you choose to travel. Most Americans involved in accidents in Greece are traveling on motorbikes. As a pedestrian, don't assume that cars will stop for you, even at a crosswalk or a red light.

$\mathcal{L}$EISURE $\mathcal{T}$IME

The only real problem with sightseeing in Greece is where to begin your odyssey—the choices are almost overwhelming. In Athens, you might begin with the Acropolis (the Hill), which looms over the city. Most major archaeological sites and museums are within only a couple of miles of the Acropolis.

From June through October, there are shows combining light, music, and narration. English performances are nightly from 9 to 9:45. While in Athens check out the renowned folk dance group Dora Stratou. The dancers appear nightly in summer outdoors at the theater on Philopappou Hill.

And don't forget to sample the excellent Greek food. Byzantino, which serves traditional fare, is the restaurant of choice for most locals in the Plaka. Varoulko Restaurant has excellent fish and seafood; it was voted one of the top ten restaurants in Athens by the city. For the unexpected but familiar, try Brooklyn Pizza. The owner couldn't find a decent pizza here, so he went to New York, hired staff, and set up his own pizza place in Athens.

Moving to the outdoors, Greece boasts one of the nine best hikes on the European continent. In April, the Samarian Gorge on the island of Crete opens to visitors. It is the most beautiful and probably the largest gorge on the continent.

Elderhostel and other educational organizations offer activities for retirees who want to exercise their minds as well as their bodies. For instance, GPSC Charters of Philadelphia sponsors an archaeology flotilla to the Cyclades. Another program is Painting the Greek Island Landscape.

The islands of Greece offer a variety of experiences, including merely soaking up the sun on a beach or visiting the site where St. John wrote the Book of Revelations. The island of Nísyros in the Dodecanese is a living, breathing (smelling of rotten eggs), semi-active caldera.

Shopping   Greece is a country where serious shoppers can get bargains. In Athens, you can get handcrafted gold very inexpensively. A highly recommended store is Byzantium at 120 Adrianou in the Plaka. If you're interested in *flokati* rugs and Persian carpets, check out Karamichos-Mazarakis Flocati. The daily Monastirakíou Flea Market has antiques at good prices. You are expected to bargain when you shop in Greece.

In the islands and the remote areas, you may actually get to watch craftspeople create their products. Local specialties include embroidery, wall hangings, leather work, icons, copper kitchenware, ceramics, silverware, and ornate utensils carved from olive wood.

Shops in most large cities and on the islands accept American Express, Visa, Master Card, Diners Club, and Carte Blanche. Traveler's checks are accepted in the larger urban areas. ATMs are also found in these areas, with the Plus and Cirrus systems the most widely used. You will need drachmas to shop in the rural areas.

Sports and Hobbies   Greece offers many opportunities for outdoor sports. Walking tours are operated by Trekking Hellas, and several companies run nature tours. For the downhill ski enthusiast, the Hellenic Skiing Federation has information on skiing in the mountains of Greece. Water sports are popular and include scuba diving, snorkeling, sailing, and yachting. There are several championship golf courses and many health and tennis clubs.

For spectators, there are weekly soccer and basketball games. In Athens, there is thoroughbred horse racing at the Hippodrome. As for hobbies, there are art classes, gardening clubs, writing courses, and even Las Vegas–style gambling in the Hotel Mont Parnes on Mount Parnitha.

ADDITIONAL RESOURCES

◈

Greek National Tourist Organization (EOT)
2 Amerikis St., Athens; tel. (30) (1) 322-3111
Olympic Tower, 645 Fifth Ave., New York, NY 10022; 212/
    421-5777, fax 212/826-6940

Emergency Contact for Foreigners
American Citizen Services Unit in Athens, (30) (1) 720-2408 or
    (30) (1) 720-3652 (after hours)
U.S. Consulate General in Thessaloniki; (30) (31) 242-906

Other Resources
Greek Embassy, 2221 Massachusetts Ave., N.W., Washington,
    D.C. 20008; 202/939-5800
U.S. Embassy, 91 Vassilisis Sophias Ave., Athens, Greece 10160;
    tel. (30) (1) 721-2951

Real Estate Agencies
Joan Rothou Real Estate Agency, 90 Athinas Ave., Vouliagmeni
    16671; tel. (30) (1) 896-3030; fax (30) (1) 896-3741
Oonagh Karanjia, Crete Property Consultants, 78 Gascony Ave.,
    London NW6 4NE; tel. (44) (171) 328-1829

Useful Web Sites
Corfu Property Agency: http://corfu.forthnet.gr/csa
Currency Converter: www.gogreece.com/exchange
Greek Embassy in the United States: www.greece@greekembassy.org
Greek National Tourist Organization: www.vacation.net.gr
Greek Realtors: www.greekrealtors.com
Mpasiakoulis Realty: www.mpasiakoulis.gr
Tourist Guide of Greece: www.vacation.net.gr/p/index2.html
U.S. Embassy in Greece: www.usisathens.gr

Ireland

by LISA MATTE

From bucolic country retreats, gentle beaches, and timeless villages in the east to the rugged mountains and wind-whipped ocean cliffs in the west, Ireland is an attractive haven for anyone looking to explore life in the slow lane. Except for urban areas like Dublin and Cork, most Irish towns roll up the sidewalks right around twilight. Social gatherings, then, move to pubs or private homes, where friends gather to share stories and sip a spot of tea or mug of stout.

Blessed with a mild climate moderated by the Atlantic Gulf Stream, Ireland sees temperatures ranging from a winter average of about 40 degrees Fahrenheit to a pleasant 65 degrees Fahrenheit in summer. July and August are usually the warmest months; May and June are the driest. Rain, and lots of it, is what keeps the Emerald Isle draped in green foliage.

Each month, more than 15,000 Americans receive their Social Security checks in Ireland. And the list of American celebrities who own homes in Ireland continues to grow. Kevin Costner, Tom Cruise, Angela Lansbury, and Julia Roberts are among the Hollywood icons who retreat to homes on the Emerald Isle.

A number of practical factors make the country an appealing retirement destination. Consider, for instance, Ireland's gorgeous physical

181

landscape and healthful environment, its incredibly friendly and hospitable natives, and a tempting list of financial inducements like tax breaks, a low cost of living, and low real estate costs.

Settling into your new life in Ireland will likely require some adjustment—mostly learning to slow down and be patient. While the Irish are friendly and congenial, some degree of caution is inherent in their nature. That means it may take a while to earn your place in the community. It's wise to be mindful and careful of what you say in pub conversations centered around religion or politics, two emotionally charged subjects that have played major roles in Irish society and culture for centuries.

By and large, the people of this country are practicing Roman Catholics. In fact, a 1991 census determined that approximately 92 percent of Ireland's 3.5 million people belong to the Roman Catholic Church. That being said, it's important to note that issues like divorce (legal in Ireland only since early 1997) and abortion (still illegal) remain sensitive topics of conversation.

While Ireland enjoys a relatively low crime rate, it's sensible to take normal precautions—especially when traveling or exploring urban centers. Pickpockets are a hazard, as are thefts from parked automobiles. Follow common-sense rules—like not going into dark alleys at night—and you'll be steps ahead when it comes to ensuring your safety.

The Culture and People of Ireland

Spend an evening in a typical bed-and-breakfast, and the innkeeper may surprise you with a sumptuous lunch, neatly packed and ready to enjoy during your next day's journey. Stop to admire a fishing boat anchored on a scenic lake and the captain may invite you along on the next day's fishing trip. Is it any wonder the Irish own an international reputation for being hospitable?

Although the Irish are notably warm and friendly toward foreigners, it may take a while to get beyond traditional pleasantries and become part of the family, so to speak. And in a country so deeply rooted in its religious affiliations, it's fairly safe to assume that moderate to conservative views are the norm.

Learn the Language Retiring to Ireland puts you one step ahead of friends and peers who choose to spend their golden years in many other countries. Why? You already speak the predominant language. And if you're lucky, you may be able to pick up just a touch of the Irish accent that makes English seem so much more lyrical coming from Irish lips.

In recent decades there's been a move to revive the native Irish language, which evolved centuries ago among Celtic tribes. It was undermined during subsequent occupations; English became the country's prevailing language around the start of the seventeenth century. While pockets of Irish-speaking people, spread over a region known as the Gaeltacht, continued to speak their indigenous language, the native tongue all but disappeared.

Study of the Irish language is now compulsory at both the primary and secondary levels, and a study conducted in 1991 revealed that approximately 32 percent of the country's population considers itself Irish-speaking. Levels of competency vary widely.

As a show of respect, make an effort to learn a little Irish. Try *dia dhuit* (dee-a-gwit) as a greeting and see what happens.

A Brief History of Ireland From early occupations by primitive hunters migrating from the European continent to invasions by Vikings and Normans, Irish society today reflects the varied traditions and cultures of its forebears.

Ireland's earliest settlers were likely hunters who arrived on the island from Britain more than 5,000 years ago. Historians believe communities of farmers and eventually metalworkers followed the hunters between 3000 and 2000 B.C.

Subsequent occupations involved Celtic invaders from Europe; Viking traders who established communities in Dublin, Cork, and Waterford; and Normans, who spread into the area after settling in England and Wales. Here's a brief synopsis of key events over the past 1,500 years:

400s St. Patrick arrives in Ireland, where he lives out his days teaching and converting the Irish to Christianity

500s–600s Ireland thrives as "a land of saints and scholars" during the early medieval period, when most of Europe endures a series of barbarian invasions

800s–900s Vikings repeatedly invade Ireland, until suffering defeat by Irish forces under the direction of Brian Boru

1100s–1500s Norman forces arrive in Ireland, eventually claiming 75 percent of the country, which then comes under control of the King of England

1500s The Protestant Reformation's establishment of the Church of Ireland ignites a series of revolts

1603 The English crown disbands the last pockets of resistance, and Ireland becomes a politically unified nation

1700s Ireland experiences a period of economic growth. The first wave of sustained Irish emigration to the New World begins

1798 Encouraged by colonists' protests against British rule in North America, the Society of United Irishmen stages a rebellion that is ultimately crushed by Britain

1846–56 The great potato famine results in the starvation deaths of 1 million people; another million Irish citizens leave the country, resulting in a 25 percent drop in the Irish population

1800s A series of efforts to reform the union between Great Britain and Ireland accomplishes little, until the Irish

Parliamentary Party gains support for limited Irish self-government; Unionists opposed to home rule organize, leading to an increasingly hostile situation

1916–18 An armed insurrection by parties opposed to home rule is defeated, but members come back to win the general election of 1918, successfully defeating the Irish Parliamentary Party that had campaigned for home rule

1920s Six counties in the northern part of the country become Northern Ireland, while the remaining 26 counties become the Irish Free State; a short civil war ensues

1948 The Republic of Ireland Act severs Ireland's final constitutional links with Britain

1955 Ireland is admitted to the United Nations

1973 Ireland becomes a full member of the European Union

1998 An historic treaty developed to address age-old tension between Northern Ireland and Ireland is signed. Guarded optimism remains prevalent, despite lingering violence.

Embrace a New Culture Ireland has a history rich in performing arts. From nineteenth-century opera composer Vincent Wallace right up to today's internationally acclaimed rock group U2, music is an integral part of the Irish heritage. Consider the Chieftains, who have filled concert halls around the world for more than three decades, and singer Van Morrison, who has been recording and touring internationally since the 1960s. And due in part to the recent popularity of the stage musical *Riverdance*, it's difficult to find anyone unfamiliar with the art of Irish step dancing.

The Irish also boast an incredible literary history. Jonathan Swift, James Joyce, and Oscar Wilde are but a handful of the great wordsmiths who hailed from Ireland. It's almost a wonder that such a small country in terms of acreage has turned out so many masterful writers—among them Nobel Prize–winners Samuel Beckett, George Bernard Shaw, and William Butler Yeats.

Moving from the cerebral to the physical, the Irish also enjoy the native sport of hurling. And, no, that's not something you do after a long night in the pub. Hurling, like field hockey, involves two opposing teams intent on navigating a ball into the other team's goal using wooden clubs. The Gaelic Athletic Association oversees seasonal play among community teams, leading to a series of nationwide finals to determine the Irish champion.

Share Your Culture   Retiring to Ireland is like coming home to some Americans, since more than 40 million U.S. citizens claim some degree of Irish ancestry. If you're one of those folks, you may discover that retaining your cultural identity is just as important as discovering your Irish roots. And despite widespread rumors that the bulk of documents necessary to conduct genealogical research were destroyed by fire in the early part of this century, information about your Irish lineage is likely intact and waiting to be discovered.

The first step for genealogical spelunkers is to find out all you can by talking to family members who remember the who, what, and where of your ancestry. Record your findings or entrust them to a responsible family member a few generations behind—a child or grandchild who is interested in family history and will in turn pass the information down the line.

The second step is to begin reviewing public records, including census returns, church registers, and Griffith's Valuation (an all-encompassing, countrywide property survey completed in the mid-nineteenth century). Further your research in Dublin at the Genealogical Office, the National Library, the National Archives, and the General Registrar's Office.

Heritage aside, it's comforting to find a bit home when you're living in a foreign land, and there are plenty of American groups in Ireland waiting to welcome you.

RECOMMENDED LIVING AREAS

County Wicklow Welcome to the "Garden of Ireland," scene of one of Oliver Cromwell's most violent massacres (1649) and also the site of the American Kennedy family's homestead in Dunganstown. Visit Glendalough in the Wicklow Mountains, where St. Kevin founded a bucolic monastery in the sixth century. A 56-acre farm in Wicklow was recently listed for $340,000. The property featured a four-bedroom home set on 45 acres with a pasture, gardens, and a lake. A two-bedroom town house in the heart of Delgany Village recently listed for $191,000.

County Clare You'll find some of Ireland's most dramatic scenery—including the astonishing Cliffs of Moher rising from the pounding Atlantic surf—in County Clare. The market town of Ennis is a good place to shop for antiques and crafts; outlets along the main street are favorites among shoppers.

A $510,000 price tag recently hung on a nineteenth-century, two-story, Gothic-style house in County Clare—originally a gentleman's hunting lodge. It has been completely restored and features three reception rooms, a study, kitchen, pantry, four bedrooms, two bathrooms, and a shower room. A coach house located on the property features a sitting room, kitchen, bedroom, and bathroom. And a separate apartment features a sitting room, kitchen, bedroom, and bathroom. More afforable is a three-bedroom cottage in the village of Quilty within a half mile of the ocean. It listed recently for $179,000.

County Dublin Dublin is famous for at least two things—stout and literary history. The Guinness Brewery is located in Dublin, as are the one-time homes of some well-known Irish writers including James Joyce, who was known to down a pint at Mulligan's Pub on Poolbeg Street. "An attractive modern house situated in a charming rural set-

188 _The World's Top Retirement Havens_

ting" is how one listing describes a five-acre property in County Dublin. The four-bedroom home is near golf courses and lakes. A one-bedroom garden-level apartment near the sea is available for $149,000.

$\mathcal{R}$ENTING IN $\mathcal{I}$RELAND

If you are looking for Irish property, you'll need somewhere to live while you're house-hunting. And after you sign an agreement to buy, it will take at least six weeks to complete the transaction.

With that in mind, it may be wise to rent a home or apartment until you get settled. Be aware, too, that the Department of Social Welfare advises people relocating to Ireland to try to secure accommodations before they arrive. Note that there's a shortage of rental properties in several urban areas.

Networking through friends, family, and acquaintances will often help you turn up prime rental opportunities. Other resources include newspaper listings and rental agencies, which usually charge a registration fee. Information on rental standards and how to find reputable rental agencies is available from Threshold, 19 Mary's Abbey, Dublin 7; tel. (353) (1) 872-6311.

As in the United States, rent is usually payable monthly. Most property owners will require an up-front deposit equal to one or two months' rent. Average monthly rental fees for a small house or apartment in the greater Dublin area range from $665 to $900. As you might expect, rents are usually lower in small towns and outlying areas.

The law requires landlords to provide tenants with a written tenancy agreement. Landlords may offer a lease, but they usually lock the tenant into the agreement for a set period of time—generally one year. Don't enter into a lease agreement unless you're fully satisfied with the conditions and rental period it obligates you to honor.

BUYING REAL ESTATE

Thanks to a booming economy Ireland is experiencing stronger economic growth than any other EU member, and property prices on the Emerald Isle are no longer the bargain they once were. That being said, it's still possible to find your dream retirement home without breaking the bank. The Irish Auctioneers & Valuers Institute found that at the end of 1997 the average new house cost $127,522. The average price in Dublin—$157,292; Cork—$116,051; Galway—$140,116; Limerick—$113,927; and Waterford—$95,232. The average cost of secondhand homes nationally was $133,387. The average price in Dublin—$175,085; Cork—$110,428; Galway—$126,241; Limerick—$98,041; and Waterford—$95, 233.

Despite rumors to the contrary, home sales by auction are not the norm in Ireland. In fact, IAVI statistics show that only six percent of property in Ireland is sold at public auction. Still, it's possible to find a hidden treasure on the auctioneer's list. Be aware, though, that bidding at auction means bidding unconditionally. Your deposit is at risk if you find you cannot complete the transaction. For information about upcoming auctions, check out the real estate pages of the *Irish Times* each Thursday and the *Irish Independent* each Friday.

Be prepared to pay a deposit—usually 10 percent of the purchase price—on the day of the auction if your bid is successful. The IAVI advises individuals who seek to purchase property at auction to have a lawyer approve the legal title to the property. You should also engage a qualified architect, engineer, or building surveyor to conduct a structural inspection of the house.

Most property in Ireland is sold by private treaty, meaning the seller establishes an asking price, then accepts bids by interested parties. This system can lead to counter-bidding and higher prices. And be mindful that your purchase is not secure until all the formal documents are signed, sealed, and delivered.

One hazard of a private treaty system is "gazumping," in which the seller accepts a more lucrative offer from a second buyer after reaching a verbal agreement with the first. The IAVI advises all prospective buyers to engage the services of a licensed auctioneer (the equivalent of a U.S. real estate agent) to be sure they get fair treatment in real estate transactions.

Banks and building societies will usually loan up to 92 percent of the purchase price of a home in Ireland. As in the United States, lenders require borrowers to meet established criteria regarding income and the ability to repay the loan. Other costs associated with purchasing property in Ireland include a stamp duty of 3 to 9 percent depending on the purchase price, survey and valuation fees, and legal fees averaging 1.5 percent of the purchase price.

COST OF LIVING

The Embassy of Ireland in Washington, D.C., reports the average cost of living in Ireland is comparable to or slightly higher than the cost of living in the United States. Some expenses, including the cost of maintaining and running an automobile, may be considerably higher in Ireland.

Remember, though, that seniors living in Ireland are usually eligible for significant discounts on some services, including public transportation. Here's what you'll pay for some typical goods and services in Ireland:

electricity	$17/month	milk	$3.95/gallon
movie ticket	$6–$7	eggs	$1.35/dozen
beer on tap	$2.75	video rental	$3.50
maid service	$4/hour	compact disc	$20
bananas	$.55/pound	woman's haircut	$15
steak	$3.25/pound		

$\mathcal{D}$AY-TO-DAY $\mathcal{L}$IVING $\mathcal{C}$ONCERNS

Ireland operates on Greenwich Mean Time, which means its clocks are in sync with those in Britain. Clocks are set forward one hour in late March and set back one hour in late October.

Electricity is 220 volts, 50 cycles. Electrical plugs are usually the flat three-pin type, but some older buildings still require round-pin plugs. Adapters are readily available in Ireland.

Irish television consists of two state-run channels, plus whatever BBC and independent programs Irish receivers can access. Individuals who use televisions in Ireland are required to obtain an annual television license, available through the local post office. The license fee is about $100.

The country's three state-controlled radio stations offer a sampling of talk and musical programming, including some call-in shows.

$\mathcal{T}$AXES

American retirees who choose to live in Ireland must pay Irish taxes. A double-taxation agreement between the United States and Ireland ensures that tax paid in one country is calculated as a credit against tax paid in the other, however.

Income-tax rates in Ireland are 26 and 48 percent, but allowable deductions may help lessen your tax bill. Americans living in Ireland are also subject to capital gains tax, value-added tax (12.5 percent), excise tax, and others. Property tax varies according to property value, although property valued below $140,000 is not taxed. Contact the Irish Revenue Commissioners, Dublin Castle, Dame St., Dublin 2, tel. (353) (1) 679-2777, for more information about taxation of U.S. nationals living in Ireland.

$\mathcal{M}$AKING THE $\mathcal{M}$OVE

Americans who intend to stay in Ireland for more than 90 days must request permission from the Irish Department of Justice within 90 days of their arrival. It's wise, though, to begin the permission process during your first few days in Ireland. If you're related to an Irish citizen, your extension request is more or less a formality—but it's still a requirement.

Begin the process by reporting to the Aliens Registration Office, Police Office, Harcourt Street, Dublin 2, or to the police superintendent's office in your community. You must have a completed Aliens Registration Form, a valid passport, four passport photographs, and evidence of sufficient funds for self-support.

If you're denied permission to remain in Ireland beyond the 90-day period, you have the right to appeal that decision. Contact the Immigration Section of the Department of Justice of Ireland, 72–76 St. Stephen's Green, Dublin 2; tel. (353) (1) 602-8202.

If you were born in Ireland, you're already an Irish citizen. If one of your parents was born in Ireland you're also an Irish citizen. If one of your grandparents was born in Ireland, or if you're married to an Irish citizen, you can apply for Irish citizenship. If you've been a legal resident of Ireland for four out of eight years in the country, you can apply for Irish citizenship. And if you meet any of these requirements, you can become an Irish citizen and remain a U.S. citizen at the same time; Irish law permits dual citizenship.

Americans in Ireland with U.S. passports must secure a valid work permit through the Irish Department of Enterprise, Trade, and Employment, Kildare St., Dublin 2, tel. (353) (1) 661-4444, before they can accept a job in Ireland.

What to Bring, What to Leave Behind You can retire to Ireland and still take a bit of home with you, because the Irish government lets you bring your household goods and your car without penalty. Your favorite chair or cherished heirlooms will also arrive in Ireland tax-

and duty-free, as long as you can prove prior ownership of at least six months and have completed the required transfer of residency forms available through the Irish embassy.

What About Pets? Ireland is rabies-free and wants to keep it that way. That means you'll face some stringent controls when it comes to toting Fluffy or Fido to your new retirement home. As long as your dog or cat meets established requirements—and you and your furry friend can stand being separated for six months during a mandatory quarantine period—it's likely you'll all be reunited as one happy family.

You can pick up an application for the importation of a dog or cat at the nearest office of the Irish embassy. If your pet is something other than a dog or cat, though, you're out of luck. Irish law prohibits the importation of any other animals. Contact the Irish Department of Agriculture, Veterinary Division, Kildare St., Dublin 2; tel. (353)-(1) 607-2000 for more information on importing household pets into Ireland.

$\mathcal{M}$EDICAL $\mathcal{C}$ARE

Free in-patient and out-patient hospital care is alive and well for U.S. nationals who are legal residents of Ireland. And individuals whose incomes meet established guidelines may be eligible for no-charge access to general practitioners through government-run programs.

Private health insurance to supplement public coverage is available through a number of sources, including the state-approved Voluntary Health Insurance Board, VHI House, Lower Abbey St., Dublin, 1; tel. (353) (1) 872-4499. Retirees who subscribe to private U.S. health-care plans should contact their insurers regarding international coverage.

$\mathcal{F}$INANCIAL $\mathcal{M}$ATTERS

A full member of the European Union since 1973, Ireland has experienced an enviable period of economic growth in the recent years. That's due in part to trade agreements established by the European Union resulting in a cohesive economic arena in which goods, services, people, and capital move freely among member nations. The result is a measurable improvement of living standards in Ireland, which have been rising for the past two decades. Total infrastructure investment between 1994 and 1999 was approximately $29.6 billion. In addition to upgrading the country's physical infrastructure, funds are also earmarked for the development of indigenous industry, tourism projects, and the improvement of training and employment programs.

More good news: A bilateral agreement between the United States and Ireland stipulates that U.S. Social Security recipients who are legal residents of Ireland may be eligible for certain Irish Social Security benefits. In some instances, it may be possible to combine Irish and U.S. Social Security contributions to meet eligibility requirements in one country or the other.

U.S. citizens who live in Ireland can receive their pensions through the U.S. embassy. Contact the International Section of the Irish Department of Social Welfare, Arus MhicDiarmada, Store St., Dublin 1, tel. (353) (1) 704-3268 for more information about Social Security benefits for U.S. nationals living in Ireland.

Ireland's Banking System   Ireland does not restrict the movement of funds into or out of the country, and you are permitted to hold foreign-currency bank accounts. Don't forget, though, to report your foreign bank account on your Irish income-tax return. And be prepared to show your passport and another form of identification when you open an Irish bank account—especially if you plan to deposit a large amount of cash. Recent legislation designed to prevent money-laundering scams requires Irish banks to verify the identities of depositors.

$\mathscr{T}$RANSPORTATION

Airports located in Dublin, Cork, and Shannon are Ireland's three international gateways. In addition to Aer Lingus (Ireland's national airline), major air carriers from around the world service Ireland's international airports. Depending on your point of origin and destination, it is sometimes less expensive to fly through London on your way to or from the United States.

Flights within Ireland are available, but it's best to weigh their cost against potential convenience and time-savings. Most flights within Ireland are under one hour, and many are as short as 30 minutes. Alternatives include bus and rail travel.

With its central location in Dublin, Irish Rail operates along a series of tracks that connect most major cities and towns. Compare service and cost with bus routes for the best value. For instance, the trip from Dublin to Cork via rail averages 3¼ hours and tickets cost about $50. The same trip via bus takes about 3½ hours with a cost of about $18. Rail travel from Dublin to Limerick takes 2½ hours at a cost of $37 per ticket, while the same trip via bus will likely take 3¼ hours at $15 per ticket.

Intra-city public transportation options vary by region, with some metropolitan areas relying largely on metered taxis. Public transportation in Dublin consists of the Dublin Area Rapid Transport rail and a network of city bus routes.

Automobile Travel   First and foremost, remember that driving in Ireland is on the left side of the road. Make sure you're entirely comfortable with that adjustment before you take to the road in search of adventure. And definitely take time to sleep a bit before getting into the driver's seat after a long overnight flight.

To get your Irish driver's license, you'll be required to pass a driving test. And everyone over the age of 70 must pass a medical exam every three years to maintain their license. If you've got your license and you're ready to hit the road, make sure your car is registered. Irish law requires automobile owners to register their vehicles with the local licensing authority and to pay an annual motor tax calculated by engine size. Drivers in Ireland are also required to have automobile insurance. Documentation of insurance and tax payments must be displayed on the car.

$\mathcal{L}$EISURE $\mathcal{T}$IME

No matter where you settle, the social center of your community will likely be the local pub. The common stereotype of a ruddy-faced, drunken Irishman is certainly an exaggeration, but pubs are still common places to meet people and discuss the day's news in Ireland. Pubs are also where you'll find musical entertainment—everything from rollicking folk tunes and heartfelt ballads to contemporary hits and classic rock.

Things to Do and See While it's unlikely you'll ever grow tired of the scenery in Ireland, there is more to the country than winding roads, rolling green hillsides, and friendly local pubs. You will want to check out some of the other attractions sprinkled about your new retirement home.

Why not start with Ireland's castles? Located just a bit north of Cork, Blarney Castle draws visitors from around the world seeking to get the "gift of gab" by kissing the Blarney Stone—a feat that requires the faithful to lean over backward from on high to smooch the revered rock.

Dating to the early thirteenth century, Dublin Castle is open to the public and a worthwhile trip. Yet another Irish castle housed generations of the same family through nearly six centuries. Now open to the public, Kilkenny Castle remained a private residence until 1935.

If you find yourself in the Dublin area around mid-March, make sure to check out the annual St. Patrick's Day Parade. Though St. Patrick's Day is a religious holiday, the enthusiasm expressed by Americans celebrating March 17 in Irish enclaves like Boston and New York has spread back across the Atlantic, and the festivities in Ireland are growing.

A few months later, it's time for the dandies to strut their stuff at the annual Dublin Horse Show. Usually held the second week in August, the show is social event in which anyone who is anyone goes to be seen. But if you'd rather see your reputation go to the dogs, check out greyhound racing in Dublin at Harold's Cross or Shelbourne Park.

Finally, Ireland is home to world-class theatrical productions. Dublin has several well-regarded theaters including the Abbey, the Peacock, and the Olympia.

Shopping   Ireland is a treasure hunter's paradise. From world-renowned crystal at Waterford to the fabulous hand-knit sweaters of Galway, shopping in Ireland is an adventure in native craftsmanship. Don't limit yourself to the urban centers, though. You'll find some of the country's finest handicrafts in villages and towns scattered across the countryside.

Look for fine Irish linen and lace in and around Limerick. You'll find charming pottery in County Kilkenny and delicate bone china in Belleek and Donegal. If it's a bargain you're after, you might want to check out the craft outlets in Cork. Search long enough and you're sure to find just the treasure you are seeking.

Sports and Hobbies   As its economy has grown, so has Ireland's reputation in the international sports arena. Olympic swimmer Michelle Smith won three gold medals and one bronze medal during the 1996 Olympic Games in Atlanta. Ireland's soccer team made the quarter-finals in World Cup competition a few years back. Other Irish athletes recognized at the international level include golfers Philip Walton and Paul McGinley, as well as horse-men Michael Kinane and Adrian Maguire.

Spectator sports popular at the national level include Gaelic foot-ball, a sort of a soccer-rugby combination; and hurling, a bit like field hockey. Horse racing and golf are also popular.

$\mathcal{A}$DDITIONAL $\mathcal{R}$ESOURCES

General Resources
Embassy of Ireland, 2234 Massachusetts Ave., NW, Washington, D.C. 20008; 202/462-3939; fax 202/232-5993.
Irish Tourist Board, 345 Park Ave., New York, NY 10154, 212/418-0800

Emergency Contact for Foreigners
Legal Aid Board, St. Stephen's Green House, Dublin, 2; tel. (353) (1) 661-5811
U.S. Embassy in Ireland, 42 Elgin Rd., Dublin, 4; tel. (353) (1) 668-8777.

Useful Web sites
www.Irishtimes.com
www.ireland.travel.ie
www.irlgov.ie/iveagh

Italy

by ROSANNE KNORR

Italy has beckoned outsiders for centuries with its classic landscapes and vast cultural heritage. Here, Europe awakened after the Dark Ages. Dante, Petrarch, Leonardo da Vinci, Botticelli, and Michelangelo all flourished here.

Modern Rome, Florence, and Venice are beautiful and cosmopolitan. The food is fresh. The wines are delightful. But, of course, Italy is not all fine art and fine living. It is a predominantly rural country, with one of the lower per-capita incomes of Europe. But once you get there, you will understand why so many people visit, then return to stay. Italy is a wonderful country for those seeking a rich and diverse experience at reasonable prices.

Some 43,000 Italian American retirees live in Italy. But anyone with a bit of capital and courage can take up residence here.

Lay of the Land Italy is a 116,324-square-mile, boot-shaped peninsula that points toward Africa and divides the Adriatic and the Mediterranean Seas. Two major mountain ranges, the Alps and the Apennines, form the peninsula's spine and the island of Sicily. More than a third of the country is spiked by mountain ranges higher than 2,300 feet. Most of the rest is hilly; only a quarter is flat.

The most important and extensive plain in Italy, the Po Valley, flattens more than 17,000 square miles. Through it run the Po River, its tributaries, and the rivers Reno, Adige, Piave, and Tagliamento. Intensive agriculture is practiced in the valley's fertile lower plain.

The country has more than 5,300 miles of coastal shoreline—from the northern Riviera to the famous beaches at Amalfi, Toarmina, and Sardinia's Emerald Coast.

Regions   Italy is divided into 20 administrative regions (*regioni*), which vary greatly in size and geography. Regions in the north include the castle-studded Piemonte, which reflects some French influence; the mountainous Valle d'Aosta, a winter-sports paradise; Lombardy, where mountains and lakes relieve the industrial landscape around Milan; Trentino-Alto Adige, where winter and summer resorts attract throngs; Liguria, an inexpensive Riviera wedged between the Mediterranean and the Alps; and the Veneto, once the territory of the Venetian empire. The north is heavily populated and includes industrial cities and intensive agriculture. Southern Italians are migrating steadily to the north.

Italy's center, which focuses on Rome and Florence, is also becoming industrialized. Center regions include medieval Emilia Romagna, which has prosperous farms; Tuscany and Umbria, with their vestiges of Etruscan civilization and Renaissance art and culture; the Marches on the Adriatic side; Latium (Lazio) and the Campania, whose hills circle Rome; and the Abruzzo and the Molise regions of the harsh central Apennines.

The south has the poorest regions: Apulia, which overlooks the southernmost part of the Adriatic Sea and flourished under the ancient Greeks; ancient and rocky Basilicata; and the southernmost province, Calabria, which was once haunted by brigands and even now has Italy's highest murder rate due to organized-crime rivalries. The south, with the two ports of Bari and Naples and some recently developed industry, still preserves some of the traditional Italian way of life.

Sicily and Sardinia, Italy's two Mediterranean islands, are also regioni. Remnants of Greek and Roman civilization can be found throughout Sicily, as can Roman remains. Sicily's climate is temperate, making it a popular resort. Mountainous Sardinia has been inhabited since prehistoric times. Throughout the island are ancient *nuraghi*, cone-shaped fortification-dwellings. Sheep and goats are raised here. Both Sicily and Sardinia are extensively cultivated, with citrus fruits and vineyards, pasture for sheep, fisheries, and a shrinking mining industry.

Climate In general, Italy has a mild Mediterranean climate, though weather varies widely from north to south. The northern and central regions have a cold January and a rainy, chilly November, February, and March. But Christmas travelers can sunbathe anywhere in Sicily. The hottest months are July and August. (Italy undergoes a vacation exodus during these months.) The average temperature in Rome in January is 49 degrees Fahrenheit; in July the average is 82.

THE CULTURE AND PEOPLE
OF ITALY

Italy has the fifth highest population density in Europe, with 57,886,000 people. The nation is mostly Roman Catholic, although the church's influence has been declining. Family life is important, and Italians tend to be warm and effusive. Each region sees itself as unique, with different dialects and regional cuisine.

Parla Italiano! While the Italians aren't as defensive about their language as the French are, you will find it easier to meet them if you speak their native tongue. Urban and educated Italians often speak good English, but country folk may not.

Italian language, literature, history, and culture courses geared to foreigners are offered in major cities. Following are a few recommended schools:

+ Dante Alighieri, Piazza Firenze 27, Rome; tel. (39) (06) 687-3722
+ Centro di Cultura per Stranieri, Via Vittoria Emanuele 64, Florence; tel. (39) (055) 472-139
+ Dante Alighieri, Centro Linguistico Italiano, Via dei Bardi 12, Florence; tel. (39) (055) 234-2985
+ Eurocentro, Piazza S. Spirito 9, Florence; tel. (39) (055) 294-605
+ Scuola di Lingua e Cultura Italiana per Stranieri, Universita degli Studi, Siena; tel. (39) (0577) 49260

A Brief History of Italy With its complicated twists and dramatic events, Italian history fills volumes. Here are a very few highlights:

735 B.C.	Rome founded
80 B.C.	The Coliseum inaugurated
44 B.C.	Julius Caesar assassinated
A.D. 800	Charlemagne, King of the Franks, crowned as emperor
1492	Christopher Columbus sets foot on America
1500s	The Renaissance elevates Italian arts and learning
1805	Napoleon crowned king; he had invaded Italy in 1796
1915	Italy joins the Allies in World War I
1924	Mussolini begins to suspend the constitutional government in favor of a dictatorship
1929	Lateran Treaty creates Vatican City in the middle of Rome
1940	Mussolini declares war against France and England
1946	Republic of Italy created
1984	Lateran Treaty is replaced, eliminating Catholicism as Italy's state religion
1996	Italy joins Europe's Euro currency system

ℛecommended ℒiving ℋreas

᷍

Many retirees prefer to live in the Lake Country in northern Italy in summer and go south to Sicily in winter. Florence and Rome are popular with those who like city life. For country living, Tuscany, the Dolomites, and other areas offer varied choices in climate, terrain, and lifestyle.

Rome The capital and largest city in Italy, Rome has been the world's most celebrated city for more than two millennia. Before Christ was born, Romans watched gladiators fight lions in the Colosseum. Today, the structure stands at the center of a mad whirl of traffic. Rome is now one of the biggest tourist cities in the world, with some of the world's most exclusive shops and the best restaurants.

Vatican City, within Rome but politically separate, represents the grandeur of the pope and the impact of Roman Catholicism. Typically, 300,000 people gather at St. Peter's Basilica to hear the pope's blessing on holy days. Among the Vatican's many attractions is the Sistine Chapel fresco, a marvel of the Renaissance created five centuries ago by an unwilling Michelangelo at the order of Pope Julius II.

The Piazza di Spagna (Spanish Steps) are a living work of art, jammed with tourists, students, beggars, and merchants selling colorful clothing, flowers, and trinkets. Many of the city's international schools are in the Via Cassia area on the outskirts of Rome, a popular area with expatriates.

Florence and Tuscany Tuscany, Italy's wealthiest and loveliest region, is blessed with golden hills, rich soil, and a treasure-trove of antiquities. Centrally located between bustling Rome and Milan, Florence is the city center of Tuscany. It's small enough to make you feel at home, and expatriates can become very much a part of its vibrant culture. Proximity to Pisa, Siena, Bologna, and Venice adds to the city's appeal.

This Renaissance city is where art was reborn around 1500. The Uffizi, Florence's fabulous art museum, features the works of Michelangelo, da Vinci, and Botticelli, among others. The Duomo (Santa Maria del Fiore) is one of the world's largest churches, containing frescoes illustrating Dante's *Divine Comedy*. The Pitti Palace houses works by Rubens and other masters.

This Tuscan city is a magnet for students, artists, and writers. It is a city of great, almost unreal beauty. But for all its fifteenth-century heritage (the city was substantially developed by the Medicis during their reign), Florence has a young heart. Young people dominate the squares and streets, their hip styles contrasting with and complementing the city's neoclassical grace.

While Florence's metropolitan area houses more than a million people, it is a surprisingly peaceful city. With no international airport nearby, you never hear the roar of jets zooming overhead, as you do in Rome and Pisa. Instead, you hear church bells.

Central to the lively daily life of the city are the piazzas sprinkled throughout the town. Piazza del Duomo, surrounding the Duomo, is the main landmark and center of town. Piazza de la Republica is the business center; its arcaded buildings house the central post and telegraph offices. Siena is the provincial capital of Tuscany. Through the ancient city gates, you're thrown back in time. This walled city looks much as it did in the Middle Ages. Cobblestone streets twist between turreted buildings. The Campo (main square) provides a breathing space from the monochromatic pink buildings surrounding it. Siena can be expensive, but you can find real estate bargains on its northern edge. For example, a three-bedroom cottage with living area, kitchen, one bathroom, studio, and spare room goes for $60,000.

Enchanting hill towns form the backbone of the Tuscan countryside. Their historical significance and medieval architecture are rivaled only by their prices. Within the Pisa–Siena–Florence triangle, cottages resembling piles of Etruscan rubble cost upward of $62,000, while semi-restored farmhouses go for $310,000 or more.

Your best bet for affordable living is in the north of the region, around Cortona and beyond Lucca, a beautifully preserved walled town with medieval churches, palaces, and belfries. Village houses can be had for $40,000 there, while large, semi-restored farmhouses average $130,000.

Umbria In central Italy, the Umbria region is less expensive than Tuscany but shares the great landscapes. Vineyards and olive trees cover hillsides, with the Apennine Mountains running through the eastern section. Small village houses overlooking the Tiber Valley can be had for $32,000; traditional Umbrian farmhouses for restoration begin at $53,000.

The Dolomites If you like hiking or skiing, you may enjoy retiring in the Dolomite Mountains of northern Italy. The area has charming Tyrolean villages near ski slopes and mountain hiking trails. The best-known village is Corvara, which is also the largest. Others include Colfosco, La Villa, Pedraces, and San Cassianto.

Cortina d'Ampezzo, in the eastern Dolomites, is Italy's most popular ski resort. Although crowded, it has some of the best ski facilities in the country. When you tire of skiing, you can ice-skate in the remnants of the Olympic stadium, shop in the town's many boutiques, or dine in one of its many restaurants. In Courmayeur and Cervinia you can ski in summer as well as winter. These towns are well known—and pricey. The Val d'Ayas is yet undiscovered and has lower ski-lift prices (and more challenging runs).

Colfosco, a small quiet ski village with numerous runs, is great for beginning and intermediate skiers. It offers little cross-country skiing and no deep-powder skiing. Its major advantage over the large, more crowded resorts is that it is part of the Alta Badia, a five-village ski association. With a Colfosco lift ticket, you have access to 75 miles of trails and 53 lifts. With the Super Dolomite lift pass, you gain access to 10 major ski areas that include 650 miles of trails and 540 lifts.

Hiking is terrific in the Dolomites, which are crisscrossed by trails. The best time for hiking is August and September, when the snow has completely melted. Don't hike in April and May unless you are an expert; the melting snow causes avalanches. The National Park of Abruzzi, near Pescasseroli, is a beautiful place to hike; trails wander through a forest of pine trees blanketed with snow.

Lake Country The Lake Country at the base of Italy's Alps is a romantic and popular destination, with steeply rolling hills and a Mediterranean touch. Olive groves and palm trees surround the warm waters. This region has long attracted the famous (Flaubert, Dickens, Dumas, Hemingway) and royalty.

Stresa, a mere hour from Milan's Malpensa Airport, offers fishing, swimming, strolling, and steamer rides on the Lago Maggiore. This misnamed lake 48 miles northwest of Milan is neither greater than the other lakes (as its name suggests) nor deeper. But its appealing western shore is less touristy than any of the other lakes. Its key attraction is the Borromean Isles, especially Isola Bella.

Lago Garda, the easternmost lake, is the largest and most frequently visited. It has Mediterranean scenery of olive groves, lemon trees, and palms. It is ringed by four cities known for art: Mantua, Verona, Trent, and Brescia.

Torbole, at the far end of Lake Garda, is the windsurfing capital of Europe. The steady breezes that blow across the lake create perfect conditions for this sport.

Lake Como, Europe's deepest lake, is too polluted for swimming, but it is lined with elegant nineteenth-century villas and crowned by snowcapped mountains. It's bordered by two lovely towns: Como and Bellagio. Como is worldly, wealthy, and refined. Its Duomo (cathedral) is one of the most famous churches in Italy. Built between 1457 and 1485, it has a spectacular rose window and houses Bernardino Luini's *Adoration of the Magi*. Bellagio, the lake district's art center, invites artists to spend a month or more developing works in progress. Located at the point where Lake Como intersects Lake Lecco, Bellagio has narrow streets and ancient buildings.

Campione d'Italia is located on the banks of Lake Lugano. This enclave of 2,000 inhabitants is part of Italy but has a Swiss economy. A two-bedroom apartment with a lake view sells for about $77,500 here. The lake resorts of Como, Lugano, and Maggiore are nearby; the big-city amenities of Milan are just 45 minutes away.

The Italian Riviera The Italian Riviera, which stretches from the French border to Tuscany, is less expensive than the French Riviera and just as pretty. It is divided into the Riviera di Levante southwest of Genoa and the Riviera di Ponente southeast of Genoa. In the little villages below the region's efficient highways are beaches, fishing ports, cheap hotels, and restaurants.

In the French part of the Riviera, the Côte d'Azur, authentic old fishing villages like St. Tropez have become nightmares—stuffed with high-rise buildings, exhaust-spewing cars, beautiful people, glitzy shops, and bad restaurants. A dozen miles away, Italy's Riviera remains authentic. The stucco is peeling, the awnings are patched, the cars are Fiat 500s instead of fat Peugeots and BMWs. Beautifully tended flowers bloom, palm trees line the boardwalk, and prices are reasonable.

Bordighera is the second resort in Italy as you drive in from France. The border town is Ventimiglia, a center of market gardening, cactus and flower production, smuggling, counterfeit French and Italian "label" merchandise, and financial *combinazzione.*

The hills of Bordighera and Ventimiglia are covered with scrub pines and cypresses, olive and citrus groves, and fields of cultivated flowers. Here carnations, jasmine, hyacinths, narcissus, violets, tulips, mimosa, and roses are grown for European buyers and the perfume industry. The gardens are full of bougainvillea, palm trees, and roses. The best palms in Italy are grown in Bordighera and supplied to the Vatican for Palm Sunday.

Bordighera, still enclosed by walls, holds steep streets and winding alleys, white stucco houses, and old chapels. It is full of good seafood restaurants. Although summer is the high season, Bordighera is a year-round resort because it is sheltered from the cold. The sea breeze keeps it cool in summer. Ventimiglia is a bit more down-market, with an array of rental cottages and apartment-hotels.

Better-known San Remo is pricier. It is the oldest resort on the Riviera and has been overbuilt. It has a casino and a yacht basin, and the hotels are affordable despite their Edwardian elegance. Inexpensive ones are located along the via Matteotti. This resort town of some 70,000 is only 21 miles from Monte Carlo and not much farther from Nice. San Remo is a prime example of just what retirement in Italy has to offer: hundreds of hotels and *pensiones* of every category, facilities for all kinds of boats, miles and miles of beaches, lavish public gardens, a fourteenth-century cathedral, swimming pools, and a nearby ski resort.

Private and romantic, Portofino is one of the most photographed places in the world. Its remarkably deep natural harbor attracts yachtsmen and jet-setters in summer. Among the celebrities who have stayed here are Lauren Bacall, Humphrey Bogart, Aristotle Onassis, and Ernest Hemingway.

The most charming town on the coast is San Fruttoso. It is accessible only by sea; you can get there by boat from Camogli. The town is surrounded by pines, olive trees, and oaks that lead down to the sea. You can walk through the cloisters and corridors of the Benedictine Abbey of San Fruttoso di Capo di Monte, which consists of a thirteenth-century palace, an eleventh-century church, and a Romanesque cloister.

At the southern end of the Riviera is one of the least crowded, most picturesque areas: Cinque Terre, with its hilltop villages of Monterosso, Vernazza, Corniglia, Manarola, and Riomaggiore perched on the rocky coast north of La Spezia. Monterosso is the largest and most crowded of the five towns. It has a beautiful beach at the southern end of the cove. You can rent boats here. Climb the hill to the Convento dei Cappuccini, which houses Van Dyck's *Crucifixion*. From Monterosso, a one-and-a-half-hour hike along a goat path leads through vineyards and olive groves to Vernazza. Another hiking trail leads to Corniglia, which has a long pebbly beach. If you're up to another hour's walk, you can follow the trail along the jagged coast to Manarola, the most beautiful of the Cinque Terre towns. Here, yellow houses balance on cliffs, and artists and writers seek their muses.

The Amalfi Coast The Amalfi Coast, a mountainous peninsula between the Gulf of Naples and Gulf of Salerno, is a land of legends. Pirates once used the secluded inlets as hideouts. Spectacular views can be enjoyed from the dizzying summits of the mountains. Serpentine roads wind through cliffside villages. Olive groves and grape vines dot the plains. In July and August, the coast becomes a madhouse, and it is nearly impossible to drive there. Spring and fall are idyllic—warm and uncrowded.

Positano, a hill-climbing village with a single road, is on the western strip of the Amalfi Drive, with its view onto the Tyrrhenian Sea and its storybook islands of sirens. Nearby is the Green Grotto, even more beautiful than the more famous Blue Grotto in Capri.

Another spectacular view is from the little town of Ravello, above Amalfi. A bus takes you to the summit via narrow, twisting roads. The cathedral of Ravello has sculptures of strange-looking animals and contains a reliquary with the skull of Saint Barbara.

Island Living Capri is a beautiful but crowded island that can be reached by hydrofoil from Naples, Sorrento, and Pozzuoli. Capri is also the name for the crowded main town. The island's most famous sight is the Blue Grotto, but more spectacular is the view from the top of Mount Solarno, where an old monastery stands. The pagan shrine of the Matromonia Cave is interesting, as are the ruins of 12 villas built by Roman Emperor Tiberius to honor the 12 Roman deities.

Sardinia is the land of *banditti*, clans, and blood vengeance. Movie stars and royalty are attracted to its luxurious Emerald Coast. Ship service is available from Genoa, Civita Vecchia, and Naples, with the overnight trip taking 14 hours. House rentals are available throughout the island. The Italian Government Travel Office has a list of agents.

A small house that sleeps four and overlooks the sea costs about $1,800 per month.

Picturesque Enna, situated on a horseshoe-shaped plateau in the center of Sicily, has aptly been called the belvedere of the island. This provincial capital of 30,000 is rich in history and pageantry. The week before Easter it is ablaze with colorful parades. The altitude (about 3,500 feet) provides cooling breezes in summer. Costs are delightfully low.

RENTING IN ITALY

Housing is in short supply in Italy, especially in major cities such as Rome and Milan. But, oddly enough, foreigners have an easier time finding a place to live than Italians do. Italy imposes strict price controls on landlords renting to Italians. Consequently, many landlords would rather leave a property vacant than let it out at a fixed low price—under laws that make it difficult to evict tenants.

Rent control laws do not apply to foreigners, which makes them attractive tenants. Landlords also figure that foreigners won't stay long, so the rent can be raised as soon as they move out. Because of this last factor, don't expect to find great bargains. Even so, properties can be found in Italy for half the rent of comparable U.S. units.

Also worth a look are residences and *pensiones* that rent attractive apartments and rooms for extended periods. You can find listings in the local Pagine Gialle (Yellow Pages).

You will find apartments far more quickly than you'll find houses for rent in Italy. And it's almost impossible to rent houses on a yearly basis. Landlords prefer to rent by the season, with prices beginning at around $240 a month. In Florence, the Agriturist Office, via del Preconsolo 10, has information about old houses for rent or sale. If your interest is Rome, the U.S. Embassy's Commercial Office there may help. The regional U.S. consulates have additional sources.

Other sources of rental information are schools and universities in the area where you want to live. Newspapers are also good sources. In Florence, *La Nazione*, *La Pulce*, and *Panorama Casa* list rentals for short- and long-term stays. Make lots of contacts, too. Some of the best rentals are found through word of mouth.

You may want to work through a rental agent, called an *immobiliari*. There are many such agencies throughout Italy, handling properties of all types and prices. Immobiliari also handle sales of apartments, houses, and land. For addresses of immobiliari, contact the Italian Embassy, 1601 Fuller St., NW, Washington, D.C. 20009, 202/328-5500.

U.S. rental agents that handle properties in Italy include At Home Abroad, Sutton Town House, 405 E. 56th St., Suite 6H, New York, NY 10022, 212/421-9165; Families Abroad, 194 Riverside Dr., Apt. 6D, New York, NY 10025, 212/787-2434; and Rentals in Italy, 1742 Calle Corva, Camarillo, CA 93010, 805/987-5278.

Or contact the tourist board in the city or area where you want to stay. They may be able to send you a list of rental agencies.

Rental Costs   Be prepared to pay two to three months' rent as a deposit and an additional two to three months' rent in advance. Afterward, you're likely to pay rent on a quarterly basis. Security deposits, sad to say, you may never recover. Be sure to identify a number of landlord candidates, then do your homework on each.

Typical rentals in Rome include a furnished, three-room apartment for about $525 per month; a nine-room luxury apartment in the city's best residential neighborhood at about $1,715 a month; and a seven-room house in a residential area at about $1,430 a month.

Lease Agreements   Allow four to six weeks to find an appropriate rental. Above all, begin your search well before summer; landlords vacation during July and August. To avoid any trick items, sign a lease only after consulting a lawyer you trust. This is where contacts with accounting firms may prove worthwhile, especially if you intend to purchase real estate for investment purposes.

Take time to do a careful inventory—even in unfurnished houses. Check for cracks, scratches, chips; test the appliances and locks; flush some paper down the toilet. In short, do a full "walk-through" with the landlord. And be sure you have all the keys; otherwise, you may have unpleasant surprises and charges later.

$\mathcal{B}$UYING $\mathcal{R}$EAL $\mathcal{E}$STATE

Italians tend to live in apartments rather than houses. Apartments are generally sold on a condominium basis. Although you'll own your dwelling outright, the surrounding land, gardens, and swimming pools are shared facilities. You and the other owners are jointly responsible for the upkeep.

Your best sources for real estate are local people. Printed information may be up-to-date and helpful, but you still need the local perspective on "best bets" and traps to avoid. Some Italian cities have American Women's Clubs that specialize in helping newcomers with housing and settling in. You may even be able to sublet a house or apartment from a family about to return to the United States. Real estate agents who deal in Italian properties include:

❦Agenzia Flora, Piazza Colombo 10, San Remo, Liguria; tel. (39) (0184) 504-566

❦Gambetti, 5 Corso Venezia, 20121 Milano; tel. (39) (02) 77551; fax (39) (2) 7601-3351

❦ Locfintur, Loc Il Cerreto-Strove, 53035, Monteriggioni, Siena; tel. (39) (0577) 301-053

Another good place to find property in northern Italy is the classified section of *La Pulce*. Advertisements are written in Italian.

The Purchase Process   Real estate agents will guide you through your purchase, most with translation assistance, and help you deal with Italian government bureaucracy. Most agents will help with paperwork, hire a notary, and, if you're renovating, put you in touch with local builders. Once you've chosen a property, a deposit of 10 to 30 percent is paid to the seller. The notary will draw up the final property-transfer document and witness the signing by you and the seller.

In Italy, a foreigner can purchase property using funds only from an external source. If money transfers are not executed quickly enough, the property and initial deposit will be lost. Since at present U.S. banks are not efficient at transferring funds to Italy, it's a good idea to use a U.S. branch of an Italian bank.

When the final transfer of property is made, Italian law requires that all parties must fully understand the details of the contract. You should either have good command of Italian, hire an interpreter, or give power of attorney to a Realtor who will act on your behalf.

Some Italian credit institutions can finance up to 75 percent of the value of a new home secured by a mortgage on the property. The minimum mortgage loan is five years, with no maximum limit.

Agency commissions are typically 2 to 5 percent of the declared property value. Notary and legal fees run 3 to 6 percent (typically between $1,300 and $3,200), depending on the area in which you are buying. You'll also pay a tax of 10 percent on the assessed value of the property (17 percent if you're buying land only).

Real Estate Prices In resort areas, apartments sell for about $78,000 to $235,000. A two-bedroom apartment in San Remo was recently advertised for $155,000. Outside resort areas, you can get a two-bedroom apartment for about $40,000. A traditional apartment (needing a little work) on the top floor of a fine old building in Apricale costs $80,000.

Properties are cheapest south of Rome, where the land and the people are poorer. Unrestored farmhouses in southern Italy can be quite cheap, but expect to pay at least half as much for restoration as for the house.

You can buy a vacation home in the Lake Country for about $57,000. A restored castle on 15 acres of land in Umbria may be found for $69,000. Villages where time seems to stand still are particularly good hunting grounds for bargains. In Perugia, in Umbria, a 1,000-square-foot stucco villa with living room, kitchen, bathroom, laundry, two bedrooms, two terraces, and 21,500 square feet of land and modern conveniences costs $150,000.

Cost of Living

Americans can live well on a modest budget in Italy. In a small, simple restaurant, a three-course meal with a liter of wine ranges from $25 to $40. Seats for open-air opera at the Baths of Caracalla cost about $15. Here's what you'll pay for some typical goods and services in Italy:

electricity	$55–$170/month	lettuce	$.75/pound
gasoline	$4.28/gallon	coffee	$5.25/pound
movie ticket	$6.25	milk	$4.80/gallon
bottle of wine	$5	chicken	$2/pound
maid service	$8.25/hour	fish	$6.80/pound
bananas	$.65/pound	video rental	$3.50
bread	$1.80/loaf	compact disc	$20
steak	$6.80/pound		

Inflation is high, however. The government plans to cut spending and raise taxes to help reduce inflation in the coming years.

Day-to-day Living Concerns

Be prepared to deal with inefficiencies in Italian mail and telephone services. In some heavily industrialized regions, the need for telephones has outstripped the supply. If you want phone service, you might have to find a residence that already has it.

Mail delivery in Italy is lackadaisical at best, horrendous at worst. An airmail letter can take up to three weeks to arrive; regular mail, a month.

Remember when dealing with business and government services, most Italians take their vacations during August. Many business and retail shops reduce their hours or close for the month, as do some government offices.

$\mathcal{T}$AXES

Italy has no wealth tax. But real estate gains are taxed at 3 to 30 percent, depending upon time held. Worldwide income-tax rates are progressive and range from 10 percent on taxable income of 3 million lire or less to 72 percent for the portion of income in excess of 500 million lire—with assorted credits, including local taxes paid.

There are two income taxes on individuals in Italy: personal income tax (IRPEF) and local income tax (ILOR). Residents are taxed on income from any source. Non-residents are taxed on income produced in Italy. For tax purposes, a resident is anyone inscribed in the record of the Office of Resident Populations, anyone who has his or her principal offices or interests in Italy, or anyone who lives there more than six months a year. Local tax does not apply to income from abroad.

$\mathcal{M}$AKING THE $\mathcal{M}$OVE

You will need a valid passport to enter Italy, but a visa is not required for stays up to three months. If, after entering, you decide you would like to stay more than 90 days, you can apply, once only, at any police station (*questura*). The extension will give you an additional 90 days. You will have to prove you have adequate means of support and that you do not want the extension for study or employment. As a rule, permission is granted immediately.

Tourists are supposed to register with the Italian police within three days of their arrival. Usually, your hotel will handle the registration. If you are staying in a private home, you will have to register in person. And you are supposed to register again each time you change guest houses. (Not many people do, though, and enforcement is lax.)

If you plan to live in Italy for more than six months, you'll need to get a visa from the Italian Embassy or one of the Italian consulates in the United States before departure. You'll need two passport photos.

In theory, foreigners living in Italy must report to the local police every three months. However, many people ignore these regulations. So the official number of retirees reported in Italy might reflect only part of the number actually living there.

If your father or mother was an Italian citizen when you were born, you may be able to get Italian citizenship. This status would give you an EU (European Union) passport and the right to work in any EU country. For more details, contact the Italian embassy or consulate near you.

What to Bring, What to Leave Behind   You can import personal belongings duty-free, including clothing, books, household equipment, a typewriter, and stereo equipment, as long as they are only for personal use.

If you plan to bring a pet to Italy, you must have a veterinarian's certificate stating that the animal is in good health and has been vaccinated against rabies 30 days before your departure date. Forms are available from all Italian diplomatic and consular representatives and from Italian Government Travel Offices. Dogs must be on a leash and sometimes muzzled when in public.

For more information, contact the Italian Government Travel

Office, 630 Fifth Ave., Suite 1565, New York, NY 10111, 212/245-4822, or the Embassy of Italy, 1601 Fuller St. NW, Washington, D.C. 20009, 202/328-5500.

$\mathcal{M}$EDICAL $\mathcal{C}$ARE

Health care in Italy is plentiful, good, and reasonably priced. A visit to a doctor costs from $30 to $85, and a hospital room costs around $175 to $350 a day.

First-aid service (*pronto soccorso*), with a doctor at hand, is available at airports, marine ports, railway stations, and all hospitals. In case of emergency, telephone 113 or 112 for the state police or the Immediate Action Service. These numbers are *only* for emergencies.

Italy is blessed with numerous thermal baths, many of volcanic origin and known for their restorative powers since Roman times. The spas are located in some of the most beautiful areas of the country. Montecatini and Chianciano are in Tuscany near Florence. The baths of Abano and Grado are near Venice. Fiuggi is a short distance from Rome, in the medieval town of Latium. Levico is in the Dolomites.

Remember, Medicare doesn't cover Americans overseas, and Italy has no medical program covering U.S. citizens. So make sure your U.S. insurance will cover you abroad.

$\mathcal{F}$INANCIAL $\mathcal{M}$ATTERS

The basic unit of Italian currency is the lira. Notes are issued for 1,000, 2,000, 5,000, 10,000, 20,000, 50,000, and 100,000 lire. Coins are 10, 20, 50, 100, 200, and 500 lire. The exchange rate is approximately 1,750 to one U.S. dollar.

You may not take more than 500,000 lire in or out of the country without official clearance. Italy has no restrictions on the amount of foreign currency imported. However, everyone entering Italy should declare the amount he or she is carrying so that the same amount may be exported.

You can change foreign money for lire at any bank or exchange office (Ufficio di Cambio). A limited amount of lire can be obtained from conductors on international trains and at certain stations within Italy.

The lira remains fairly steady against other European currencies, but not against the dollar. You'll probably get a better exchange rate for your traveler's checks than for cash.

The Banking System   The Bank of Italy has recently freed its control over individual banks. Italy's premier merchant bank, Mediobanca, has recently been sold to the private sector (the Agnelli family), and commercial banks are being allowed to set their own interest rates and compete for customers as they please.

With a huge public debt to service, funds are tight in the lending sector. The prime rate is about 17 percent, and small businesses typically pay 20 percent. Venture capital is almost nonexistent.

The high interest rates benefit savers, who typically earn from 15 to 16 percent on deposits. Italy's savings rate is even higher than Japan's— 22.7 percent compared to only 17 percent for the Japanese.

Banking customers get other conveniences as well. Most Italian banks are part of the Bancomat system. Customers receive a card they can use to withdraw money at member banks.

TRANSPORTATION

Italy's railway system is good and covers the country well. The Italy Railcard offers special travel deals. For example, an eight-day pass costs $168, a 30-day pass costs $290. For information contact CIT in the United States at 800/248-7245; in Italy call (39) (6) 479-4340. Air networks are also extensive. Alitalia is the state airline for domestic and international service.

In large cities such as Rome and Florence, you won't want a car. Between the traffic and the lack of parking and garage space, you'll be happier taking public transportation. Florence, in particular, is a walking city. In fact, it's a magical city for walks, with surprises around every corner. Bicycling is also a good way to get around. You can rent a bike for a few dollars a day or buy a used one. Outside of the big cities, you'll want a car to explore the small towns, vineyards, and countryside.

$\mathcal{L}$EISURE $\mathcal{T}$IME

Italy is a cultural extravaganza of prehistoric sites, sculpture, architecture, art, and music. You can visit the Uffizi Gallery in Florence, the Sistine Chapel in Vatican City, and the Colosseum in Rome. You can attend the opera in Milan or the world-renowned international biennial exhibition of visual arts in Venice. You can browse countless art galleries, large and small.

At small trattorias and sidewalk cafés, you can eat pesto made with the freshest olive oil, garlic, and pine nuts. You can visit vineyard regions, stopping to taste the delicious results of the harvest. Get a good guidebook and plan for years of enjoyable exploring.

Shopping Milan is Italy's fashion capital, but you'll find beautiful ladies' wear, leather goods, and textiles throughout Italy. Small shops offer pottery, jewelry, and specialty items. Street stands offer fresh produce, glassware, scarves, housewares, and a wide range of artwork.

Sports and Hobbies The most popular sport in Italy is football (soccer). Water sports and winter sports are enjoyed at seaside and mountain resorts.

If you are an artist, take advantage of Florence. Many art schools here are open to foreigners. Three of the most accessible are Centro di Cultura Lorenzo di Medici, Scuola Leonardo da Vinci, and Scuola Dante Aligheri. All are fine schools and relatively inexpensive.

ADDITIONAL RESOURCES

Italian Embassy, 1601 Fuller St. NW, Washington, D.C. 20009; 202/328-5500

Italian Government Tourist Office, 630 Fifth Ave., Suite 1565, New York, NY 10111; 212/245-4822, fax 212/586-9249

U.S. Embassy, Via Vittorio Veneto d121, 00187 Rome; tel. (39) (6) 46741

Useful Web Site
www.italyemb.nw.dc.us/italy/index.htm

Mexico

by JOHN LYONS-GOULD

Why retire in Mexico? To stand in the ancient streets and romantic courtyards of San Miguel de Allende, in the striking shadow of the Sierra Madre range. To enjoy the commercial and cultural riches of Guadalajara, Mexico's second largest city. To play on one hundred miles of shoreline bordering Lake Chapala in the town of Ajijic, an old fishing village with a new country-club atmosphere. And so much more. You will have a hard time finding another country with Mexico's variety of livable spaces and wealth of things to do and see.

Fleeing harsh northern climates, thousands of snowbirds flock to Mexico every winter. They, and those who choose to retire here year-round, come for the high quality of life and relatively low cost of living. They are lured by the natural beauty of the region and welcomed by a rich and traditional culture.

The conversion to Mexican ways of life will not come without challenges, and, as any foreign country, Mexico is not for every retiree. But, when all is said and done, this extraordinary country of over 90 million people (geographically about one-quarter the size of the continental United States) is a favored retirement spot for a number of compelling reasons.

The vast Central Highlands, which encompass about two-thirds of the nation's 762,000 square miles, offer retirees some of the finest weather in the world, with sunny days, low humidity, and moderate rainfall in most areas. The cultural climate in Mexico is equally attractive. In this traditionally conservative society—with its backdrop of Roman Catholicism—respect for others is a way of life. Crime rates are significantly lower in most Mexican cities than in the United States.

Contemporary Mexico is a dynamic, rapidly modernizing society where you'll find international airports, satellite TV, and even Wal-Mart (thanks to NAFTA). But life is still simple and inexpensive here. You can buy comprehensive medical insurance in Mexico for less than $300 a year, and most medical costs are 30 to 50 percent lower than in the United States. And don't let fears of getting sick discourage you. You can drink the water and eat the salad in most restaurants without fear—at prices 50 to 60 percent lower than in the United States. Whether you cherish the cosmopolitan rush of the world's largest city or crave the Old World history of a colonial village, Mexico can accommodate your needs in style.

The Culture and People of Mexico

Travelers and expatriates alike continue to marvel at the hospitality and warmth of the Mexican people, even with the numbers of foreign retirees and other expatriates increasing. Mexicans generally enjoy doing business with Americans and place a high value on family and honesty. English is often spoken, especially in the Central Highlands, where over 50,000 *Norteamericanos* reside.

Family units are strong in Mexico, as are family businesses. Many gringos compare the economic environment (with no welfare system) to that of the United States in the 1950s. Violent crime is nearly nonexistent, and property crime is low compared to most U.S. cities.

Learn the Language The Spanish language is beautiful and relatively easy to learn. Knowing at least a modicum of Spanish is a prerequisite to living and doing business in Mexico. And the more you know, the more comfortable you will feel in your new home. You can sign up for Spanish classes in Mexico for as little as $30 a week or hire your own tutor for $5 an hour.

Don't know where to start? Try the Universidad Autónoma de Guadalajara, Ave. Patria 1201, Lomas del Valle, tel. (52) (3) 641-7051, ext. 2251, for intensive four-week courses three times a year. Or take Spanish Alive, a 14-day immersion course, and learn in style. The $2,000 fee includes tuition and supplies, luxury accommodations, full breakfast, and free transportation. Contact La Puertecita Boutiquéotel, Santo Domingo 75, Col. Los Arcos, San Miguel de Allende, Gto.; tel. (52) (415) 22250; fax (52) (415) 25505.

A Brief History of Mexico The who did what, when, where, and why of Mexican history can be a bit confusing, especially to foreigners. Just take note of a few high points and fill in the rest for yourself as you explore the country.

A.D. 300–900	Years of the Mayan empire
1325	Founding of Tenochtitlán (modern Mexico City) by the Aztecs
1521–1650	Conquistadors introduce Christianity
1821	Mexico wins independence from Spain
1857	Mexican constitution is proclaimed
1867	Mexico's last emperor is captured and killed; General Porfirio Díaz's corrupt dictatorship lasts for 35 years.
1910–1930	Political confusion. Pancho Villa, Zapata, Madero, Huerta, Obregón, and another constitution later, the political climate starts to calm.

1970–1976   Peso is devalued; the bad economy fuels rumors of military takeover
1976–1982   President Portillo institutes economic reforms after great oil and gas discoveries in Mexico
1982–1988   Peso tumbles again due to huge external debt
1988–1994   Strong economic recovery and promise of NAFTA
1994   Mexico's first "clean" elections challenge ruling PRI party

Enjoy New Traditions   With more than 50 distinct Indian groups, Spanish descendents, and mestizos (people of mixed Indian and European descent), Mexico offers visitors a rich and varied culture. This variety is reflected in music, dance, and more. For example, mariachi music originated in the state of Jalisco, and no wedding would be complete without it. In the southern state of Chiapas, you're more likely to hear marimba music, played on wooden xylophones from Africa. And throughout Mexico, you can hear traditional Spanish songs and dances called *corridos*.

In the United States we eat our hats. In Mexico, they dance around them. *Jarabe tapatio*, also known as the Mexican hat dance, is the country's national dance. The most popular dance is the *viejitos*, or Dance of the Little Old Men of Michoacán. Other dances include Spanish forms such as flamenco and salsa and Mexican rain dances in honor of the Aztec god Tlaloc (performed with carved drums and reed flutes).

Bullfighting is alive and well in Mexico and so is the "macho" image that the sport embodies. Cockfighting is also popular—and legal—here. Fiestas are another important part of the country's persona, including Día de Los Muertos, Christmas posadas (complete with piñatas), Semana Santa (holy week), Cinco de Mayo, and some five thousand other celebrations.

Develop Your Own Cultural Identity   While you may feel like an explorer charting new territory as you chase your dreams in a foreign land, you won't have to go it alone—especially in Mexico. More than

30,000 expatriates live in Guadalajara itself. There are over 80 organizations in that city and the surrounding area that can assist you in your transition. Get out a little, make a few contacts, and you'll be amazed at how quickly you begin to find your niche in Mexico.

The American Society of Jalisco, Apdo. Postal 5-510, San Francisco 3332, Colonia Chapalita, Guadalajara, Jal.; tel. (52) (3) 121-0827, offers memberships for $30 and less. Publications like *Retire in Mexico*, *Guadalajara Reporter*, *The News*, and *El Ojo Del Largo* cater to the U.S. retiree.

$\mathcal{R}$ECOMMENDED $\mathcal{L}$IVING $\mathcal{A}$REAS

San Miguel de Allende—All-around Best Place to Retire   San Miguel de Allende, one of the best-preserved colonial towns in Mexico, has some 2,500 U.S. expatriates living in villas perched high atop its ancient streets and romantic courtyards. Artists and craftspeople thrive in this town, 180 miles from Mexico City and surrounded by rich farmland near the base of the Sierra Madre.

You can become a student of massage, French cooking, violin, horseback riding, Spanish, oil painting, or pottery at one of two prestigious art centers in the city: Bellas Artes and the Instituto Allende. Every day you'll hear music—from rock to classical and jazz—in local restaurants and nightclubs. Fiestas are too numerous to name, and wine flows freely in the plazas during special events. But amid all the merriment, you won't see a single traffic light, neon sign, or billboard; the whole town has been declared a national monument.

A world-class retirement destination, San Miguel boasts an international airport in León, a new hospital, luxury homes, and a 330-acre housing development around a new championship golf course. Housing in San Miguel is not cheap, but prices have fallen to more reasonable levels in the past decade. The mild and dry climate is hard to beat, the culture is rich and lively, and Mexico City is not far away.

Housing prices start at around $50,000 for a condo. A typical home with three bedrooms, two-and-a-half baths, an open patio, a living room with a fireplace, a kitchen, servants' quarters, and a garage costs about $80,000 to $90,000.

Guadalajara—Best City Living Guadalajara is the second-largest city in Mexico and an important commercial center and travel destination. If you're looking for city living with traditional charm, this is your place. Many retirees report that they feel safer in Guadalajara than in any other city in the world.

The Spanish settled the area in 1542, and Guadalajara was the first city in Mexico to fall to the revolutionary Miguel Hidalgo during the War of Independence. The city is still steeped in traditional culture. You can live in its historic center near the Degollado Theater, the Cabanas Cultural Institute, and the Museo Orozco (which houses over 100 paintings by native son Jose Clemente Orozco). You can visit centuries-old cathedrals after a long siesta, enjoy the elegant buildings and plazas over lunch, and see the city from a different perspective aboard *calandrias* (horse-drawn carriages).

Guadalajara is located in the warm, temperate highlands northwest of Mexico City, where average rainfall is 20 to 40 inches a year and winters are usually dry. Nearby you'll find desert, pine and oak forest, and deciduous jungle. The city itself offers a full schedule of soccer matches, bullfights, basketball games, and cock fights. The climate is perfect for golf, and there are a number of well-maintained championship courses in the area.

Houses in the Guadalajara area run anywhere from $39,000 for a quaint city home to $299,000 for a luxurious colonial mansion. Contact Re/Max Guadalajara, Carretera Oriente 52, Apdo. Postal 111, Ajijic, Jal. 45920; tel. (52) (3) 642-8202; fax (52) (3) 642-8198, for information on real estate.

Ajijic—Favorite Lakeside Living The Nahuatl Indians founded this onetime fishing village ("the place where water springs forth") in the early 1400s. The Spanish colonized the area in 1652, ushering in the dominant architecture and cobblestone streets in the city's *zócalo*, or central plaza. You'll find a large selection of retirement homes with good amenities spreading out from the city's center to the hills. Average temperatures are in the mid-70s, with a moderate summer rainy season.

Ajijic, bordering Lake Chapala, is a favorite among retirees for its perfect balance of Old World Mexico and modern amenities. Community and social organizations catering to retired expatriates thrive here. A two-hour drive takes you to Puerto Vallarta and the Pacific coast. Ajijic itself offers a host of outdoor activities including golf, tennis, horseback riding, water-skiing, sailing, and fishing.

A large three-bedroom home with vaulted brick ceilings, traditional tile floors, and a sunny, high-walled courtyard costs about $90,000 here. New developments like La Huerta—The Orchard Village and Las Palmas—Villas by the Lake feature secure luxury living at $110,000 to $125,000 for up to 2,000 square feet. Contact Ajijic Real Estate, Calle Morelos 4, Apdo. Postal 555, 45920 Ajijic, Jal.; tel. (52) (376) 62077; fax (52) (376) 62331, for more information.

Guanajuato—Favorite University Town The Jesuits built the town's university in 1732 for the children of wealthy Spanish silver-mine owners. Today the school draws students from all over the country. The mining families also built opulent mansions and elegant churches like La Valanciana, which still stands.

The town is located along the banks of the Rio Guanajuato, in a narrow canyon three and a half hours from Mexico City. This mountainous terrain was home to the first battles in the fight for Mexican independence, and you will see monuments everywhere commemorating the struggle.

The meandering river that cuts through town creates a gridwork of winding streets and interesting plazas. Local builders used stone from the surrounding hills to construct well-made houses—painted in bright red, gold, coral, and blue. Housing prices vary widely, depending on condition, size, and proximity to the university.

RENTING IN MEXICO

Renters in Mexico can easily locate pleasant, well-constructed apartments that range from $300 for one-bedroom units to $700 for two-bedroom homes in gated communities. But rents as low as $200 and as high as $1,500 are not uncommon, depending on the level of amenities. Rents are usually higher in winter, when snowbirds flock to Mexico. Here are some typical rental listings for Guadalajara:

* Chapalita furnished apartment, ground floor, one bedroom, with telephone, kitchen, parking, and security, close to grand plaza; $350 a month
* Residential Victorian apartment, two blocks from Plaza del Sol, two bedrooms with security and some furniture; $400 a month
* Single, furnished apartment with telephone on Aurelio L. Gallardo; $225 a month

How to Find Good Rental Properties In most areas, the local newspapers are your best bet for finding rental properties. *El Ojo del Lago* in the Lake Chapala/Ajijic area is a good resource. Around Guadalajara, look for listings in the *Colony Guadalajara Reporter* and *The News*.

For the best listings by far in San Miguel, head to the UPS office—really! And everywhere, don't forget to wander the streets looking for signs and to ask locals for tips on good rentals.

Things to Keep in Mind Most important when renting: always sign your lease in pesos. Contracts made in foreign currency are not legally binding in Mexico. As with most transactions in Mexico, you can bargain about rent. Mexican landlords, for the most part, like gringo tenants, because they typically pay their rent on time. Note that Mexican law protects renters, making eviction almost impossible.

Before you rent, make sure to ask the following questions: Does the property come with phone service? How many electrical outlets are there and where are they located? Is the water heater automatic?

Are there good screens on all doors and windows? How noisy is the area? What are your neighbors like? Does the property come with an *aljibe* (underground water reserve with a pump)?

$\mathcal{B}$UYING $\mathcal{R}$EAL $\mathcal{E}$STATE

Buying real estate or property in any foreign country is not something that should be taken lightly. In Mexico some restrictions apply only to foreign buyers, financial practices will be unfamiliar to you, and you'll encounter water and sewage concerns particular to a developing country.

So take your time. Research and visit areas you think you might like. Talk to people who live there. Rent before you buy. And when the time comes, find trustworthy professionals to help you through the buying process.

Should You Buy Property in Mexico? Yes, with a qualification. Prices are lower in Mexico than in the United States, even with the recovery of the peso and a stabilizing Mexican economy. There are plenty of good deals to be had, as long as you are willing to rent first, work with a real estate agent, and investigate Mexican law pertaining to foreign purchasers. Home construction is generally of high quality—concrete, steel, brick, stucco, and tiles.

Be careful when selecting a real estate agency—ask for recommendations and make sure the company is licensed. Every legal document must be executed before a notary public to be valid in Mexico. Make sure you find a good one (again, ask for referrals). You don't need a lawyer to buy property in Mexico, but you do need to understand restrictions on foreign purchasers. Contact the American Society of Mexico, the American Chamber of Commerce, the U.S. embassy, or a U.S. consulate for more information.

Most real estate transactions in Mexico that involve foreign purchasers are made on a cash-only basis. So talk to your notary about trust and direct-deed ownership options before you buy. Also note that a Mexican will is recommended for all property owners in Mexico. Finally, look at a number of properties, be prepared to work with more than one agent, and be sure to hire an independent appraiser.

COST OF LIVING

The average retired couple can expect to live on about half of what it would cost for a similar lifestyle in the United States (about $1,000 a month in most places). Most products are significantly less expensive in Mexico, except for real estate and certain imported specialties.

A seafood dinner in a quality restaurant costs around $7, and you'll pay only 15 to 18 cents a pound for many fresh, delicious fruits and vegetables. Here's what you will pay for some other everyday items in Mexico:

electricity	$10/month	bread	$.25/loaf
gasoline	$1.60/gallon	steak	$3/pound
movie ticket	$2	tomatoes	$.65/pound
six-pack of beer	$1.75	coffee	$3.75/pound
maid service	$25/month	milk	$1/gallon
bananas	$.15/pound	eggs	$1.10/dozen

DAY-TO-DAY LIVING CONCERNS

Although you won't find all the comforts of home in Mexico, you will be pleasantly surprised by the general state of technology and modern conveniences here. Mexico's telephone system, Telmex, offers direct-dial service to other countries, as well as operator assistance. Expect to pay about $15 a month for standard telephone service. The country is also linked worldwide by Telex and fax.

Service has improved tremendously since Telmex was privatized, but problems still occur, especially in the rainy season when lines might be down for extended periods. If your phone needs repair, bypass the phone company and hire a local repairman. Better yet, buy a cellular phone.

Water? Make sure your property has plenty of it, especially if you are buying a home in a dry region. As a general rule, don't drink tap water unless it is boiled or filtered first, and make sure to eat only at restaurants that use purified water. You can buy bottled water easily in most places; special "water vendors" travel regular routes each day in many sections of Mexico.

Electric current is the same in Mexico as it is in the United States and Canada. Average costs for electricity in Guadalajara run $15 a month, and propane gas for cooking costs another $10 a month.

$\mathcal{T}$AXES

The good new is that pensions and other funds from abroad are exempt from Mexican income tax (although you'll pay U.S. taxes on them). Another good-news bulletin on the tax front: during your first year of residence in Mexico, you can take a one-time exemption from the general import tax on household items, autos, and other personal belongings. There's also no such thing as an inheritance tax south of the border.

The Mexican *predial*, or property tax, is currently .08 percent of the assessed value of the property—extremely low in comparison to U.S. rates. Rates are discounted if you pay the whole sum in advance annually.

MAKING THE MOVE

Remember, you are moving to a foreign country. So don't hesitate to get legal or other assistance if you are not sure about your rights or responsibilities. And before you begin the process of applying for resident status in Mexico, be forewarned. Because decent-paying jobs are at a premium in economically strapped Mexico, it's very difficult to win the coveted FM-3 visa designation that allows foreigners to work here. You should also remember that applying for residency in Mexico can be a complicated, time-consuming exercise—you'll need plenty of patience and a keen sense of humor.

Becoming a Temporary or Permanent Resident   The basic visa for temporary living and traveling in Mexico is the FM-T, or Tourist Card, which allows you to stay in the country for up to six months as long as you don't work (writers and artists may work in Mexico on an FM-T, as long as they don't sell any products in the country). You can acquire the FM-T upon entrance into Mexico fairly easily, provided you have proof of citizenship, such as a passport, birth certificate, or voter's registration card. You can renew the FM-T at any time by leaving and reentering the country.

If you want to spend more than three months in Mexico or work in the country, it's time to apply for another type of visa. Designed for people who want to live part-time in Mexico but not necessarily make it their permanent home, the FM-3 No Inmigrante Visitante allows you to stay in Mexico for up to five years. You must have a monthly income of at least $1,500, plus $500 for each dependent (half this amount if you own property in Mexico). You may own and operate a vehicle with foreign license plates, and you will receive a logbook to present to customs each time you cross the border.

Anyone who wants to reside permanently in Mexico must obtain an FM-2 Inmigrante Rentista visa. You must have an income of at least $1,800 per month and $900 a month for each dependent. As a permanent resident, you will be exempt from Mexican tax payments on income from abroad, exempt from inheritance taxes if you own property in certain Mexican states, and eligible for the one-time exemption from the general import tax. Contact a Mexican consulate for details regarding any of these exemptions.

You may not work in Mexico under FM-2 status until after your fifth year, when you are eligible to make a declaration of immigration. *Inmigrado* status confers on you most of the rights and privileges of Mexican citizenship, excluding the right to vote. Inmigrado status does not require you to give up your U.S. citizenship.

What to Bring, What to Leave Behind It is generally a good idea to bring anything that would be hard to find or too expensive to replace in Mexico. Tools, especially quality automotive tools, are one of the best examples. If you have them, bring them. Also, plan to bring your car if you are going to live in Mexico under an FM-T or FM-3 visa and maintain a U.S. or Canadian driver's license.

Do *not* bring furniture. It is an expensive and time-consuming process that involves a lot of paperwork. Many apartments and houses come already furnished, and you can pick up plenty of reasonably priced furniture throughout Mexico.

What About Pets? Pets are important to many retirees. Can dogs, cats, and parakeets be safely transported to Mexico to live with their owners? Answer: Yes. You can bring Fido with you into the land of the Maya.

But be forewarned: You will be required to present several documents describing the pooch's health and vaccinations. For more details, write or call the Mexican Consulate, 8 E. 41st St., New York, NY 10017; 212/217-6400.

MEDICAL CARE

If you're like most retirees, obtaining good medical care at reasonable prices will be an absolute must, regardless of the country you choose. The good news about Mexico's health facilities is that the major cities offer excellent care (especially areas with large foreign colonies). Another plus is that many Mexican dental and medical schools are staffed by U.S.-trained doctors and dentists.

The bad news is that it may be difficult to find adequate medical facilities in the more remote regions of Mexico. Remember also that Medicare and Medicaid will not cover your treatment in Mexico; look into Mexican national health care instead.

Hospital de la Fe at Libramiento a Dolores Hidalgo 43, Mesa del Malanqui, San Miguel, is an excellent medical facility—thanks in large part to the influx of U.S. expatriates in the region. The 16-adult-bed facility also offers three nursery beds, three pediatric/maternity beds, and state-of-the-art operating and delivery rooms staffed by 23 doctors and 28 nurses.

IMSS Medical Insurance   Here's some more good news on the health front: Mexico runs its own form of medical social security, known as the Mexican National Health Insurance Plan. Foreign retirees can sign up for the plan for just under $300 per year, with no deductibles or copayments.

Coverage includes a wide range of services such as laboratory tests, doctor visits, eye examinations, dentistry, prescription drugs, emergency services, and hospital and surgical care. The doctors and clinics are good, but you may have to wait a few days for an appointment unless it's an emergency.

Apply for coverage at the Instituto Mexicano Del Seguro Social (IMSS) in your area. You'll undergo a complete medical review in a local clinic and possibly a physical examination. You may want to bring a translator if you don't speak Spanish. There is a six-month waiting period after you apply, and people with serious or pre-existing problems can be rejected.

Availability and Cost of Care In addition to IMSS, Mexico has plenty of good private medical clinics and hospitals where you won't have to wait in line for a doctor. It's also heartening to know that most doctors in Mexico still make old-fashioned house calls 24 hours a day.

Reports of an hour-long physical exam on a Friday night for $20 are not uncommon. An office visit including EKG will run you about $40, blood work about $24, and a chest X ray about $16. Dental appointments in the Guadalajara area run $25 with X rays, and filling a tooth will set you back an additional $25. Medicine is also inexpensive in Mexico, with a typical prescription that costs $60 in the States costing only $16 south of the border.

$\mathcal{F}$INANCIAL $\mathcal{M}$ATTERS

There's no such thing as a *stable* emerging economy, and the ups and downs of the Mexican peso are well documented. The experts argue over the short- and long-term outlook for economic growth in Mexico, the extent to which the North American Free Trade Agreement will impact the economy, and when Mexico will arrive with a truly global economy. Your guess is as good as theirs in most cases.

The days of the 1994 peso devaluation and slashed housing prices are, for the most part, gone, but there are still plenty of good deals and many good investments for retirees in Mexico. In general, NAFTA has loosened trade restrictions, allowing superstores like Sam's and Wal-Mart to open here and offer new products.

Mexico's Banking System Most retirees will be delighted to learn that, for the most part, the Mexican banking system closely parallels the system used in the United States. Reliable, failure-proof banks offer checking and savings accounts—along with the safety deposit boxes and certificates of deposit you are used to back home. Some banks allow you to have retirement and Social Security checks deposited directly into your account. You'll also enjoy FDIC protection, a high rate of interest, and free checks.

Opening a bank account is also very similar to the process in the United States. However, checks from U.S. or other foreign banks can take as long as six weeks to clear, and it can also take a long time to wire funds to a Mexican bank.

Automatic teller machines are common in well-traveled areas of Mexico, and you're better off paying with cash than checks. Most Mexican stores will not accept checks, no matter how much you plead with the management.

What Should Retirees Do with Their Money?   Exchange rates are currently about 7 to 8 pesos per U.S. dollar. But pesos are always a bit risky; do yourself a favor and keep most of your money in dollars.

Simple money management can go a long way in Mexico. Save money while prices are low, rely on compounded interest, and invest smartly (avoid risky offshore investments). Mexico generally welcomes foreign investment, and a recent change in the law allows foreigners to own 100 percent of Mexican corporations.

Check with some of the retirement organizations in Mexico for up-to-date recommendations on banks that provide special investment and trust services for foreigners. Promex Bank is generally recommended. Lloyd's Bank, (52) (5) 252-1376, also offers excellent investment, banking, insurance, and travel services. Clients pay $2 a month for investment services and receive *Lloyd's Economic Report* every month. The financial group Multiva also offers a wide range of financial services in both English and Spanish.

Advice for Entrepreneurs   For the most part, Mexicans like doing business with straightforward and reliable Americans. If you want to start a business in Mexico, establish a network of Mexican business advisors, including an attorney and a certified public accountant. Plan to spend at least $5,000 on start-up costs.

Remember that things are different here. Not only is the mail slow and telephone service not as reliable as you're used to, but appointments are very loose. Businesses often open late and shut down for long siestas. Most people do not return phone messages.

$\mathcal{T}$RANSPORTATION

In the more developed areas, traveling around Mexico isn't very different from traveling in the United States. Several airlines (including Mexicana, Continental, and American) fly in and out of the country each day; most connect to regional destinations at Mexico City. Mexico also features more than 5,000 miles of well-maintained toll roads, including five major routes that crisscross the country.

The Mexican Tourism Secretariat maintains a fleet of mechanics in green trucks (Green Angels), who patrol main highways. Service is free, except for parts and gasoline. The angels stop working each evening at nine, so plan accordingly.

Mass Transit Mexico's bus system is incredibly cheap, with frequent departures and reliable service to most cities. First-class buses even have stewards serving soft drinks and snacks, with no-frills buses about 50 percent cheaper. But the buses are also noisy and crowded, and long trips can be uncomfortable. The best way to see the country—though a bit slower—is to travel along scenic train routes.

Taxis are government regulated and affordable, but be sure to agree on a rate before you enter the cab, and make sure the meter is working. Like their compatriots in other areas of commerce, Mexican cab drivers enjoy haggling over fares. The best strategy is to offer about half of the first price you're given, then politely argue your way to a compromise.

Automobile Travel Do not drive in this country unless you pick up Mexican car insurance from spots along the border or from rental-car companies—you do not want to see the inside of a Mexican jail. Gas stations in Mexico are full-service, and tipping the attendant is customary. Payments are cash only, and most stations close by 10 p.m.

Always carry your current driver's license, insurance papers, and proof of ownership. Because roads are often rough and poorly marked, avoid driving at night, especially long distances.

*L*EISURE *T*IME

Mexico is truly diverse—from the Gulf of Mexico to Pacific Ocean beaches, from vast Chihuahuan deserts to the heights of the Sierra Madre, from the southern rain forests to the arid Central Highlands. And that's just geography. Mexico is also home to a variety of Indian and Spanish cultures, with different traditions and many dialects. For those in search of recreation and sightseeing, pick a place to start—and enjoy.

Things to Do and See In one of nature's most spectacular migrations, several million monarch butterflies congregate every year in the fir forests of Michoacán to feed on the milkweed plant and escape northern winter temperatures. For best viewing, hire a naturalist guide and climb the mountain paths to see these creatures during February or March.

Adventurers who prefer an urban setting should take a taxi ride through the elaborate system of tunnels lying beneath the colonial city of Guanajuato. While you're in Guanajuato, stay at El Castillo de Santa Cecilia Hotel, an authentic castle complete with moat and fortress.

In San Miguel, pamper yourself at one of Mexico's finest spa hotels, La Puerticita Boutiquéotel and Spa. While you're at it, splurge at one of San Miguel's four-star restaurants, Julian's. Have the chateaubriand for $8, and don't worry—you can drink the water. In Guadalajara, dine at La Troje and enjoy mariachi music, traditional *cantadors* (Latin singers), and folk dancers.

If you're up for a drive to the southern tip of Mexico, visit the beautiful Triunfo Biosphere Reserve, named for an inactive volcano and protecting 300 species of birds. Or visit Puebla, the City of Ceramic Tiles, near the snowcapped mountain of Popocatépetl, where the battle of Cinco de Mayo was fought against the French.

If you have more time, go scuba diving off the island of Cozumel, tour the oldest Spanish city of Veracruz, shop for candied fruit at 6,000 feet in the colonial city of Morelia, or relax in a hammock on the beaches of Puerto Escondido after a morning of surfing. If you still haven't done enough, take the Chihuahua al Pacifico rail line along the rim of the deepest spot in North America, Copper Canyon in the Tarahumara Range of the Sierra Madre.

Shopping Those who live in Ajijic or Chapala and want to do some serious shopping can take a bus tour to Guadalajara. Closer to home, watch for market days and enjoy bargains on everything from housewares to groceries to jewelry to livestock. Don't mind the crowds, noise, and smells—enjoy the adventure.

As you travel, expect to bargain for great deals on silver, rugs, pottery, paintings, clothing, artifacts, minerals, and more. Collecting just about anything is cheaper and easier in Mexico than north of the border.

Sports and Hobbies The Pacific coast offers world-class fishing, sailing, snorkeling, diving, and a host of other activities. Inland, in San Miguel for instance, you can enjoy exceptional golf, tennis, horseback riding, yoga and dance classes, string quartets, birdwatching, bridge, theater groups, and an American Legion post. Soccer (*fútbol*) is *big* in Mexico, so learn the customs of the sport if you haven't already.

$\mathcal{A}$DDITIONAL $\mathcal{R}$ESOURCES

Mexican Ministry of Tourism, Presidente Mazaric 172, Colonia
   Polanca, Mexico D.F. 11587; tel. (52) (5) 250-0151 (emergency
   line)
Mexico Retirement and Travel Assistance, 6301 S. Squaw Valley Rd.
   Suite 23, Pahrump, NV 89048, tel. (52) (3) 641-1152.
Re/Max, Carretara Oriente 52, Apdo. Postal 111, Ajijic, Jal. 45920;
   tel. (52) (376) 61511.
Sanborns Insurance Services, P.O. Box 310, McAllen, TX 78503,
   800/222-0158

Useful Web Sites
http://quicklink.com/mexico/
www.virtualmex.com
www.livingoverseas.com
www.eden.com

A estender os olhos,
Não podíamos ver senão terra e água:
Terra que nos parecia muito ...
PERO VAZ DE CAMINHA

Portugal

by LISA MATTE

Retiring to a foreign country means different things to different people. Retiring in Portugal means, at the very least, sampling some of the very best Mother Nature and human beings have to offer: Golden vineyards, sun-drenched orange groves, and sleepy fishing villages tucked into coastal nooks and crannies. Cool Atlantic beaches in the north. Balmy Mediterranean surf to the south. Coastal islands boasting a year-round subtropical climate. Medieval castles, historic villages, and modern cities. There is something for everyone in Portugal.

Sure, retiring to Portugal may require some degree of adjustment in terms of cultural differences, but settle in and you'll discover that the natives are most decidedly friendly. In fact, the people of Portugal are some of the most hospitable folks in the Western world. But warm welcome aside, Portugal has become a popular retirement destination among Americans for a variety of practical reasons.

Sun worshippers seeking respite from the long, cold winters of the northeastern and central United States will find something close to Nirvana in the Algarve region of Portugal, where sunshine warms coastal Mediterranean resorts an average of 3,300 hours each year.

Located on the southwestern corner of the European continent, Portugal's Costa de Lisboa boasts a year-round temperate climate ranging from a springlike 57 degrees Fahrenheit in winter to a pleasantly moderate 75 degrees Fahrenheit during summer. Further north along the coast, retirees will discover similarly balmy climates in the Costa de Prata and Costa Verde regions.

Venturing inland, the mountainous region of Montanhas is a haven for folks who prefer a more diverse climate. Temperatures in this natural paradise range on average between 57 and 78 degrees Fahrenheit, but temperatures in the upper elevations have been known to drop well below freezing. This relatively cool and dry climate makes Montanhas the ideal location for outdoor sports. Snowfall at higher elevations allows winter sports aficionados to take to the slopes at somewhat modest ski resorts. Most are perched amid the Serra da Estrela, Portugal's highest mountain range, topping out at 6,535 feet above sea level.

Another plus for retirees is Portugal's reputation for looking after its elders in terms of medical and social programs. Residents are privy to well-regarded health coverage at low costs. In addition, most larger communities feature a state-administrated medical care facility. Social clubs and organizations provide an outlet for friendly mingling and good-natured sports competition among seniors.

While expatriates can expect some minor annoyances—such as occasionally unreliable telephone service in outlying areas—the benefits of retiring to Portugal far outweigh the liabilities. Transportation is relatively efficient and reasonably priced. Food is fresh and bountiful. Transnational newspapers including the *International Herald Tribune* and *USA Today* are readily available, and the Portuguese television system features at least a dozen international channels.

The Culture and People

Perhaps the best reasons to settle in Portugal are its "human resources." Often described as Europe's friendliest citizens, the Portuguese are famous for their warm hospitality and easygoing nature. Make an effort to understand the country's cultural etiquette and you'll find yourself quickly enjoying your new home.

Emanating from a traditional and somewhat conservative heritage, Portuguese hospitality is evident in its citizens' friendly and unhurried approach to life. While this trait contributes to the livability of the country, it can also lead to unexpected (and sometimes aggravating) service delays. Remember to remain calm and polite in frustrating situations. Courtesy is a well-regarded asset in this traditional culture.

Learn the Language While English is a common second language in Portugal, American visitors who intend to become residents are well-advised to learn Portuguese to expedite their transition. Like French and Italian, Portuguese is a Romance language derived from Latin. Individuals who speak one or more of those languages will have an easier time expanding their linguistic skills to include Portuguese.

A Portuguese-English phrase book will help ease awkward communications for a short time, but anyone thinking seriously about retiring to Portugal should consider taking a Portuguese language class. If you must speak English, use the phrase "Fala ingles?" ("Do you speak English?") to open conversation.

The Centro Audio-Visua de Linguas at Praca Luis de Camoes 36, 1200 Lisbon offers an eight-week Portuguese language class for foreigners. Portuguese tutors are available for hire, and you'll find that watching Portuguese television is another good way to polish language skills.

A Brief History of Portugal Modern Portuguese society is the result of centuries of turbulence and political upheaval. At various times, this far-western slice of Europe was claimed by everyone from Celtic tribes and Phoenician traders to Greek patriots and the Roman Empire.

Even today, remnants of six hundred years of Roman rule remain evident in the form of ancient roads and bridges—still in use throughout the country. Agriculture, too, recalls the legacy of Roman occupation. Harvests reflect the Roman introduction of wheat, barley, and olives to the region.

Portugal was conquered by one group after another until the dawn of the Age of Discovery in the early fifteenth century. It was during that glorious 100-plus-year period that Prince Henry the Navigator gave Portugal its moment in the sun. Here are some other historical highlights:

1394	Prince Henry the Navigator is born into the Aviz dynasty, destined to transform Portugal into a wealthy maritime power
1420–1460	Prince Henry is named Grand Master of the Order of Christ as he proceeds to expand Portugal's trade routes and convert indigenous peoples to Christianity; one of Prince Henry' s sailing vessels successfully rounds Cape Bojador on the West African coast, thereby proving that the cape is *not* the end of the world
1494	The Pope settles ongoing disputes between Portugal and Spain by dividing the New World between the two nations, "giving" Asia, Africa, and Brazil to Portugal
1580	Portugal's dominance in the New World is challenged by Spain, whose rulers claim Portugal as their own
1640–1654	Portugal ousts Spanish rule and aligns itself with England, establishing an alliance that remains strong to this day
1700s	Portugal is ruled by a series of absolute monarchs while fending off attacks by French and Spanish forces
1800s	A series of coups d'etat and dictatorships mark an end to a period of relative stability in Portugal

1928–1968	Antonio de Oliveira Salazar steps into the limelight as minister of finance before being named prime minister in 1932. Though widely unpopular, Salazar maintains firm control of Portugal's government until his death in 1968.
1968–1974	Dr. Marcelo Caetano succeeds Salazar as dictator. He is ousted during the revolution of 25 do Abril— an almost bloodless revolution sometimes called the Revolution of Flowers because many soldiers placed carnations in their gun barrels.
1974–1996	Portugal again weathers a prolonged period of political instability until the 1996 election of Socialist Party member Jorge Samaio to the presidency
Present	Portugal remains cautiously optimistic about its future under the fiscal and political direction of Samaio and Prime Minister Antonio Guterres.

Embrace a New Culture Portugal's checkered past has left its mark on the present. Monuments, archaeological finds, and cave paintings recall its legacy. Relics dating to Roman rule blend with a strong Celtic influence in northern regions, while signs of Arabic presence remain notable in the south.

Music, drama, and film festivals of both local and international acclaim take place each year throughout the country. Talented musicians, dancers, and actors dressed in elaborate costumes take center stage on the national front. Municipalities also host local festivals featuring music, dancing, and parades in observance of various saints' days.

Reminiscent of the troubadour style of singing popular in the Middle Ages, Portugal's folk music recalls its agricultural history with a foot-tapping rhythm complemented by the sounds of guitars, harmonicas, and woodwinds. In contrast, *fado*—Portugal's most popular style of contemporary music—features "bluesy" melodies performed by a solo singer and accompanied by the guitar. Head to small cafés frequented by locals to sample traditional versions of these melancholy songs.

While Americans are most likely to use tiles for utilitarian purposes, Portuguese painted tiles—called *azulejos*—are considered works of art. Dating to the Moorish occupation during the Middle Ages, such tiles grace the walls of Portugal's buildings—from churches and castles to bars and restaurants. Handcrafted ceramics, finely woven carpets, and delicate embroidery are other popular forms of artistic expression among the Portuguese.

One image you are likely to see gracing everything from decorative tiles and carpets to pottery and fabrics is a sign of good luck. This ubiquitous icon is a flamboyantly colored rooster. Legend has it that just as a condemned man was being dragged to face his fate at the gallows, a roasted bird sprang to life, jumped up onto the judge' s table, and proclaimed the prisoner innocent of all charges, thereby saving his life.

On the sports front, soccer has become a national obsession in Portugal. Traditional spectator events like bullfighting remain popular with the Portuguese, despite disapproval expressed by animal rights groups. Announcements during bullfighting season (March to October) assure naysayers that the bulls will not be killed. Be forewarned, though. A typical two-hour episode *is* bloody and the bull *is* speared. And while laws governing Portuguese bullfighting prohibit a public kill, it is widely believed that bulls are destroyed after the fights.

A highly religious country, Portugal is home to people who worship in a variety of forms and churches. The dominant religion is Roman Catholicism.

The shrine in Fatima is dedicated to the appearance of the Virgin Mary to three shepherd children on May 13, 1917. The Virgin is said to have instructed the children to return to the site on the 13th day of each of the following six months. On October 13 that year, close to 70,000 religious faithful gathered at the site where, it is said, they witnessed an extraordinary display of light and the miraculous cure of ailments suffered by those in the crowd.

Sharing Cultural Identities Remember those daring Portuguese explorers who set sail for territories unknown and charted ocean trade routes around the globe? Retiring to a foreign land can be a bit like setting off on a high-seas adventure. Like those Portuguese sailors of yesteryear, you'll bring a bit of yourself along in the form of social customs, cultural traditions, and native language—no matter where you land.

For that reason, it's comforting to note the existence of American clubs and organizations that will help ease your transition. You'll also find chapters of the Lions Club and Rotary Club. In addition, Americans gather at a variety of recreational clubs devoted to golf, bridge, tennis, and yachting.

Recommended Living Areas

The Algarve One hundred miles of gorgeous sun-drenched beaches stretch along the southern coast of Portugal, where the sun shines more than 3,000 hours a year. This region, known as the Algarve, is dotted with Moorish villages featuring charming whitewashed houses interspersed with modern resorts catering to European travelers.

While tourists have discovered the Algarve, the region has managed to retain much of its Old World charm. Women draped in shawls still wash clothes in the river. Donkeys carry baskets overflowing with fruit and pull carts loaded with pottery. Fishermen mend their nets on the beaches. Chickens and pigs forage in the gardens. And Portuguese life goes on.

Until recently, Portugal—the Algarve in particular—was a property hunter's Mecca. But word has spread and prices are on the rise, as hordes of British and West German retirees have settled in the Algarve in recent years. The days of finding a fisherman's cottage by the beach for next-to-nothing are over. The good news, though, is that property prices and the cost of living in Portugal are still lower than just about anywhere else in Europe.

Retirement homes in this vacationers' paradise come in all shapes and sizes. A one-bedroom apartment in Portimão with nice views and a large balcony was listed recently for $27,000. A renovated two-bedroom house in the center of Lagos had an asking price of $56,000. And a four-bedroom luxury villa in Villamoura, a private tennis community, was listed at $234,000.

Faro, the capital city of the Algarve, is also the region's center of transportation, connecting the Algarve to the rest of the country via bus, rail, and air. Recreational opportunities abound. Sailing, scuba diving, horseback riding, golf, and tennis centers are located throughout the region. And visiting grandchildren won't want for entertainment, not with three enormous water parks and the Zoomarine aquatic park to keep them amused.

Costa de Lisboa Dubbed Portugal's "Sunshine Riviera," Costa de Lisboa boasts a year-round temperate climate. Winters are springlike, and summer days are cooled by refreshing Atlantic breezes. Drawn to this pleasant weather, foreigners from around the world flock to the Costa de Lisboa. Fortunately, though, the Portuguese population here is so established that it is capable of absorbing that influx without sacrificing its own charm and tradition.

Lisbon, the capital city of Portugal, is set among seven low hills just six miles from the Atlantic coast. Occupied at times throughout history by Phoenicians, Greeks, Carthaginians, Romans, Visigoths, and Moors, Lisbon is a cultural melting pot where established tradition combines with contemporary society to create a lively city of international acclaim.

Other cities of note within the region include Estoril, a cosmopolitan resort featuring scenic beaches, luxurious hotels, three golf courses, and the largest casino in Europe; Cascais, a one-time sleepy fishing village that has developed into a favored getaway destination; Sintra, one of the oldest towns in Portugal and longtime summer residence of Portuguese royalty; and Ericeira, a charming fishing village where visitors relax on long stretches of beach and in sandy coves.

Villages and towns throughout the region boast magnificent castles and churches worth exploring. You will also find plenty of social entertainment. Head for a local pub to sample Portugal's national music—the haunting fado. Try your luck at Estoril Casino, or join the jet-set crowd at an area nightclub.

Looking for sports activities? The Costa de Lisboa is a favorite water-sports destination and is home to nearly a dozen golf courses, including the Quinta da Marinha, designed by renowned golf architect Robert Trent Jones. In fact, golf is so popular throughout the Costa de Lisboa that some of its top residential neighborhoods are golf communities. Located on the north coast of Lisbon, the 550-acre Praia d'el Rey features an 18-hole golf course and clubhouse surrounded by an assortment of villas, townhouses, and apartments.

Recent listings offered a two-bedroom apartment in Praia d'el Rey for $77,500 and a townhouse for $124,000. At the other end of the spectrum, a four-bedroom home with a one-bedroom tenant's house and an assortment of amenities including a Jacuzzi and swimming pool was listed at $1.2 million.

Costa de Prata Nestled between the sea and mountains, the Costa de Prata is a region of breathtaking beauty. Charming villages, bountiful vineyards, and ancient castles are tucked away among hushed forests, whispering streams, and sleepy lagoons. Located between Lisbon to the south and Oporto to the north, the Costa de Prata (Silver Coast) is all that its name implies.

This land, where the silver-blue waters of the Atlantic Ocean kiss Europe's western coast, is also home to an array of architectural treasures including the Batalha Monastery, a classic example of the Portuguese Manueline style. The famous Castle of Almoural, surrounded by the waters of the River Tagus, is also here. As is the Alcobaca Monastery, a Gothic treasure listed by United Nations as an international monument. In addition to boasting a history rich in art and tradition, Costa de Prata is home to Fatima—the site of an appearance by the Virgin Mary to three shepherd children in 1917.

The international airport at Lisbon is the most convenient arrival point for travel to the Costa de Prata. Settle into your new abode and explore the region. Check out the town of Coimbra and its university— one of the oldest in Europe. Relax on a sandy beach in the shadow of a towering cliff. Sample regional culinary delights like roasted suckling pig, lobster, and fish stew. And don't forget your clubs because—like other regions of Portugal—the Costa de Prata features an assortment of golf courses. A recent real estate listing for Costa de Prata advertised a two-year-old, three-bedroom house outside Lousa with a view of the Serra Lousa mountains. The price was $216,000.

Costa Verde   Another golf enthusiast's delight awaits prospective re- tirees in the Costa Verde, where a rolling countryside and lots of open space combine to create the ideal landscape for golf courses. But don't concentrate on your golf game to the extent that you miss the region's other treasures.

Located in the far northwestern corner of Portugal, the Costa Verde has been described as "a region of remote enchantment, emerald green pine forests, brilliant blue waters, and long stretches of golden sands." Take in that scenery while enjoying one of the region's fine wines and port.

With an average year-round climate between 49 and 68 degrees Fahrenheit, the Costa Verde is indeed a little slice of paradise. And it's an accessible bit of paradise due to the international airport at Oporto.

RENTING IN PORTUGAL

The Embassy of Portugal, located in Washington, D.C., advises Americans considering retiring to Portugal to plan an extended visit to the country and to seek direction from a reliable real estate agent be- fore making housing decisions.

While rental fees fluctuate depending on size and location, the embassy estimates average rent for a two-bedroom apartment in Lisbon at $550 to $700 per month. Average rents in suburban and rural locations are usually lower, but the same does not hold true for rental fees in seaside resort areas.

How to Find Good Rental Properties Rental listings are available for viewing on the Internet at a variety of sites, including www.cite.pt. Initiate a simple search to see what comes up and where the links lead. Don't have Internet access at home? Head for the local library. Most community libraries offer Internet access.

Another good place to look is the Portuguese National Tourist Office, 590 Fifth Ave., Fourth Floor, New York, NY 10036-4704; 212/354-4403. This office offers a prepared list of sources for information about rental property in Portugal.

*B*UYING *R*EAL *E*STATE

No barriers are placed on foreign ownership of land in Portugal. The Portuguese Office of Tourism does, however, advise prospective buyers to double-check regulations before finalizing any purchase, as laws are known to change. The American embassy in Lisbon, Avenida das Forcas Armadas, can provide a list of recommended real estate agents.

In addition, the tourism office (known in Portugal as ICEP, or Investimentos, Comercio e Turismo de Portugal) suggests retirees interested in purchasing a home or land in Portugal first secure the necessary authorization from the Banco de Portugal at 4 Rua Febo Moniz, 1100 Lisbon.

The *Anglo-Portuguese News* is a good source for reviewing real estate listings. Request a copy by contacting Nigel Batley, *Anglo-Portuguese News*, Ave. de Sao Pedro 14-D, 2765 Monte Estoril, Portugal.

The Buying Process   Until Portugal became a member of the European Union, foreigners had to purchase houses in cash, unless the developer offered mortgages. Today foreign buyers are allowed to import money through any Portuguese bank. Importing money, though, triggers notification of the transaction to the Bank of Portugal, and foreigners who import cash must tell the bank how they plan to use the money.

Prior to finalizing the transfer of property, the buyer must pay a Property Transfer Tax (SISA)—usually 15 percent of the purchase price—to the Inland Revenue Office. The SISA does not apply to villas and apartments sold for less than $55,500 or to land purchases. One way to reduce or avoid the SISA is to purchase land, then hire a contractor to build a house. Taxes are not levied on money paid to builders.

A word of caution: Be wary of anyone who suggests you declare a lower-than-actual purchase price to reduce your SISA tax levy. Portuguese tax authorities have established a computerized system through which they can compare purchase price declarations with actual purchase prices. Getting caught can cost a bundle in terms of penalties, the actual tax due, and interest on the unpaid tax.

Before you sign anything, make sure you are dealing with a bonded, government-registered agent. Be aware that not all builders are reputable. Unless you speak fluent Portuguese, it's best to find a builder or Realtor who is well versed in English or find an interpreter you trust. When building, engage a lawyer to execute a contract that includes provisions for payments at various stages of construction. Consider holding back 10 percent to guarantee the final cleaning and any last-minute details.

COST OF LIVING

Figures released recently by Eurostat indicate that Portugal has the lowest cost of living of all the members of the European Union—roughly half that of Germany and France and slightly lower than Spain and Greece. That same cost-of-living study suggests that a basket of goods purchased for $5.60 in Portugal would sell for $8.62 in the United States, $11.62 in Germany, and $14.99 in Denmark. Here's a list of everyday items and their approximate cost in Portugal:

electricity	$45/month	tomatoes	$.30/pound
gasoline	$1/gallon	coffee	$7.50/pound
movie ticket	$4	milk	$1.05/gallon
beer on tap	$1	chicken	$1/pound
maid service	$4.50/hour	eggs	$1.25/dozen
bananas	$.40/pound	video rental	$2.75
steak	$7/pound	compact disc	$20

$\mathcal{D}$AY-TO-DAY $\mathcal{L}$IVING $\mathcal{C}$ONCERNS

Portugal operates within the same time zone as Great Britain (a relatively recent change), which puts it an hour behind neighboring Spain. Clocks are set forward one hour on the last Sunday in March and back an hour on the last Sunday in October.

Electricity is 220 volts, 50 cycles. Electrical plugs usually have two round pins, and adaptors are required for U.S. appliances.

Portuguese television consists of a combination of state-run, independent, cable, and international channels. In addition to state-run and independent stations, radios in Portugal pick up several English-language stations including the BBC World Service, Voice of America, and Radio Australia.

Portugal enjoys a relatively low crime rate when compared with other European countries, but it's wise to take commonsense precautions. Pickpocketing and purse snatching are not uncommon in tourist areas. On a health note, while bottled water is readily available throughout Portugal, tap water is usually safe to drink.

$\mathcal{T}$AXES

The Portuguese government bases its personal income-tax structure on the global income of a private individual after all applicable deductions. The tax applies to all people who live in Portuguese territory, and both Portuguese citizens and aliens are subject to the same tax rates.

A tax treaty between Portugal and the United States, established in January 1996, prevents dual taxation. For more detailed information about the current tax situation in Portugal, contact the public relations division of the Portuguese Ministry of Finance at 4, Rua D. Duarte, 1100 Lisbon; tel. (351) (1) 886-0581, or at 87-D, Rua do Carmo, 1200 Lisbon; tel. (351) (1) 347-3310.

$\mathcal{M}$AKING THE $\mathcal{M}$OVE

Portugal requires all foreigners (except nationals of other European Union countries) who intend to settle in the country for six months or more to secure a residency visa. Americans visiting Portugal for periods of up to 60 days need only hold a valid passport.

Applications for residency visas must be submitted to an office of the Portuguese consulate at least six months prior to anticipated arrival in Portugal. Applications must be accompanied by a series of documents, including a declaration of the purpose of application, proof of financial means (retirees may submit letters from banks or other financial institutions), criminal-record certificate, medical certificate, notarized copies of relevant passport pages, and any applicable references in Portugal.

After receiving visa approval, applicants are required to present their passports at a consulate office, where they will be granted a 90-day visa allowing them entry into Portugal. When they arrive in

Portugal, applicants must contact the nearest Servico de Estrangeiros to request a permanent residency card. While living in Portugal under the 90-day visa, applicants can request a Baggage Certificate from the consulate to clear the way for tax-exempt importation of household goods.

Employment   Retirees who intend to reenter the workforce once they're settled in Portugal must first apply for a work permit, which they can get from their prospective employers. The Portuguese embassy suggests Americans who want to work in Portugal first contact American firms with offices in Portugal. A list of those companies is available from the World Trade Academy Press, Inc., 50 E. 42nd St., New York, NY 10017, or the Bureau of International Commerce, U.S. Dept. of Commerce, Washington, D.C. 20230.

What to Bring, What to Leave Behind   It is not practical to import televisions or other major appliances from the United States into Portugal because of the different electrical current. Furniture and other household effects may be imported, as long as the owners of the property are establishing residence in Portugal, have owned the items for at least one year, can show that the items were furnishings in their previous residence, and do not already have a furnished home in Portugal.

A numbered list of household goods you wish to import (including a Portuguese translation of that list) must be submitted to an office of the Portuguese consulate. The consulate will then issue a Certificate of Baggage to be presented with the individual's passport to customs authorities.

You can import an automobile into Portugal and keep it under foreign registry for up to 180 days. Americans (except those who are residents of other European Union countries) who are planning to remain in Portugal for more than 180 days can choose to register the car in Portugal and pay applicable customs duties or to export the car at the end of the 180-day period.

What About Pets? Most household pets (with the exception of some psittacine birds) may be imported into Portugal with prior approval of the Board of Cattle Breeding. Pets must be accompanied by a certificate of good health issued by a veterinarian at their point of origin. A visa issued by a Portuguese consulate may also be required. In very rare cases, retirees may secure authorization for the importation of psittacine birds.

MEDICAL CARE

Medical care in Portugal is less expensive than comparable care in the United States. While public hospitals offer first-rate service for approximately $30 per day, charges at private hospitals are usually a bit higher. Helicopters are available to transport patients in need of emergency medical assistance to health-care facilities in Lisbon, including the British Hospital, which has an English-speaking staff.

Few American health-care plans offer coverage in Portugal. Check with your provider regarding the availability of overseas medical coverage. Foreign residents who contribute to Portugal's national insurance program are eligible for coverage under that plan. Annual premiums for Portuguese health insurance average $150 per person.

FINANCIAL MATTERS

Since becoming a full member of the European Union in 1986, Portugal has experienced an almost uninterrupted period of economic growth and development. Between 1986 and 1992, Portugal had an annual gross-domestic-product growth rate of 4.6 percent. While a recession affected Portugal's economic growth in the mid-1990s, the country appears to be back on track. Optimistic once more, analysts are predicting continued growth of 3 to 4 percent annually through the end of this century.

Infrastructure improvements planned or in process include a $1.8 billion investment in the country's highway network plus a $3 billion investment in other major and secondary roads, a $1.4 billion investment in Lisbon's Metro transit system, and a $1.5 billion investment in the country's railroad system. These improvements coincide with an ongoing renovation project at Lisbon's international airport.

Banking With a Portuguese resident's card, you are eligible to open a non-tourist bank account. Forms are available in bank offices. American banks with offices in Portugal include First National, City Bank of New York, Chase Manhattan Bank, Morgan Guaranty Trust Company, Bank of America, Manufacturers Hanover Trust, and Chemical Bank of New York.

While residents and non-residents may bring unlimited amounts of Portuguese currency into the country, they must declare any foreign currency exceeding the equivalent of $5,500 upon entry. Money can be exchanged at banks, which are open from 8:30 to 3 Monday through Friday. Private exchange bureaus are another option, but shop around because fees and exchange rates may vary.

Investing The Portuguese government is actively pursuing foreign investors—a fact that may be of particular interest to retirees seeking to become entrepreneurs. Benefits offered to foreign investors include promises of security, protection of assets, and rights on par with Portuguese companies; access to fiscal and financial incentives; and the right to form a corporation with 100 percent foreign capital.

One investment option open to entrepreneurial retirees in Portugal is the purchase of land for commercial use. For information about the purchase and development of property for tourist, commercial, or industrial use, contact the Portuguese Institute of Foreign Trade, 101 Avenida 5 de Octubro, 1000 Lisbon.

$\mathscr{T}$RANSPORTATION

Airports located in Lisbon, Porto, and Faro are Portugal's three international air gateways. In addition to TAP (Portugal's national airline) and Portugalia, major carriers servicing one or more of those airports include Alitalia, British Airways, Delta, KLM, Lufthansa, Sabena, Swissair, and TWA.

Flights from one destination to another within Portugal are available, but it's best to weigh their cost (which varies) against convenience, because distances between regions are relatively short by U.S. standards. Alternatives include using one of the country's bus companies or hopping aboard a car operated by the state-run railway system.

According to tourist-office data, express bus service from Lisbon to Oporto costs about $10 per person. Rail passage via express train between the same cities runs $32.50 per person for first-class and $19.95 for regular seating. Tickets on local trains are significantly lower, at $19 for first-class and $11.90 for regular seating.

Intra-city transportation alternatives vary by region, with Lisbon's mass transit being the most highly developed. This is due in large part to the recent upgrade of the city's Metro (underground system), completed for Expo '98. People in outlying areas rely primarily on bus and taxi service.

Automobile Travel   Driving in Portugal may require some adjustment—unless you've recently relocated from Boston or New York, where drivers are notoriously aggressive. Speeding is rampant and so are signs of road rage—such as tailgating. The frustration can be compounded by antiquated back roads (dating to the country's Roman occupation) and donkey carts meandering along at an Old World pace.

Once you've learned the ropes, it's time to get a Portuguese driver's license. Your first step, though, is to secure a Portuguese identity card. The process includes getting a translation of your American driver's license through the American consulate, undergoing a medical exam, and making a visit to the regional transportation center.

*L*EISURE *T*IME

Portugal is an overwhelmingly Roman Catholic country, and most public holidays and festivals revolve around religious celebrations. Public holidays are New Year's Day, Good Friday, Anniversary of the Revolution (April 25), Labor Day (May 1), Luis de Camoes (Portugal's most renowned writer) Day (June 10), Feast of Corpus Christi (June 21), Feast of the Assumption (August 15), anniversary of the Proclamation of the Republic (October 5), All Saints Day (November 1), Restoration of Independence (December 1), Feast of the Immaculate Conception (December 8), and Christmas. In addition, many regional fairs and festivals take place throughout the year.

Things to Do and See A relatively small country in terms of acreage, Portugal is unusually diverse when it comes to things to see and do. The question is where to start—in its modern urban centers, charming rural villages, or lively beach resorts?

Oporto, Portugal's second largest city, is the home of the country's port wine trade. There you can visit the cellars of well-known wineries. Espinho is a modern beach resort and casino center well worth visiting.

Explore the Roman ruins at Milreu in the Algarve. Wander through the medieval castle of São Jorge in Lisbon. Enjoy delicious local seafood at a cozy restaurant in the quaint fishing village of Ericeira. Or make a pilgrimage to Fatima.

Shopping Portugal is home to a variety of fine craftsmen who make their living selling items—some works of art—in markets throughout the country. In addition to fine wines, the Costa Verde is known for its copper craftsmen, wood-carvers, and weavers who create woolen fishermen's sweaters. Craftspeople in the Algarve are renowned for their pottery, and the coppersmiths of the Costa de Lisboa carry on a tradition dating to ancient Rome.

Hand-painted azulejos are a popular fine craft created in and around Lisbon, and the Costa de Prate (Silver Coast) is home to intricate silver filigree. With the exception of large shopping centers, which remain open all day, most shops are open daily from nine to one and three to seven.

Sports and Hobbies   Thanks to its nearly 500-mile coastline, Portugal is a water-sports enthusiast's paradise. Swimming, surfing, sailing, windsurfing, and water-skiing are just a few of the ways you can enjoy the beach.

If your idea of fun means being *on* rather than *in* the water, Portugal offers an abundance of prime fishing spots. Freshwater anglers can take to the lakes, rivers, and streams in the country's northern provinces in search of salmon and trout. Big-game fishermen can sign on for a deep-sea fishing charter in search of marlin, swordfish, and tuna.

Golfers are sure to find a course to their liking in Portugal, where more than 30 golf courses—some designed by internationally acclaimed architects including Robert Trent Jones and Frank Pennink—dot the landscape. In southern regions, you'll play against a backdrop of sparkling blue water and magnificent white-sand beaches. Inland courses are designed to enhance the rolling vistas lined by fragrant pine, orange, and pomegranate trees. Farther north, you'll find golf courses set amid wide-open plains and adjacent to mountain forests.

A tourist-office sporting guide describes Portugal's tennis courts as being "air-conditioned by the Atlantic." That's true. Indeed, many of the country's top tennis centers are located in coastal communities where breezes from the Atlantic Ocean help moderate the climate. Horseback riding is another popular pastime throughout the country.

As far as spectator sports are concerned, bullfighting remains popular in Portugal. *Futbol* (soccer) is fast becoming a favored alternative. In fact, most towns field local teams during the regular soccer season, which runs from September to May.

$\mathcal{A}$DDITIONAL $\mathcal{R}$ESOURCES

General Information
Embassy of Portugal, Consular Section, 2125 Kalorama Rd. NW, Washington, D.C. 20008; 202/328-8610, fax 202/462-3726.
Portuguese National Tourist Office, 590 Fifth Ave., New York, NY 10036, 212/354-4403
Portuguese Trade and Tourism, 1900 L St. NW, Washington, D.C. 20006, 202/331-8222

Emergency Contact for Foreigners
U.S. State Department Citizens Center, 202/647-5225 (202/647-4000 for 24-hour assistance)

Other Resources
"A Guide to Buying Property in Portugal." Russell & Russell, 9113 Wood Street, Bolton B11EE, England
Living in Portugal, A Complete Guide, by Susan Thackeray. Robert Hale Limited, Clerkenwell House, Clerkenwell Green, London EC1, England

Useful Web Site
www.portugal.org/

Spain

by LESLIE DORAN

Spain has long been a favorite retirement destination for Europeans, but there are also more than 60,000 Americans currently living in Spain, and 8,000 of them are receiving Social Security benefits from the United States. The wonderful climate and year-round sunshine, combined with a low cost of living, make Spain especially attractive to retirees. When you add in the wealth of culture and easy travel to other European countries, retirement in Spain becomes even more appealing.

The country is as big as Utah and Arizona combined, and it enjoys a dry, temperate climate in summer and cooler, rainier winters. The landscape varies, from the mountains of the Pyrenees to the verdant valley of Gran Rey to the beaches of the Balearic and Canary Islands. The coastline of Spain, mostly in the southeast, spans 3,000 miles and provides plenty of space for beach activities.

The capital of Spain, Madrid, is located in the middle of the Iberian peninsula at 2,120 feet above sea level, making it the highest capital in Europe. It is the heart of the country, and its inhabitants are called Madrileños. Madrid is a very social city with an active nightlife; many Madrileños don't go to bed until 3 a.m.

Some of the world's greatest artists are Spaniards: El Greco (okay, he was originally from Greece), Goya, Velázquez, Dalí, and Picasso. Their vibrant paintings grace the Prado, the Reina Sofía, and the Thyssen-Bornemisza museums in Madrid (known collectively as the Golden Triangle of Art).

The time is right, economically, to find a little piece of heaven in Spain. The cost of living is low and property is plentiful, with a wide variety of lifestyles to choose from. So whether you prefer peaceful rural life, pampered coastal tourism, or active city living, act quickly and wisely with your retirement income and let Spain show you the home away from home you always wanted.

The Culture and People of Spain

The Spanish people are warm and friendly, but the hours they keep are very different from those here in the United States. Siesta is a daily occurrence, and most business doors close from 1:30 to 4:30. With recent increases in tourism, more shops are staying open in the afternoon. Some visitors say that Spain reminds them of the United States 40 or 50 years ago. A slow pace and relaxed ambiance dominate throughout the country.

Spain is blessed with a low crime rate, but some tourist areas have witnessed a recent increase in pickpocketings and muggings. Travelers are instructed to keep copies of their driver's licenses, airline tickets, and passports in a safe place.

Spanish is the official language of Spain. In some of the larger cities many employees speak English, but in the rural areas they do not. In the southern parts of Spain, near the coast, many Spaniards speak some English.

Learn the Language You will need to master at least a moderate amount of Spanish to get along here. The language is not difficult to learn, especially if you are motivated. The local people will appreciate your efforts, and you will find you have more choices if you speak the language. You can take taped or college courses while still living in the States, but if you want to develop an authentic accent, you might consider taking classes in Spain. Colegio Federico Garcia Lorca offers summer and holiday courses costing $240 for two weeks of study.

If you move to Madrid, your English-language skills could help you pay the bills. The newspaper *Segundamano* prints an entire section of job listings for English-language teachers. You could earn up to $16 an hour and practice your Spanish at the same time.

A Brief History of Spain Spain's history is marked by the ebb and flow of the many peoples who came and lived within its borders, leaving their imprint on the language, culture, and faces of the citizens. The Celts invaded from the north, the Italians from the west, and the Moors from the south. As you travel around the country you will see the physical evidence left by Spain's forebears at museums, monuments, and monasteries. Here is a brief timeline of historical highlights:

1200–500 B.C.	Iberians come into Spain
900 B.C.	Celts move in from the north
200 B.C.–A.D. 400	Romans take over, bringing Christianity and the basis for the Spanish language
500	Visigoths invade Spain
700	Moors take over most of Spain
1478	The Inquisition begins, initiated by the Pope
1492	Columbus discovers America, and the Moors are forced out of Spain
1588	England destroys the Spanish Armada
1808	Napoleon invades Spain and puts his brother on the throne

1876   Spain becomes a constitutional monarchy
1939   Franco takes over as dictator and rules for 36 years
1955   Spain joins the United Nations
1975   Juan Carlos becomes king
1986   Spain becomes a member of the European Union

Enjoy New Traditions   Spain is the second largest country in Europe, and its inhabitants have a huge appetite for life and celebration. It has several distinct regions, each with its own unique fiestas and traditions.

The Galicians, descendants of the Celts, sport the bagpipes that are usually associated with Scotland and have their own language, Gallego. The Basques speak Euskera, which has linguists stumped as to where it originated. The Catalans, from around Barcelona, speak Catalan. These groups all speak Spanish as well, but their diversity adds to the richness of Spain's culture.

Spain has other traditions that deserve attention. Dance is an art form that Spaniards perform with gusto. The stomping feet, clicking castanets, and swirling skirts of flamenco are recognized worldwide. As for fiestas (always a good excuse to dance), Spain has more of them than any other country.

Develop Your Own Cultural Identity   The many Americans living in Spain have formed numerous expatriate organizations. For example, the American Women's Club of Madrid meets monthly, with more than 250 members who take part in philanthropic activities.

For those who want to learn more about Spain, Elderhostel offers classes several times a year. Some examples are Spanish Painting: Golden Age, Modernism and Abstract; Prehistory to Picasso; Monarchy and Exploration; and Spain's Northern Capitals and Pathways of Culture. For more information contact Elderhostel International, 75 Federal St., Boston, MA 02110-1941.

RECOMMENDED LIVING AREAS

Costa del Sol The Andalucia Province of Spain, known as Costa del Sol, offers a large tourist population at its center. Toward the mountains you'll find remote villages where the pace is slower and more in step with desirable retirement life. The weather is wonderful, and the sun shines 300 days a year—ideal for those who want to be outdoors, gardening, golfing, hiking, biking, or just lazing around. The region has plenty of high-quality golf courses with spectacular views.

There are great towns to explore in Costa del Sol, like Granada, the old Moorish capital. Ronda, a town favored by the aristocracy, boasts gravity-defying cliff houses, and Seville is the hometown of Don Giovanni. Córdoba has sites that are important to both the Jewish and Moslem religions—the Sinagoga of Córdoba and the Mezquita mosque.

The International San Pablo airport in Seville and the airport in Málaga provide air service for this popular region. Properties are available, from established expatriate-planned communities to old, refurbished farmhouses ready for renovation. Prices range from $29,600 for a secluded cottage with five rooms and three outbuildings to $177,631 for an old mill with a four-bedroom house and its own swimming pool.

Marbella is the second most popular tourist destination in Spain and is considered the most exclusive spot on the Costa del Sol. The city enjoys an almost ideal setting, with sun, blue skies, and the Mediterranean sea as constants. The two main beaches are La Fontanilla and El Fuerte, and they draw large crowds.

Despite the influx of vacationers, Marbella still manages to maintain its appeal, mostly due to the charm of the old village at its center. There are whitewashed houses and narrow alleyways leading to the central Plaza de los Narangos, named for the surrounding orange trees. The Paseo Marítimo, the refurbished port, has outdoor restaurants and vendors selling pottery and other crafts.

Property in the area varies from modest apartments at $21,700 to small cottages for $80,000. Then there are the palatial homes that sell for half a million dollars or more. For more information on listings contact the Property Center of Marbella, 31 Avenida Alhambra, Aloha Pueble, Marbella 29660; tel. (34) (95) 281-4060.

Málaga, the main town on the Costa del Sol, is not as flashy as Marbella but is home to an airport and a train station. Málaga is also the center for business and commerce in the region, which makes it all the more surprising that housing and the cost of living are not expensive here. Málaga has long been a seaport, and today it is a regular stop for most Mediterranean cruises.

Málaga is blessed with a beautiful natural setting. The town is nestled between the ocean and the mountains at just under 2,000 feet. Many small communities nearby offer good real estate opportunities within easy distance of shopping and entertainment.

There are homes in the Málaga area to suit every need. A renovated two-bedroom farmhouse with white stucco walls and a red tile roof, living room, fireplace, kitchen, and views sells for $50,000. Maybe you would like to build a villa. If so, count on spending around $65 per square foot. Altogether you could end up with a bill of $75,000.

Contact the following agencies for information:

* Andalucian Property Center, Paseo de Larious, 1 Edif Los Remedios, Málaga 29740; tel. (34) (95) 254-5565
* Country Properties S.A., 21 Plaza Almijarar, Competa 29754; tel. (34) (95) 251-6178
* Images of Andalucia, Tara, Ctr. Colmenar, Solano 29170; tel. (34) (95) 211-1178

Mallorca and Menorca—Favorite Balearic Isles   Mallorca is the largest of these two islands and home to the provincial capital, Palma, which houses the main airport for the area. The island has a population of 350,000, over half of the total in the Balearic Islands.

Tourism in Mallorca really took off in the 1960s, and Palma's concrete jungle contrasts sharply with the rest of the island's serene natural setting. The island's northwest portion contains many white-sand beaches and groves of olive and lemon trees. The inland area is dotted with lazily circling windmills, used to draw water for the fig and almond orchards.

Mallorca draws the rich and famous to play on its beaches and in its bars and discos. The temperate climate and scenic beauty acts as a magnet for many artists. Writers such as George Sand and Santiago Rusiñol have let the world know of Mallorca's attractions.

It is possible to build a residence in Mallorca with the assistance of a legally appointed architect and civil engineer. After choosing the land, you can build a medium-size house with a pool, garden, and basic amenities for around $250,000. A similar existing house would cost around $115,000.

Properties on the market now include a small, rustic house with a fireplace, garden, pool, and view of the mountains for $215,000. A four-bedroom, two-bathroom house with a terrace runs $200,000. Contact Vida Balear Real Estate, 9 Paseo Masitimo, Palma de Mallorca 07014; tel. (34) (97) 145-0422, for more information.

Menorca, the second largest island, has a much smaller population of 65,000. The sleepy little island bears the unmistakable stamp of its British rulers in its Georgian-style architecture, especially in the city of Mahón. It shares a transit system with its neighbor, Mallorca, consisting of both planes and ferries. Since Menorca got a later start in the tourist trade, it has avoided a lot of development problems by learning from the other islands. There are no high-rise hotels or condos to mar the scenery.

Menorca is still unspoiled and undeveloped in many areas, yet it boasts attractive living facilities. The people are friendly, and many speak German, due to a recent influx of European vacationers. The beauty of the island is represented by Ciutadella, the former capital and harbor town set on lush, green hills. The old town nestles close to the harbor and has winding, narrow streets with whitewashed homes and churches. The new capital, Mahón, has an even more impressive harbor that is over three miles long. The town's architecture features a royal citadel across from Borne Square and an obelisk that commemorates the defeat of the Turks in 1558.

The best thing about Menorca is the number and quality of properties available. It is here that Americans will get the best value for their dollars. Inland, a villa with six bedrooms, three bathrooms, a workshop, pool, and guest apartment lists for $162,500. A farmhouse with eight bedrooms, two garages, and stables is on sale for $390,000. A two-bedroom, one-bathroom house with sea views costs only $42,500.

Contact one of the following for more information: Bonnin Sanso, 14 Carrer Nou, Mahón, Menorca 07701; tel. (34) (97) 136-3462; bonnin@infotele.com.es, or Pedro de Amilibia, Fincas la Isla, 22 Sa. Ravaleta, Menorca 07701; tel. (34) (97) 136-5985.

RENTING IN SPAIN

If you are looking to rent in Spain, you are in luck. It is possible to find appealing and modestly priced temporary housing in most of the country. Rents will range from as little as $300 a month for an apartment to $3,000 for a luxury flat in the Costa del Sol.

It is a good idea to rent in the part of the country where you think you want to live long term. Ask locals about good Realtors and the best neighborhoods.

Something to keep in mind: be sure to sign the lease in pesetas, since it is always to your advantage to deal in local currency. You should also hire a lawyer to check the legalities of your rental agreement.

How to Find Good Rental Properties   A good source for rental properties in Spain is the classified section in local English-language papers. Word of mouth is also one of the best ways to find bargains. Tell the local postmaster, baker, barber, or bartender that you are looking.

You can also contact Eagle Globe Property, 27 Avda. Condes de San Isidro, Fuengirola 29640, Malaga; tel. (34) (95) 246-6177, or Marbella Property Index, tel. (34) (95) 277-6808, for information.

Average Rental Costs and Listings   Your needs and lifestyle will drive the cost of a rental. During the winter months in the south of Spain, rents will naturally be higher. Some sample properties include:
- A Mallorca studio with loft, fully furnished for $1,200 a month
- A luxury villa on a 10-acre hilltop with a pool, tennis courts, TV, a beautiful view of the Costa del Sol, and an English-speaking staff for $4,000 a month
- A Costa Brava villa with utilities and cleaning included for $800 per month

*B*UYING *R*EAL *E*STATE

Now is the time to buy property in Spain, just before the peseta becomes the Euro (the new universal European currency). Prices are reasonable, even in resort areas, but there are some restrictions. As a foreigner, you can't buy land in areas that have strategic or defense importance. Restricted areas include the regions bordering France and Portugal.

To purchase property you will need a Spanish bank account, a lawyer to check the contract, and a notary to check on the land title. You must also insure that all previous taxes and utilities bills have been paid and that there are no liens against the property. It could take as long as four to six weeks to complete the purchase process. Various fees and taxes will increase the price of the property by 10 percent.

When you buy real estate in Spain, it is also wise to make a Spanish will. In the case of death, especially when out of the country, the document will make it easier to transfer the Spanish property to your heirs.

COST OF LIVING

The cost of living in Spain is relatively low, especially outside of the main cities, where you can go to local markets for fresh produce and fish. Going out for dinner can cost as little as $6.50 for a meal that includes an appetizer, entrée, wine, and dessert. The following are everyday items and what you can expect to pay for them in Spain:

electricity	$30/month	tomatoes	$.75/pound
gasoline	$3/gallon	coffee	$3/pound
movie ticket	$5	milk	$2.50/gallon
six-pack of beer	$2.50	chicken	$2/pound
bottle of wine	$6	fish	$5/pound
maid service	$7/hour	video rental	$2.75
bananas	$.50/pound	compact disc	$15
bread	$.50/loaf	woman's haircut	$10–$20
steak	$5–$6/pound	man's haircut	$5–$10
head of lettuce	$.70		

DAY-TO-DAY LIVING CONCERNS

Spain offers all the comforts that you are used to in the United States. Modern appliances are readily available, and because Spain's electrical current is different than that of the United States, it's a good idea to purchase new appliances when you arrive.

Daily living costs are low, and service and utility charges are minimal. The average water bill for a medium-sized household might be as low as $100 a year.

Telefónica, Spain's telephone company, is the sole provider in both Spain and Portugal, where it is called Telecom Portugal. Local calls run about 16 cents each.

$\mathscr{T}$AXES

Permanent residents of Spain—individuals who spend more than 183 days per year in the country—are taxed at a rate above 50 percent. However, Spain has a tax treaty with the United States that allows dual residents to pay the lower tax. Taxation on capital gains made in Spain ranges from 20 to 50 percent. In addition, Spain has a value-added tax (VAT), which is levied on all goods and services at a rate of 6 to 10 percent.

There is some good news on the tax front. With a residence visa, you can import household and personal items duty free. Additionally, annual property tax is only 0.7 percent of the value of the property, which is generally lower than in the United States.

$\mathscr{M}$AKING THE $\mathscr{M}$OVE

A U.S. passport is the most important document you will need when traveling to Spain; be sure to keep it in a safe place. You will need it to enter the country, as identification, to change money, and to rent or lease a car. With your passport you can stay in Spain for 90 days without a visa or other certificate. If you stay longer, you will need to apply for a residency permit. No matter how long your stay, when you arrive in Spain it is wise to register with the American Embassy in case of an emergency.

Becoming a Temporary or Permanent Resident   If you decide to become a long-term resident of Spain, you will need to apply to the Ministry of the Interior. This is done at the local police station. To apply you will need the following: an application form, your valid passport, a medical certificate, 20 passport photos, proof of your financial independence or a pension of at least $500 per month, and a police certificate showing that you have no criminal record. The process can take up to a month and will cost about $75. While the application is being processed, your receipt is your guarantee, allowing you to remain in Spain. You must carry it with you at all times.

If you want to become a Spanish citizen, you will have to enlist the services of a Spanish lawyer—and that's just a start. The easiest way to become a citizen is to marry one—otherwise it takes 2 to 10 years to officially become a Spaniard. There are advantages to becoming a Spanish citizen, including unrestricted movement between all EU countries. But before you take that step, consider the whopping 50 percent Spanish income tax.

What to Bring, What to Leave Behind   Most retirees who move to Spain buy most of what they need in Spain. Small electrical appliances should be left in the States.

Cars in Spain are reasonably priced, but you can also ship your own vehicle for about $1,000. The exact cost depends on the make, model, and year of the car. Hual North America, 2310 Broening Hwy., Suite 165, Baltimore, MD 21224; 410/631-5708, is an experienced company that can answer specific questions about shipping your car.

What About Pets?   For retirees with pets, there's good news. There is no pet quarantine in Spain. You must present a certificate from your veterinarian stating that your animal is in good health and has had its rabies vaccine. The document must also be certified at the nearest consulate of Spain.

*M*EDICAL *C*ARE

Spain's public-health system is good and available to anyone who works in Spain. It was established in 1986. About half the nation's hospitals—those that provide complex and advanced procedures and surgeries—are part of the national system. The balance of the hospitals are run privately, mostly by the Catholic Church or the Red Cross. There is an ample supply of doctors throughout the country, but there is a shortage of qualified nurses.

Before leaving home, you should take a couple of preventive and prudent steps. First, get a complete physical to assure your good condition. Make sure that your immunizations are current and get extra supplies of all medications that you take regularly. Get prescriptions from your physician for refills and make sure the medication is listed in its generic name. Always carry medications in their original, labeled containers and transport them in your hand-held luggage. If you have a chronic medical condition, wear a MedicAlert bracelet or necklace.

Medical Insurance Retired Americans living abroad will find that Medicare and Medicaid are not available to them. As part of your pre-trip list of things to do, locate a private insurance plan and get covered. There are many insurance companies to choose from, and several specialize in coverage for travelers. The key is to shop around well in advance of your departure. Be sure that any policy you choose includes emergency medical evacuation coverage. This coverage provides for transportation from rural areas to major health-care centers, including emergency return to the United States. Sanitas, tel. (34) (91) 585-2400, is an insurance program recommended by *International Living*.

FINANCIAL MATTERS

Spain's entry into the European Union has required the country to open its economy and revise economic policies. The Spanish economy was in a recession in the early 1990s, but a modest recovery began in the mid-1990s. To meet EU requirements, Spain must continue to reduce the government deficit and lower inflation. Progress in 1997 was measured by a lowering of the inflation rate to about 2.5 to 3 percent and the deficit to about 3 percent. However, the unemployment rate is still up at 22 percent after a slight decrease in the mid-1990s.

Spain's Banking System   The Spanish banking system is much like that in the United States. Banking hours are 8:30 to 2:30 Monday through Saturday, but banks close on Saturday in summer. Some branch offices stay open later in the afternoon.

To open an account, bring your passport and another form of identification. You can open both checking and saving accounts, and the saving accounts will pay about 4 percent interest. There are no limits on moving personal money in or out of the country. All branch offices offer foreign-currency exchange services, and automatic teller machines are common throughout Spain.

What Should Retirees Do with Their Money?   Several large American banks, including Citibank and American Express, have branches in Madrid and other large cities. These are good places to deposit your retirement income. You may wish to use a local Spanish bank for an account of pesetas. Check with local expatriate organizations for recommendations on regional investment opportunities.

Spain does have some incentives for foreign investors. Foreigners have the same rights as Spaniards when setting up a business in Spain, but that isn't saying much. You should employ a local accountant and lawyer to help you with business interests.

TRANSPORTATION

Traveling in Spain is not much different from traveling in the United States. Cars drive on the right side of the road. Spain has two kinds of highways, *autopistas* (toll charged) and *autovias* (no toll). Gasoline is easy to get but expensive, as in most of Europe.

Spain is blessed with three small airlines that pride themselves on customer satisfaction. Iberia Airlines is the largest and has package deals with American, Continental, and Delta. It also offers a Visit Spain ticket, costing $250 to $300, that makes traveling to several destinations even more economical.

Mass Transit For travel within Spain consider the Spanish State Railway (RENFE), which is very economical and has comfortable express trains. RENFE offers a discounted pass called the Flexipass, which must be purchased in the United States. Call Rail Europe at 800/4-EURAIL for more information. Bus transport in Spain is inexpensive, countrywide, and comfortable for short distances. Stations are not easy to spot in Spain since they can be at bars, cafés, or hotels. A disadvantage of taking the bus over long distances is the lack of bathrooms. Taxis will get you around quickly and efficiently in most cities. Rates are inexpensive. Foreigners are urged to use only registered cabs.

Automobile Travel You must have a current U.S. driver's license and insurance coverage to drive in Spain. It is also recommended that you bring an International Driver's Permit. To get an IDP contact your local AAA office. You'll need a valid U.S. license, two passport-sized photos, and $10.

City driving in Spain should be avoided at night, especially on Friday and Saturday, because of inebriated drivers. In the country, dangers take the form of wandering farm animals and badly marked roads. A good time to drive through cities is between 3 and 5 p.m., when people are taking siestas.

*L*EISURE *T*IME

Go back in time. Travel to Santillana del Mar to see the caves of Altamira, called "the Sistine Chapel of Prehistoric Art." Flash forward to Barcelona's new Museum of Egyptology, where over 250 artworks and artifacts are housed. The museum also maintains over 3,000 volumes devoted to Egyptology.

Only one hour from Madrid lies a special paradise. El Palacio de la Granja was built as a summer palace by Philip V. Its formal gardens and grandeur were created in an attempt to imitate Versailles. The palace contains one of the world's most incredible collections of Flemish tapestries.

At a fourteenth-century castle near Toledo you can learn to cook Castilian cuisine or Arabic dishes at the Parador of Córdoba. Unique weeklong courses are offered by Paradores of Spain and include housing, instruction by Parador chefs, and sightseeing excursions.

To sample a great fiesta, go to Seville during its annual April fair. The six-day extravaganza showcases Spanish dance, folklore, culture, and sports. It's an orgy of sounds, colors, and food.

Shopping Bargain hunters will enjoy Spain. Leather goods include shoes, luggage, bags, coats, and gloves. Fine handcrafted embroidery, lace, and jewelry are commonly displayed by local artisans, and prices on most items are very good. Pottery and porcelain, like the famous Lladro figurines, are sold at a fraction of what they cost in the United States.

In both the major cities and the countryside, flea markets are great places to get treasures. Bargaining with the vendors only adds to the Spanish shopping experience.

Sports and Hobbies Spain's most popular spectator sports are soccer and bullfighting. Some would insist that bullfighting is more of an art, full of theater and dance, like a ballet. It is not for everyone, though, and those who object to the cruel treatment of animals should stay away. If you do choose to go, make sure you get seats in the shade and bring something soft to sit on. Soccer is the national sport, and fans are enthusiastic, but not to the dangerous degrees that have caused problems in other countries.

If you wish to participant in sports, there are plenty of activities to choose from. Coastal residents enjoy sailing, fishing, and swimming. Southern Spain boasts 59 golf courses, giving aficionados an embarrassing number of choices. The mountains offer hiking and bicycling in summer and skiing in winter.

ADDITIONAL RESOURCES

Tourist Offices of Spain
666 Fifth Ave, 35th Floor, New York, NY 10103; 212/265-8822;
  oetny@okspain.org
845 N. Michigan Ave., Chicago, IL 60611; 312/642-1992;
  spainil@ix.netcom.com
San Vicente Plaza Bldg., 8383 Wilshire Blvd., Suite 960, Beverly
  Hills, CA 90211; 323/658-7188; espanalax@aol.com
1221 Brickell Ave., Suite 1850, Miami, FL 33131,
  oetmiami@ix.netcom.com

Emergency Contact for Foreigners
Embassy of the United States of America, 75 Serrano, Madrid
  28006; tel. (34) (91) 587-2200

Useful Web Sites
American Club of Madrid: www.go-spain.com/acm
General information: www.spaintour.com/
Marbella Online Magazine: www.abosulute-marbella.com
Official Board of Spanish Tourism: www.tourspain.es
Si Spain: www.SiSpain.org
Tourist Office: www.okspain.org
U.S. embassy in Spain: www.embusa.es

Thailand

by ROSANNE KNORR

Imagine retiring to a fantastic land of richly hued orchids, trumpeting elephants, storytelling dancers in elaborate costumes, and Buddhist temples trimmed in gold. You can do it in the kingdom of Thailand, a country that presents itself with dramatic effect. Even Hollywood was enthralled and made the country, under its former name of Siam, into a household word with the 1956 movie extravaganza *The King and I.*

Contemporary Thailand is a land of contradictions and contrasts. It can be as modern as the businessmen in three-piece suits who staff its contemporary office towers or as traditional as the robed Buddhist monks who maintain its centuries-old temples. Thailand is technically a kingdom, in which the royal family is regarded with awe and respect, yet the absolute monarchy long ago ceded its power to democratic forces. Perhaps most remarkable, though Thailand is small and is located in Southeast Asia, which has seen its share of civil strife, the country has never been a dependency of another nation.

Thailand is a long finger of land in Southeast Asia that lies mainly within the Indochinese Peninsula, though its southern portion reaches into the Malay Peninsula. Its neighbors are Malaysia on the south; Burma on the southwest, west, and north; Laos on the northeast; and

Cambodia on the southeast. The Gulf of Thailand and the Andaman Sea create seacoasts on the southeast and southwest respectively.

Long and narrow, the country spans about 1,100 miles north to south and about 500 miles east to west. The northern and western portions are dominated by mountains. The ranges along the Burmese border rise to more than 8,500 feet at Doi Inthanon, the highest point in Thailand. Another mountain system traverses the country's central areas.

In contrast to the heights are the coastal plains and low-lying rice paddies. A vast alluvial plain stretches between the central and western mountain areas. This plain is fed by Thailand's main river, the Chao Phraya, which runs through Bangkok. As might be expected, the river's fertile delta holds the nation's best farmland. This, combined with its proximity to the capital, easily makes the delta the most densely populated section of the country.

The Khorat Plateau covers an area north and east of the central mountain range. Low, but barren, it makes up about one-third of the country and is bordered by the Mekong River Valley.

Rich in natural resources, Thailand mines coal, gold, lead, tin, precious stones, and other metals and minerals. Its densely wooded upland areas produce valuable teak wood for export. Massive jungles and swamps provide other tropical trees that are prized for their wood, including rattan, ebony, and rosewood. Thailand's tropical climate also supports exotic plants and fruits, including orchids, lotus, gardenias, hibiscus, bananas, mangoes, and coconuts.

The famous Siamese cats, as evident by their name, are indigenous to Thailand but are bred and shown throughout the world. Wildlife is abundant, including elephants, tigers, rhinoceroses, leopards, water buffalo, crocodiles, snakes—including some poisonous varieties—bright birds, and fishes.

Thailand's climate is tropical, although conditions vary according to location. Rain is no stranger to Thailand, which can see massive downbursts. Rain is especially prevalent from late spring through fall, when the winds blow from the southwest, bringing moisture with them.

June through October, temperatures range from about 78 degrees

Fahrenheit to 98 degrees Fahrenheit. In winter, the winds shift to the northeast, bringing drier weather and lower temperatures, which range from about 56 to 92 degrees Fahrenheit. Inland areas are warmer than coastal areas and the high mountain elevations.

THE CULTURE AND PEOPLE OF THAILAND

Thais make up approximately 75 percent of the country's population. The largest minority group is Chinese, with about 4 million people, or 10 percent of the total population. Thailand includes other minority groups, including the Malay-speaking Muslims in the south and various hill tribes in the north. The country has also had an influx of Cambodian and Vietnamese refugees, mainly in the eastern areas.

About 95 percent of all Thai people practice the Buddhist religion. In fact, the head of the Buddhist hierarchy, called the supreme patriarch, is generally a member of Thailand's royal family. Thailand has about 18,000 Buddhist temples and 140,000 Buddhist priests. The religion permeates society and is part of daily life for many people. Almost all Buddhist men in Thailand enter a *wat* (monastery) for at least a few days or months to study and reflect.

Other religions are represented in Thailand but play a much smaller role. Muslims, most of whom live in the area north of Malaysia, make up approximately 4 percent of the Thai population. In addition, the country has some small Christian and Hindu communities.

Perhaps as an offshoot of their Buddhist heritage, Thai people believe strongly in dignity and self-control. Children must attend school between the ages of 7 and 14, though the facilities available are often insufficient for the number of children. Nevertheless, the literacy rate in Thailand is nearly 90 percent, higher than that of most countries in Southeast Asia. The country's largest universities are Chulalongkorn

University in Bangkok and Chiang Mai University in the north. The Asian Institute of Technology in Bangkok provides technical training.

Thailand has aligned itself in many ways with the West. Thai women, unlike women in some other Asian cultures, are active in the professions, business, and the arts. Teenagers have adopted American jeans and T shirts.

Learning the Language   The main language in Thailand is Thai, which is difficult for Westerners to learn. The written language uses a non-Roman alphabet, and spoken Thai is based on five tones. Several regional dialects complicate matters further. However, English is a popular language in Thailand and is taught in many schools and often used for business dealings. Other languages spoken include Chinese, Lao, Malay, and Mon-Khmer.

Even if you don't learn Thai fluently, if you plan to live here it's important to learn numbers and key words for daily life and emergencies. Before driving, be aware that though some road signs are written in Thai and English, you'll often see signs only in Thai. Learn the basics before taking to the road.

The Arts of Thailand   Thai music, drama, and dance are intricate and sensual. Musical arrangements usually involve a combination of woodwind and percussion instruments that are grouped in five- or ten-piece ensembles.

Dances have adapted from Indian techniques and involve gestures and swaying body motions that tell a tale. Performers wear elaborate costumes and headgear for exotic and dramatic presentations.

A Brief History of Thailand

First century B.C.   Yunnan is colonized by Tai-speaking peoples from western China.

1200s   The Mongol conquest of Thailand

late 1200s   The Tai form a political unit, from which the name Thai originates

1851–1868	Rule of King Mongkut, who invites European advisers to help modernize the country
1917	Thailand enters World War I on the side of the Allies
1932	The absolute monarchy is overthrown by military and political leaders, creating a constitutional monarchy.
1942	Thailand declares war on the United States and Great Britain under a pro-Japanese government, which is overthrown in 1944
1946	Thailand is admitted to the United Nations

ℛecommended ℒiving ℐreas

Thailand is mostly an agricultural country, interspersed with provincial towns and beach resorts, with one large city, Bangkok. Most of the Thai population (77 percent) lives in the countryside. Except for resorts, rural areas are not popular with foreign retirees; rural life can be a bit rough on the edges, with little access to social and cultural events or good medical care. Most retirees choose Bangkok, Chiang Mai, or resort centers.

Bangkok Bangkok is the bustling capital and far and away the largest city in Thailand, with a population of almost 6 million. One reason for Bangkok's success is its location on the Gulf of Thailand, which makes it the country's chief seaport. The city is the cultural hub of Thailand, as well as the main starting point for travel to other cities and the Thai countryside.

The river Chao Phraya divides Bangkok into two sections. On the right bank is the old quarter of Thonburi and its canals. On the left bank is the central business area, with the capital buildings, luxury hotels, and palaces. Its Ratchadamnoen Klang is a broad main avenue, said to be patterned after Paris's Champs-Élysées.

The National Library, Thailand's largest library, is located in Bangkok. The National Museum houses ancient artifacts that show how Thai culture developed. The sumptuous house of Jim Thompson, now a museum near the National Stadium, encompasses a collection Thompson gathered as he traversed the country from the late 1940s to the 1960s. The collection includes arts, crafts, and ceramics, and the grounds hold a lovely garden.

Among the most famous architecture in Thailand are the wats in Bangkok, including Wat Phra Kaeo, the eighteenth-century temple of the Emerald Buddha. Another spot that is not to be missed is the Vimanmek, the restored palace home of King Chulalongkorn (1868–1910). Now a museum dedicated to the king, the building is the largest teak construction in the world.

Tourism, as one might imagine, is a major business in Bangkok. Unfortunately, along with the exotic architecture and culture, Bangkok has attracted an increased population that brings with it pollution, noise, and streetside poverty. One must find a peaceful retreat within the city—usually behind walls or down a quiet street. To avoid traffic jams, most expatriates live in central Bangkok, with restaurants, shops and cultural events accessible by foot or public transportation.

Furnished apartments are plentiful in the central, Sukhumuit, and Sathorn areas of Bangkok. Many of these are serviced apartments that you can rent for one- to three-month stays while you're looking for a more permanent place. Location is of ultimate importance since Bangkok traffic precludes easy travel, and you'll want to be close to your favorite shopping and entertainment spots. New apartment buildings are going up rapidly in Bangkok, and many offer amenities including swimming pools, parking facilities, and security guards. Other options are condominiums, town houses, and single-family de-tached homes with gardens and pools. Large houses are called villas. They often sit in narrow lanes but have gardens and privacy walls.

Most expatriates live in central Bangkok, where you'll find shop-ping, restaurants, and nightlife. The most popular area is Sukhumuit, which offers a good supply and range of housing. The Ploenchit/

Lumpini area is more expensive than most, but it's convenient to the central business district and major shopping areas, luxury hotels, Lumpini Park, movie houses, and restaurants.

Suburban Bangkok is popular for its cleaner air, and the neighborhoods often have newer accommodations that include many contemporary amenities. But what is gained in amenities is lost in the hassle of commuting to central Bangkok.

The section of north Bangkok near the airport and the International School of Bangkok offers single-family homes, condominiums, and town houses. East Bangkok near the Bagna Trad Highway and Sri Nakarin Road has complexes of single-family homes, popular with expatriates, with facilities such as swimming pools and clubhouses. New housing is plentiful along the eastern seaboard in Pattaya, about 80 miles southeast of Bangkok.

Housing prices in Bangkok are reasonable and diminish the farther one goes from the central part of the city. Luxury two-bedroom apartments overlooking the Chao Phraya rent for $1,135 to $1,662 per month. The cost includes daily room service, water and electricity, health and sports facilities, and the use of a shuttle bus to town. A classical Thai house on a quiet cul-de-sac in the Sukhumuit neighborhood, with four bedrooms, lofty ceilings, polished wooden floors, and a garden, rents for $1,940 a month. In Sathorn, a two-bedroom home with an office—completely furnished and including cleaning service—goes for just $690 a month.

Chiang Mai   Not nearly as large as Bangkok, Chiang Mai offers a population of just over 100,000. It is the largest town in northern Thailand and one of the more pleasant towns of the kingdom, located 435 miles northwest of Bangkok. Founded in 1296, Chiang Mai is an accessible town and easy to traverse by foot or bike. Certainly, these human-scale means of transportation make it easy to stop for a moment to enjoy Chiang Mai's gardens and temples, of which it has more than 300. The town is also known for its artisan culture. Its specialized craftspeople create beautiful articles in gold and lacquer, as well as traditional Thai umbrellas. Chiang Mai is a regional center for education, with four universities that offer many courses in English. Four international schools train children from kindergarten to ninth grade in English. As a result, Chiang Mai offers many job opportunities for qualified people who want to teach English to the local population.

Chiang Mai offers a wide range of rental housing. A two-bedroom apartment rents for $609 a month. A roomy three-bedroom rents for $750. A fully furnished country bungalow just 10 minutes outside Chiang Mai, with two bedrooms and two bathrooms, can be rented for just $415 per month.

$\mathcal{R}$ENTING IN $\mathcal{T}$HAILAND

Most accommodations in Thailand are rentals, and housing can be found directly through newspaper listings, postings on apartment gates, real estate agents, and tips from other expatriates and household staff. Bangkok offers the broadest range of accommodations, including apartments, condominiums, town houses, and individual homes. Once you find a place to rent, you can normally move in within 10 to 30 days of signing the lease. Landlords are responsible for the real estate commission. Many apartments come furnished, though you will need to provide your own kitchen utensils, linens, television sets, and other personal items. Before renting, make sure the air-conditioning—a necessity in the Thai heat and humidity—works. Check for proper water pressure and verify that you will have a phone line. If you need to set up phone service, you'll wait anywhere from a day to two months.

Rents and Fees The cost of your lodging will depend on its size, location, modernity, and amenities. Utility costs may be included in the rent, but this should be stipulated prior to signing the lease. In most cases, the tenant pays for electricity and water. Some units also charge for cable TV. Maintenance fees are also included in the rent.

Rent is paid monthly. In furnished accommodations, the payment is split into three portions: premises, furnishings, and management services. The landlord typically pays the local property tax but its cost will be included in the rent. The tenant deducts a withholding tax on each part of the rent and pays it directly to the government. Corporations leasing furnished accommodations for employees pay a value-added tax, but non-working retirees do not.

Lease Agreements In general, leases in Thailand are short and are written in English. You do not need a lawyer to look over the lease, but be sure that you understand all the terms before signing.Leases typically run for one to two years, with a month's rent payable in advance. Two to three months' rent is the usual security deposit, which is lost if you break the lease within the first year. Two-year leases specify a 10 percent rent increase for the second year.

BUYING REAL ESTATE

With the exception of condominiums, foreigners cannot buy or own property in Thailand, unless they have a Thai spouse. Therefore, most retirees in Thailand rent their accommodations. The current regulations that prohibit property ownership by foreigners is under review, however. So if you're interesting in buying property in Thailand be sure to investigate the most up-to-date ruling.

COST OF LIVING

Thailand can be inexpensive, but be aware of a disparity between prices for locals and those for foreigners. Sometimes foreign buyers pay three, five, or even more times the local price. You'll be able to bridge this disparity as you learn the language and begin to buy at local markets instead of tourist sites.

Street vendors entice passersby with an array of rice, noodles, fish, meat, soup, and banana fritters. You can also enjoy take-out food and casual outdoor restaurants. Menus are often written in three languages: English, Chinese, and Thai. If your taste runs toward Western-style cooking, such restaurants are available but are much more expensive than those serving Thai cuisine.

Most edibles are inexpensive in Thailand. You can eat well in one of country's many food courts for just 55 to 85 cents. The best deals in the markets are on local fruits and vegetables. Imported goods will be more expensive. Here's what you can expect to pay for some everyday goods and services in Thailand:

electricity	$15–$20/month	steak	$2.10/pound
gasoline	$2.40/gallon	coffee	$1.35/cup
movie ticket	$2.20	milk	$3.96/gallon
wine	$8.30	chicken	$1.10/pound
maid service	$50–$60/month	fish	$.69/pound
bananas	$.10/pound	video rental	$1
bread	$.70/loaf	compact disc	$5.40

$\mathcal{D}$AY-TO-DAY $\mathcal{L}$IVING $\mathcal{C}$ONCERNS

If your Thai isn't what it should be, you'll be able to read your news in English in the *Bangkok Post* and *The Nation*. If you speak another language, Bangkok offers more than 18 dailies in Thai and Chinese. Magazines are also published in Thai, English, and Chinese, and several weekly papers serve the areas outside of Bangkok.

In Thailand, the electrical current is 220 volts, 50 cycles, versus 110 volts, 60 cycles in the United States. The plug shape is continental, with a round pin arrangement, though other types of plugs are used. You can buy adapters and transformers that will allow you to use your American appliances in Thailand. However, adaptors change only the current, not the cycles, so computer printers and anything else with a motor will not run properly on them.

Electricity is expensive in Thailand, and the power supply is unreliable. Be sure to protect voltage-sensitive appliances, especially personal computers, TVs, and VCRs, with surge protectors or an uninterrupted power supply.

Broadcasting systems also differ from those in the United States, so your TV and VCR will not work in Thailand unless they incorporate a multi-service system. These multi-service devices are very expensive in Thailand but can be purchased more cheaply in the United States.

Phone service is good in Thai cities, although it may take awhile to get a phone line installed in your apartment. If possible, ask your landlord to have a phone line installed before you sign your lease. Public phone booths take one- and five-baht coins (about 36 bahts equal $1). Main post offices have facilities for long-distance calls.

A few health and safety precautions: Be aware that water is not of good quality in Thailand. Bottled water is available in stores, and most expatriates have it delivered. Also be aware that drug use is popular in Thailand, especially in certain areas of Bangkok and at some beach resorts.

$\mathcal{T}$AXES

Americans who live in Thailand for more than 180 days during the calendar year are considered residents of the country and are therefore liable for Thai taxes. As a retiree, your foreign non-employment income is exempt from taxation if you do not bring it into Thailand. You will pay income tax if you are employed by a Thai company, however. Thai employers make Social Security and Labour Compensation Fund payments for their staffs.

The area of taxation is complex. When planning your stay in Thailand as a resident, consult a professional tax advisor about your specific tax situation. For additional information, contact your local IRS office or IRS International in Washington, D.C., at 202/874-1460.

$\mathcal{M}$AKING THE $\mathcal{M}$OVE

Americans can visit Thailand without a visa for 30 days with only a valid passport and proof of a confirmed ticket to leave within that time. For a stay of more than 90 days, you must obtain approval from the Immigration Division in Bangkok. You can apply through the Royal Thai Embassy or consulate or, if you wish to work, your company can apply directly to the Immigration Division.

Paperwork   To obtain a visa, you must show a valid passport, an application form signed by each applicant in the family, and two passport-size photographs, color or black-and-white, face forward. A tourist visa costs $15 and permits you to stay for 60 days. A non-immigrant visa costs $20 and is good for 90 days. A transit visa costs $10 and permits a maximum stay of 30 days; it's good for your transfer to a third country only, and a photocopy of your confirmed onward air ticket must be submitted when applying. You must pay fees for visas with cash or a money order, and you should not apply for a visa more than three months before your visit to Thailand.

What to Bring, What to Leave Behind   Most appliances can be brought into Thailand tax-free, however you'll need adaptors and transformers to use them (see Day-to-day Living Concerns). Many apartments come furnished, so you may not need to bring many household items with you. In particular, don't bring valuable items that can be damaged by high humidity, heat, mold, or mildew.

Bringing your car from the States is not advised. The import duty is high, as is the shipping cost. Used cars are easy to buy in Thailand and are a much better option.

If you plan to become a resident of Thailand, you will be required to surrender foreign currency to an authorized bank or to deposit it in a foreign currency account. Foreign visitors who are merely traveling through Thailand do not have to surrender their currency.

What About Pets? There are no quarantine requirements for pets coming to Thailand, however you should contact the Thai consulate before you leave for the most current information. In general, you'll need a health certificate issued by an accredited veterinarian within 10 days of your departure. The health certificate must be endorsed by the USDA/APHIS Veterinary Services federal veterinarian in the state where the certificate is being issued.

An original certificate showing proof of rabies shots more than 30 days and less than 180 days prior to your flight is required. Routine immunizations are also required. Finally, you will need an import permit to bring your pet into Thailand.

Before taking a pet to Thailand, however, consult your veterinarian about the animal's health. Your pet will need to adapt to the high heat and humidity. Rabies is prevalent in Thailand, and dogs returning to the States often face a long quarantine.

MEDICAL CARE

In Bangkok you'll be able to find English-speaking doctors and dentists who are well trained, though in outlying areas they may not be prevalent. Office visits with a generalist cost about $6 to $8. You'll usually be asked to pay for doctor and hospital services immediately in cash. The U.S. embassy can provide recommendations for doctors, dentists, and hospitals.

Hospitals in general are well equipped, and care is good and in expensive. Among the most popular hospitals with expatriates in Bangkok are the Samitiveg Hospital, Bangkok Nursing Home, Bumrungrad Hospital, and Adventist Hospital. For the most part, their staff members speak English.

Pharmacies are called dispensaries in Thailand, and you can find a wide range of internationally known pharmaceuticals, sold without prescription. If you purchase without a prescription, however, make sure you get a brand name; some generic Thai and import brands can be of poor quality.

Health Insurance　Medicare doesn't cover Americans overseas. You may be able to use your U.S. health coverage, but probably not. Your best bet is to purchase an expatriate health-insurance policy offered by one of several companies, many based in Britain. Policies that provide coverage only in Europe and Asia are much less expensive than those that cover you in the United States.

$\mathcal{F}$INANCIAL $\mathcal{M}$ATTERS

The unit of currency in Thailand is the baht, which is divided into 100 satang. The government issues 25- and 50-satang coins and 1-, 5-, and 10-baht coins. Notes come in 10, 20, 50, 100, 500, and 1,000 baht. One U.S. dollar equals about 36.1 baht.

Major credit cards are accepted at most large retail stores, hotels, restaurants, and travel agents in Thailand. A surcharge of 3 to 5 percent or more is usually applied. A more economical means of getting cash is to use your Plus, Star, or Cirrus system card at an automatic teller machine, found at most major banks. You can also get money, for a fee, from credit cards at exchange booths and banks. Traveler's checks are available at banks for a fee of about seven baht per check and a tax of three baht per check—a total of about 28 cents per check. Money exchange booths accept every major currency, offer competitive rates, and are open 24 hours. However, most will not exchange baht for other currencies. Banks will exchange baht for other currencies during normal banking hours or at their exchange windows.

The Banking System Thailand's chief financial institution is the Bank of Thailand, which issues all currency. Several commercial banks and foreign banks also serve Thailand. U.S. banks maintaining branches or subsidiaries in Thailand include Chase Manhattan Bank and Citibank.

You can open a savings account if you have an address in Thailand. Personal checks are not commonly used in Thailand except by businesses. To transfer large amounts of money from your U.S. account, have it wired into your account in Thailand.

*T*RANSPORTATION

Travel in Thailand is easy by water, air, and land. The Bangkok port is one of the most modern in Southeast Asia and provides services for its landlocked neighbor, Laos. The Chao Phraya river, which splits Bangkok in two, is navigable for about 50 miles; water taxis and ferries make stops along the route.

Thai Airways is the main supplier of international and domestic flights in Thailand. Domestic flights are reasonable in price. For example, a flight from Chiang Mai to Chiang Rai on Thai Airways costs about $30 round-trip. Other airlines, including Singapore Airlines and Air France, also serve the country.

The railroad system in Thailand is owned and operated by the state, and most lines radiate from Bangkok. Travelers can take first- or second-class trains. For the most part, service is convenient.

Buses are plentiful in Thailand. The air-conditioned buses are more comfortable and more expensive, but worth it. Taxis are amazingly cheap—so cheap that people sometimes use them for major trips across the country. You can rent a bicycle rickshaw for short trips. A *tuk-tuk* is a scooterlike vehicle on three wheels that carries two passengers. Tuk-tuks can be hazardous in heavy city traffic, however.

Driving in Thailand   It's not advised to bring your own car to Thailand, since shipping costs and import duties are high. You can easily lease or purchase a vehicle when you arrive, and the used-car market is especially good in Thailand.

A highway system links Bangkok with provincial cities. The worse traffic is saved for Bangkok itself, since the city's infrastructure has not kept up with growth and new constructon. (An elevated rail system is under construction in Bangkok but is not expected to ease matters until after the year 2000.)

Drivers from countries whose licenses are not printed in English must obtain an international driving permit. If you live in Thailand for more than three months, you must obtain a Thai license. Third-party insurance is not mandatory in Thailand. Though few drivers are insured, it's recommended that you carry damage and liability insurance.

Driving on highways in Thailand is generally easy. Gasoline prices are on par with those in the United States. Roads are marked with international signs, interspersed with Thai-only signs, so plan on getting a good map. Avoid driving in rural areas at night, due to reckless drivers and occasional highway robberies. And remember to drive on the left side of the road. Road maps are printed in both English and Thai. To purchase one, contact the Roads Association of Thailand, Department of Highways HW, Si Ayutthaya Rd., Ratchathewi, Bangkok 10400; tel. (66) (2) 246-1971 or (66) (2) 246-1122 ext. 2276.

ℒEISURE 𝒯IME

Visit orchid farms and pineapple plantations. See elephants—or even ride on the back of one. Stroll through flower markets and sample the exuberant array of tropical fruits and vegetables. Visit the fish market in Bangkok's Maba Chai and the floating market of Damnoen Saduak. There are endless ways to enjoy yourself in Thailand.

Of course, you'll want to visit the rich array of temples and palaces that offer a look at the amazing architecture, sculptures, and artistic heritage of Thailand. In Bangkok, the Grand Palace combines Thai architecture with Western influences, along with a Chinese Garden. The Emerald Buddha Temple is the only temple inside the palace and is famous for its Thai mural painting and lustrous inlaid pearl door. The entrance fee (about $4 for non-residents) includes a visit to Wimanmeek Hall, a museum that displays gifts the Thai royal family received from abroad.

For a bird's-eye view of Bangkok, climb to the Golden Pagoda on top of a man-made mountain. It's located in Wat Sra'ket' at the entrance to Rachadamnern Avenue. Then get a good guidebook to Bangkok and start exploring.

Outside Bangkok, you'll want to see the Ancient City in Samutprakarn, a nearby province. The Ancient City is the largest outdoor museum in Thailand, and it includes replicas of all the important palaces and temples in Thailand.

At Nakhon Pathom (35 miles west of Bangkok), you'll see the highest temple in Buddhist territory (417 feet). Its dome of gold tiles is visible from miles away. In northeast Thailand you'll see spectacular scenery and geological features on steep climbs that often lead to temples. At Prasat Hin Khao, southwest of Buriran, you can visit the Phanom Rung temple complex, which is more than a thousand years old. Perhaps best of all is the 360-degree view from this mountaintop site. And when you're done touring Thailand, you can cross a border or two to visit Singapore, Malaysia, Kuala Lumpur, or the Cameron Highlands.

Shopping You can browse open-air markets and small shops in Thai cities and villages for exotic bargains. In Bangkok, a wide variety of department stores and malls offer Western-style goods. Supermarkets and specialty food shops abound.

298 The World's Top Retirement Havens

You'll also find tourist markets with goods from China, Laos, and Vietnam. Chantaburi, four hours by bus from Bangkok, is known for its sapphires and rubies. In Chiang Mai, artisans work in gold and and lacquer.

Sports and Recreation   The beautiful beaches along Thailand's southern coast may entice you to simply relax to the sound of the surf. All water sports are popular here, including water-skiing, scuba diving, windsurfing, and deep-sea fishing.

Sports facilities, including swimming pools, tennis courts, and fitness centers, are often found in residential apartment complexes. Other popular sports include jogging, biking, basketball, rugby, and cricket. Golf courses, both public and private, are found in and around Bangkok.

For more exotic activity, Thailand's tour operators offer internationally famous jungle trekking. You'll scout the region's flora and fauna, plus discover ancient cultures. At Chiang Mai and Chiang Rai, treks include visits to native mountain tribes.

For those who prefer to spectate, soccer is the most popular sport in Thailand. Thai boxing should not be missed. The activity combines a sporting event with the culture's traditional music.

ADDITIONAL RESOURCES

General Information
Royal Thai Consulates General
  700 N. Rush St., Chicago, IL 60611; 312/664-3129
  205 SE Spokane Ave. Suite 350, Portland, OR 97228-5516;
  503/232-7079
Royal Thai Embassy, 1024 Wisconsin Ave. N.W., Washington,
  D.C. 20016

Tourism Authority of Thailand
  3440 Wilshire Blvd. #1101, Los Angeles, CA 90010; 213/382-2353, fax 213/389-7544
  303 E. Wacker Dr. #400, Chicago, IL 60601; 312/819-3990, fax 312/565-0355
  5 World Trade Center #3443, New York, NY 10048; 212/432-0433, fax 212/912-0920
U.S. Consulate General, Chiang Mai; tel. (66) (5) 325-2629
U.S. Embassy, 95 Wireless Rd., Bangkok 10330; tel. (66) (2) 205-4000, fax (66) (2) 254-1171

Useful Web Sites
http://asem.inter.net.th/thailand/thaiweb.html
http://usa.or.th/embassy/consul.htm
www.nectec.or.th/WWW-VL-Thailand.html
www.thaiembdc.org/

$\mathcal{G}$ENERAL $\mathcal{I}$NFORMATION FOR $\mathcal{R}$ETIREES AND $\mathcal{E}$XPATRIATES

Health Insurance Companies
AARP Health Care Options
  800/245-1212, operator 36
Access America
  800/955-4002
American Express Travel Protection Plan
  800/234-0375
Columbus Health Insurance
  www.expatexchange.com/columbus/index.html
International SOS Assistance
  800/523-6586
Medex
  800/537-2029
Tompkins Financial Group, Expatriate Health Insurance Protection
  http://home.iSTAR.ca/~tompkins/expathealth.html
Travel Assistance International
  800/821-2828
Travel Insured International
  800/243-3174
TravMed International Traveler's Assistance Association
  800/732-5309
Universal Travel Protection Insurance
  www.noelgroup.com

Web Sites for Americans Living Overseas
American Automobile Association
www.aaa.com/vacation/idp.html
American Citizens Abroad
www.aca.ch
Association of Americans Resident Overseas
http://hometown.aol.com/aaroparis/aarohome.htm
Escape Artist
www.escapeartist.com/going/home.htm
Expat Exchange
www.expatexchange.com
Overseas Digest by William Beaver
http://overseasdigest.com
Senior News Network:Travel
www.seniornews.com/travel.html
Transitions Abroad
www.transabroad.com
U.S. government information services
www.state.gov
U.S. government travel warnings
http://travel.state.gov

Retirement Resources
American Association of Retired Persons
601 E St. NW, Washington, D.C. 20049; 800/424-3410;
member@aarp.org
Elderhostel
www.elderhostel.org
Third Age Living
www.thirdage.com

$\mathcal{A}$BOUT THE $\mathcal{A}$UTHORS

John Bigley has contributed travel articles and photographs to many consumer and trade publications. Along with Paris Permenter, he has authored 14 travel guidebooks, including *CitySmart Guidebook: Austin* (John Muir Publications, 1997). John is a member of the Society of American Travel Writers. He makes his home in central Texas.

Leslie Doran is a freelance writer based in Durango, Colorado. Her articles and book reviews have appeared in *Builder/Architect* magazine, *Colorado Homes & Lifestyle*, the *Durango Herald*, *Durango Magazine*, *Garden Railways*, *Mystery News*, and other publications. Leslie is cofounder of the Durango InkSlingers, a local writers' organization.

Rosanne Knorr left the hectic world of advertising to discover her own retirement haven in France. She has written six travel books, including *The Grown-Up's Guide To Running Away From Home*, which inspires and informs adults about moving overseas. Rosanne currently lives in the Loire Valley with her husband, John.

Jeffrey Laign has written several books, and his articles on travel and health appear regularly in dozens of magazines and newspapers. Laign and his family live in Fort Lauderdale, Florida.

John Lyons-Gould is a freelance writer and editor and a former English instructor at Humboldt State University in California. His articles and poetry have appeared in various publications. He lives in New Mexico with his wife and two sons.

Lisa Matte writes a monthly family travel column for the *Boston Herald*, and her work has appeared in many regional, national, and international travel publications. She is the author of *CitySmart Guidebook: Boston* (John Muir Publications, 2000).

Paris Permenter, writes about national and international travel for numerous consumer and trade publications. Along with husband John Bigley, she has coauthored 14 books, ranging from Caribbean guides to resort cookbooks. Paris is a member of the Society of American Travel Writers and lives in central Texas.